TALES OF A
BLACK
GAYSHA

TALES OF A BLACK GAYSHA

CHRISTIAN RICHARDSON

ARCHWAY
PUBLISHING

Archway Publishing books may be ordered through booksellers or by contacting:

Archway Publishing
1663 Liberty Drive
Bloomington, IN 47403
www.archwaypublishing.com
1 (888) 242-5904

ISBN: 978-1-4808-8376-5 (sc)
ISBN: 978-1-4808-8377-2 (e)

Library of Congress Control Number: 2019915775

Print information available on the last page.

Archway Publishing rev. date: 01/25/2020

From my Heart to yours:

To all of you who have encouraged me to move forward with telling my stories. To all of you have helped to mold me into the person I am today. Not only my family and friends, but those strangers who I've met along the way who have given me sound advice, hugs or even a smile. To all of you who give a middle finger to society and its rules. To all of you that have continued to push and has never given up despite the odd's being against you. Most of all, this book is dedicated to all of US, who have ever been judged by the unjust and made to feel like we were any less of a person because we march to the beat of our own drum and do as we please. I dedicate this book to you.

From my mouth to God's ears,
I Love you and Thank you so much,
- Christian

CONTENTS

KEY CODES

Bish, Bih, Bich – Friendly term of endearment, that's LESS offensive than "BITCH"

Brick (Hard) – referring to a man's penis

Chile/Chyle – "Child" referring to female's

Clocked'T – Recognized or Noticed a certain thing or situation without saying it out loud

Fish – referring to a female

Heffa – referring to Female's. Sometimes in an affectionate manner.

Hunni (Honey) referring to Female

LMAO – Laughing My Ass Off

LOL – Laughing Out Loud

SMH- Shaking My Head

Sugga (Sugar) – Referring to male's. Sometimes in an affectionate manner.

CRAIG'S CHOCOLATE BEAR

Good morning, Love,

I'm laying here on the floor of this huge apartment in Texas. I can't help but realize I am in the right place for now. Not to mention, my god-sister is temporarily stationed here, and I just love hanging out with her and her kids. They just bring me so much joy. She's such a rock star mom and she's always willing and ready to do anything for her babies. Gotta love that about any mother. She's so dope. I can honestly say, I'm so proud of her and the woman she's become. She and I talk about everything. We just laugh, love and talk. Although, I didn't tell her I'm feeling some kind of way (sexually frustrated that is). She already thinks I'm a freak. I mean, I am and I'm okay with that, but I don't need to verify it to her. She totally gets a kick out of my antics.

But Baby! When I tell you it's *dry* down here. WHEW! However, in all fairness, I haven't really been looking lately because of work. When I did happen to go out, it was just some low-key flirting with a few fellas; a little bumping and grinding at bars, but that's about it. I need to do something *fast*! Hell, I'm cute, young and have somewhat of a high sex drive. *giggle* Yes, I thought about the whole sex toy thing, but I honestly hate toys. Ugh! I need a damn body attached to that meat. Lord knows there are some fine ass soldiers here on this base! I definitely need to get up with one or a few. Hmph.

Love, why did I decide to call Alex and tell him about my little "situation."? This fool! Not only did he set me straight, but he held no punches either (of course as only he could do). So, I was telling him about me and my "dry spell," so to speak, and Lord, why did I tell him that? He cackled at me and let me have it. Oh my God. Let me tell you about this joker. He told me I should either download an app or post an ad on "Craigslist" (RIGHT! Me?!? Yeah right!). He told me it would help me to meet some fellas and find some folks to hang out with (other than my sis and her kids). You know, he was right. I started thinking how much I need some life and night action. So, after talking to Alex for forty-five minutes, I decided to place my ad and I downloaded the proper app. I mean hey, why not? I posted an ad just to see what kind of responses I would get. I would love for that "BIG TEXAS MAN" to roll through and shut it down! I mean, since I've heard so much about them, let's see if Texas can represent.

#Pause if you don't have a drink, go get you one and take a sip. *#Continue*

The internet ads and Texas came through baby! OH.MY. GAAWD! YES! YES! YEEEEEES!!! No sooner than I posted the ad, within forty-five minutes I had a slew of responses. I was like, *Well damn!* I requested a Bear over 6ft and a straight up FREAK!

OH-ME-OH-MY! Once I was done weeding through all the bullshit, I managed to come across a few that were completely too good to be true.

Since I'm somewhat of a rebel and I do what I want anyway, I decided to push the envelope. The fella that I responded to first was this big six-foot-three chocolate bear of a man that was about two hundred fifty pounds, sexy belly, bald head, with a hell of a thick beard ("Beardy" as I call them) and some thick fingers. Whew! He was just handsomely sexy. After a few emails between us, he informed me that he was down with the freak session as long as I can keep it between us. He wasn't out and he was military. I said, "Of course! Just the way I like'em. Ow!"

We exchanged phone numbers and I texted him my address. Now, Love, you know me; you know I was nervous as hell. Like, *oh my gag, what the hell did I just do?* You know I had to go hop in the shower and wash my ass real good. But then, I was like, *No, let me slow down.* I want to remember every pleasure about this experience. I made sure I showered with my "Hey Big Zaddy" flirty body wash. No sooner than I hopped out the shower and was rubbing my body down with lotion, my phone rang. It was him, calling to tell me he was at the front gate and to buzz him in, and I did just that.

Love! I could not believe I was about to do this. *Yes. Yes, I was!* I was freaking out! OH.EM.GEE! You know I was running around, making sure everything was in its place and decent, spraying air freshener. Just making sure it's clean and tidy (you know, I'm all about presentation, honey). I put on my terry cloth robe, leaving it slightly open, while tying it very loosely. You know that sexy, playful innocent look. As soon as I gave myself a final once over, he knocked on the door (Oh, my God)! I took a couple of deep breaths, said a little prayer. Praying he was not crazy, looked like his pictures and was not on no bullshit. "Lord, please don't let him be on no bullshit. AMEN!" I took some deep breaths and said *Here goes nothing; got damn it.*

Love, I opened that door and OH-MY-GOOD-ALMIGHTY-APHRODIETY! This man was *damn* fine! The pictures didn't even do him justice. When he smiled at me and said, "So, wassup?" I instantly blushed and was turned on even more. He had a deep baritone voice and he smelled *so damn good*! *Ah*! And you know how much I love a good-smelling man. Whew, Lord! Be still my culo (Pearl Clutching moment).

I smiled back at him, then let him in. I could feel my body temperature rising instantly. As I locked the door behind him, I asked him if he wanted anything to drink.

"Sure, I'll take some water, if you have any." So of course, that means he wanted bottled water. And you know I always have more than enough. *GIRL!* Let me tell you about this sexy freak!

#Pause Speaking of water, take a sip of your drink again because *here we go*! #Continue

As I'm giving him the water, of course my robe comes undone

(NO, I did NOT do that on purpose. I promise I didn't. Then again, I didn't tie it that tight on purpose). He sipped his water, put that bottle down, and came right over to me and started kissing my neck.

Right on my damn spot! Baby! The way my knees buckled! I'm in my head, screaming, "GIIIRRRRLAAAA!!!" Like, what is he doing to me and how the hell did he know? Naturally, I started moaning and was in full on "DO IT 2 ME" mode (#Janet). He was just kissing me, my neck and body so damn passionately; and it had me *weak as hell*! Then this motherfucker had the nerve to whisper in my ear, "I'm about to make your body mine." All I could muster up was a passionate moan, in the key of sensual *Okay'ness*. He had me *gone*! Nobody has *ever* made me buckle and become instantly turned on like that since "Hubbz" (and girl you know how he and I used to put holes in walls and go at it). Hmph. Anyway we managed to make our way to my bedroom as he made me giggle a little bit. I kept trying to pull away from him, but he would not let me. He kept me close to him with one hand while he undressed himself with his other hand. I'm like, *This dude is not playing with me right now!* Like seriously.

As I managed to break free from his grasp and fall back onto the bed, this man was undressed and READY to ROCK. Honey LISTEN! When I looked up at that BIG, CHOCOLATE, BEAUTIFUL BEAR BODY that was standing before me; and I know I should NOT have; but I thanked GOD for him! Whew GLORY!

#Pause Who the hell thanks God before some lustful sex. *Shit! I did!* And I was not ashamed. Thank you God for eyesight, and the senses for me to experience all this BIG BEAUTIFUL MAN IN ALL HIS GLORY! Yes God! *#Continue*

As he crawled onto the bed on top of me, he started on my neck again, but this time he said, "Oh, my God, you smell so damn good, I could eat you!" and BITCH! He did just that. He rolled me over on my stomach and went to work! Well damn! Every single-damn-thing he did, he did it with *passion*. It was like his sex game was strictly passion.

#RealityCheckPause: You must be careful with these kinds of things. That's how one falls in love with the sex and think you're

falling in love with the man. The sex is so good and he's so in tune with your body, you think its love. When the reality of it is, he's just good at sex. PERIOD. You're in deep LUST, not LOVE. I totally understand it. I KNOW the difference and my "heart is NOT in my vagina". So there's no attachment. *#Continue*

OH-YES-SIR! He kissed and licked every inch of my body. I'm so glad I went to get a Manni and Pedi done a couple days prior. He had my toes all in his mouth. I'm thinking, *Wait a minute! You betta go head and get all of it!* When I tell you this joker sent me O-VAH! And not one fuck was given on his part either. His oral skills were *epic*! I mean, like he had my body talking and responding to his every action. Again, not since "B" has my body done this. I had to stop and push him off me quite a few times. It quickly became too much, and I was getting loud.

I didn't want my neighbor to hear me. Especially the one upstairs. You know he's nosy and curious (he's another story). Anyways, you know I had to reciprocate with the oral skills, right (smiling)? I was not about to let him show me up. Love, why did he come up looking like a damn glazed doughnut? Face was all shiny and a mess! I said *damn*! He put in *work*! So, um yeah; I definitely had to return the favor. He had my legs shaking and my back arching. The whole time he was pleasing me, all I could think was, *OH, GAWD, I LOVE ALEX*!

I pushed him off me and said, "Now it's my turn. I'ma fix your ass." I rolled over so that I was on top. I kissed and licked his body from his sexy hairy chest all the way down to the bottom of his belly button. Wait, though. *Why* did his "V" smell like "Versace Blue". *Yes!* You know that's my shit right there! Not everybody can wear it though. Even though they THINK they can. TUH! It smelled so good on him. That was even more reason for me to rock his got damn world and give him that killer "JAWBONE" action.

Honey, when I tell you I went in! I tried to suck him inside out. I sure the fuck did! I was working my mouth and tongue on him so damn good he was running. You already know how juicy my mouth is. Baby! I had his damn toes throwing up gang signs annnnd popping! I had his legs locked and his eyes were closed while he was cursing! BOOM! Ooooohhh baby I got that ass now, mutha'fucka! I was tryn'a suck his damn soul out!

He made me stop and said, "Oh you trying to bitch me out and make me cum fast."

I laughed and said, "No, that was payback."

That's when this MF gone tell me, "Oh, so you got jokes." He rolled over so that now he was back on top. He pulled me to him and then it was on! He goes right back to my spot. He figured out, that if he hit's my spot right, my body would react. Not only did my body react, but my back arched and up went my legs (*swoon!*). I'm thinking, *What the hell is this Sex Voodoo he got goings on?* Now, Love, you know damn well ain't nobody been in the cookie jar since "Big Daddy." But this MF!- he was *so* smooth with it. I could not believe this was happening. It was just so many emotions running through my mind and body. Everything was heightened and my body felt like it was on one thousand. Girl, I know! I know, I know. Hmph. All I could do was just go with the flow and be in it. Whew, Lord! My favorite kind of sex is *passionate sex*. The things that can happen, the amount of ecstasy on top of euphoria...amazing!

He managed to wrap my legs around his waist and proceeded with some frottage. Which, by this time, you already know my body was sensitive to his touch.

We did the frot game for like two minutes while we kissed, and then and rolled me over on my stomach. Now this is where his skills came into play (with his big slick ass).

#Pause Take a sip heffa! *#Continue*

He began kissing me on my neck and down my spine. As he was kissing me (and licking me) of course, naturally, my back arched. *Bitch! Why* did he slide right on up in me! Please don't ask me how he did that shit so slick and quick like, but he did. *He did! He diiiiid!*

You know damn well my snap back does not allow that kind of activity so fast. You know me boo, you gotta work my thick ass over first. And you know what, that's exactly what that old slick bastard did! Baby, listen! When I tell you he was on one thousand along with me. Oh Yes Ma'am! Oh no but Catch this GAG; how about my iPod was docked, right?! Why did "Lil Kim" come on? I was like, *Wait a minute! Why is the devil playing with me like this TA'DAY?* I lie to you not! That damn "Hardcore" album. And I swear, I think it made him even hornier and harder.

I could feel his hips grinding to the beat of the songs. I was like, *you know what?* Honestly, though, it was a turn on (giggle). You know I like a man that can dance and groove with me. Yeah, he definitely had me in a trance. Once I finally got in the groove of things, it was just...Wow! I mean, he did everything perfect. Did I mention he had my legs in the air with his hands in my hair? Come on now! *Yes, he did* (high-five)! When I tell you all my "Domestic Housewife" T's was gone out the window.

I straight up turned into that "Freak Fuck Monster" I try not to let out! He was so good with his skills, he made me cum twice. I tell you no lies! Those orgasms were so damn good I would have gladly let him have me without checking his credit. Yes, that serious! You already know. When I tell you, I now understand why these simple ass heffa's be "dick'matized" and hard pressed. He damn sure would have had me fighting and snatching hoe's bald over that sex game. GOOD GAWD (Shaking my head)! After we were done almost an hour later (yes, a freaking hour), we were lying there soaked in sweat and I had water legs. We laughed, then he said, "You mind if I take a shower?" he asked.

"Hell no! Gone and wranch ya balls off."

He laughed. "Join me?"

"As soon as I get the feeling back in my legs, I sure will."

As I was laying there looking at him, he actually seemed a bit shy. Like his people interaction skills were very lowkey, unless it was intimate or something he can shine at. For example, that sex session. So, as he made his way into the bathroom, I attempted to gather myself and go swig a glass of wine (I ain't want no damn water). I drunk my wine and I chased it with a little bit water anyway. Then, I heard him yell, "Where you at?" I went into the bathroom and stepped into the shower. I was washing my face and letting the water fall over me, as I felt him when he started kissing me on my neck and I didn't think anything of it. Come to find out, he wanted to go for round two?

I said, *"Pause!* Hold up, Playa, you were very good and very pleasing, but I do NOT have any more strength left in me. My legs are still weak right now as it is. I promise you; you wore me out." Of course I was lying. LOL. Are you kidding me!? I just needed a minute.

He leaned in to kiss me and he pressed my chest up against the wall. Then he slapped his hard meat against my ass, then said "What am I supposed to do with this?"

"Oh, come on! Are you serious?"

He laughed at me and said, "It's your fault."

"Um! I didn't do anything. You asked me to join you, so I did."

"You so sexy and I just can't get enough of you. Just help a brother out one last time."

Man, listen! I lathered up these hands and gave him one old soapy hand-job! I hit his ass with that "Kung-Fu" grip action and he nutted in like two minutes.

I'm so glad we were in the shower. Right down the drain it went. The gag was, his legs buckled, and he fell in the shower. His simple ass almost pulled my damn shower curtain down and everything!

"You set me up! You could have warned a brutha. That shit was *fire*! Damn!"

"Whatever, you told me to handle it, so I did."

We got out the shower, I dried off and put my robe back on. He dried off then laid back in the bed. I just looked at him, then I laughed and made my way back to the kitchen. I heard him when he got up. He came in the kitchen to get some water. He had his bikini briefs on (they looked so fucking sexy on him, too) and nothing else. He drank his water and looked in the fridge to see what else I had. Mind you,

I'm just standing there, looking at him with my lovely lustful after sex glow I had going on. He was just so sexy to me. I loved everything about him and his body. I was literally getting turned on again just looking at him (I know right). Needless to say, we went for round two! Oh Shut up. I know what I said. Judge ya daddy, heffa. HA!

This time, the sex only lasted about fifteen minutes. He laughed and said he had nothing left. Give him about thirty minutes and he'll be ready again.

"Uh, no, sir! You gots'ta go! You will not occupy all my time today."

He laughed and said, "You're right, but I was damn sure gone try." He got in the shower again, this time I did not join him. When he got out, he made his way over to me, opened my robe again, and we just kissed for about another five minutes.

I told him, "This better be it. I am not here for more sex." We both laughed. Then like clockwork, I mounted him again and BAM! Round 3. UGH! I lie to you not. Clearly we both had some pinned up sexual energy we needed to get out. And we did just that. LOL! WHEW!

After we finished the 3rd time, he said to me, "I don't know what it is about you, but I love that I feel so comfortable with you. We can connect sexually and intimately. I've never done this with anybody before."

"So, wait; you're into the whole app hook up thing?"

"Well yeah. No commitment and I do as many as I want for as long as I want, whenever I want."

"Oh, okay. I see. Well, I'm new to this and you're my first."

"No way. You for real?"

"Yes. Very much so."

"Oh, shit! That's wassup. Glad I could be your first."

So we chatted a little longer. We talked about family, work and life. Then he got up, showered yet again and got dressed. This time while he was showering, I ran to the other side of my apartment to clean up. LOL. I came back once he was actually dressed. As he went into the kitchen and grabbed another water while checking his phone. He grabbed his keys off the key hook then said, "A'ight, walk me out."

As we are walking out the door, he grabbed me, pulled me towards him with some force, opened my robe, sucked my nipple, and kissed my chest, while making his way up to my lips and kissed me so passionately, yet again. Then, he whispered in my ear, "We are definitely gone do this again."

I blushed and said, "Okay, as I bit my bottom lip and gazed at him so lustfully.

As he released me, he closed my robe, kissed me again and said, "You're a great partner and I'll definitely be back. Don't give my shit away or next time I'm'a spank that ass."

Mind you, I'm still standing there with that lustful after sex glow satisfied look on me all while thinking, *If this mutha'fucka don't carry his ass on some where! Got me turned on like this! Who the fuck does he think he is?* The only thing that came out my mouth was, "Okay, Pa, you got it". He smiled at me, kissed me again, then walked down the steps to his truck and pulled off.

Baby! Yesterday was a day! After he left, I cleaned up, cooked dinner and chilled the rest of the day. My sis and the kids came over for dinner. Of course by then I had already cleaned up thoroughly. My sis is nosy as hell. The last thing I need is for her ass to catch on and ask questions. After dinner, we went and sat by the pool for a few minutes. So today, I guess I'll go text my god-sis again and hang out with her for a few minutes. I'm loose as a noodle and he knocked that edge off. Hell, I was loose and good yesterday. LOL. Texas did NOT let me down. I can't wait to tell Alex about this. He is going to flip and have a field day with this one. I said alright for the Internet ad. BLOOP! I'm supposed to hang out with the fellas next weekend in Austin. I'll keep you posted on that one. I can only imagine what that's going to be like. They're clowns.

I gotta go, Love
Talk to you later.
Eskimo Kisses.

6ᵀᴴ STREET & MASERATI BOUNCERS

Good morning, Love:

So far, I'm enjoying my stay here in Texas, now that I'm officially over the "hump," so to speak. Whew, Lord, I laugh at the thought of it all. It is possible that one rendezvous opened the flood gates. I definitely think so.

Tonight, I was invited to hang out in Austin with my co-worker D., along with some of his buddies. He's from California. He seems cool, so far. You know I keep my guard up just a little bit and always ready to rock if need be. Gotta keep my eye on folks nowadays. Anyway, his friends are cute, too. One of them is light skinned with GORGEOUS eyes! He's a cute little round-bodied, scoop-ball-head joker. The other one is in the military; small framed little fella, but also handsome. Not my type, but baby his benefits sure did make him my type. HA!

Now, you know I had to show up and show out, right? I pulled that white linen and fresh black Cole Han loafers out the closet. I kept it cute, light, and simple, with my "Classy Fella" flair, and topped it off with the "Snobby" delight. Oh baby I didn't give them too much.

So, of course, I rode with the fellas and the little one drove. Hunni, he opened that little BMW up! The skyline was lit up and glowing; it was simply beautiful. But, then again, he drove so damn fast. Before I could blink, we were there! I'm thinking "Dayum! Next time have some stop light with your driving," I kept it cute because I didn't want to appear unappreciative.

We pulled up on 6ᵗʰ Street, which looked like Washington, DC's Adams Morgan on steroids. The valet opened my door to let me out, and I could not help but smile and be excited. I felt like Janet (Jackson) when she got out the car in her "Alright" video, walking into the theater, looking like Dorothy Dandridge, so flawless, dressed in all white, covered in love, diamonds and smiles. I was channeling that feeling. Don't ask me why Love, that's just what popped into my head.

The weather was perfect. Not, too hot, not, too cool. It was just right. As we walked inside, I was getting so much attention from so many different flavors of men. Tall ones, short ones, thick ones, skinny ones, butch ones, rugged ones, fellas from USA, fellas from the UAE. *Whew!* I just wanted to play crouching tiger hot cooch on all of them. You know I was ready to shake a titty at all of them hunni! Hmph.

The first little lounge we stopped at was CUTE! Once inside, I had to slide in the restroom and do a check. From all those looks, I had to make sure I didn't have a boog or something. I love that whenever I doubt myself or feeling slightly insecure, here comes a female to reassure me that I am "just so cute!" I love it! That's exactly what happened.

As I was coming out of the restroom, this young lady about mid-thirties told me how cute I looked and how she just knew I was not from here. I smiled, hugged her, and said, "You're right!" We laughed and chit-chatted a little bit.

"I saw that look on your face," she said, "trying to figure out why people stopped to look at you when you walked in."

I smirked and nodded.

"It's because you have this glow and bright aura around you, sweetie. That's how I knew you were NOT from here."

Of course, I was blushing and slightly bashful with some embarrassment.

She hugged me again. I think she just wanted another hug because she hugged me again before she walked away. She smelled so good! Oh, my God! She was very cute, too. She was GORGE, to be perfectly honest. You know I *love* me a pretty piece of fish, hunni.

Like if J.Lo and Eva Longoria were to have a love child, it would have been her. She was way cute, wearing her bad-ass Giuseppe-Zanotti Fish Bone heels. I could NOT let her leave without me bringing attention to get shoes either.

"Hold up, heffa. Let me see them ankles."

She laughed so loud and said, "Oh, my God! You're a gay! I LOVE YOU EVEN MORE NOW!"

We both cracked up.

"I'm a shoe whore to the fullest," I told her with a tilted head. "Doesn't matter who the designer is; if it's cute and comfortable, PUMP ON! Worry about the price later." We chatted a little bit longer, then I told her I needed to go back to my crew.

She was so cute and fun; very sweet and loveable. I brought her a drink and then went to reconnect with the fellas. I found them back outside already, in front waiting on me. Naturally, they wanted to know who she was and why I didn't bring her to meet them. I rolled my eyes at them, then smirked. As we continued to make our way down the sidewalk to the main lounge where they wanted to chill at, I was walking and checking out the sights and, low and behold, what do I see?

Yes, my car crush. An all-white Maserati chrome finishes with slight tint. It had me at hello! You know I was excited. Nipples got hard, mouthwatering; I was forty-five seconds from making it clap and putting it on the glass. Yes, God! Love, I literally stopped in my tracks.

"What the hell is wrong with you?" asked D. "That ain't yours!" I laughed and responded with, "Not yet anyway."

As we are crossing at the corner of Trinity Street to go into the lounge, I was still looking at that Maserati; I wanted to see who was driving it. The window was slightly cracked, as I was trying to peek in to see who it was. It appeared to be an older White gentleman (silver fox), and from what I could see, he was fine! Whew, Lord. We locked eyes; he winked at me and smiled.

That was all I needed! I was ready to toss these titties in a circle and give it all to him! I was so damn busy looking at him and the car, I didn't even notice how close we were to the door and bumped right into the bouncer and damn, he was fine, too! He was a big burly six-foot-five joker with a bald head, scruffy beard, muscles and a sexy belly with pretty chocolate skin, wearing a Winnie the Pooh style T-shirt! Love, you know I don't have no sense, so when he grabbed me and asked, "You good?" I giggled and said, "Well, I am now. Thank you."

He laughed and looked at my ID. "DC, huh?"

"Yes, sir."

"That's wassup. What brings you to the Lone Star state?

"Work."

"DOD?"

With my flirty smile, I said, "Yes, sir."

"Stop calling me sir. My name is Sye."

"Okay, fine, Sye! Any more questions, Sye?"

"Nah, you good. I'll catch you later."

"Okay Sye, I'll wait on it".

Girl, you know damn well I was blushing and giggling like a damn fool! I had to gather my ass together real quick; he was not going to have me acting like a little chicken head. But I damn sure loved the idea of him checking for me, though. As we walked in, I noticed the layout of the place right away. It was really nice. The main bar and the chill area was downstairs along with the re-strooms etc. It was a very intimate setting and not too overdone.

Even the screens were mounted on the walls in the perfect an-gles. I go to the restroom to check myself one more time and who the hell do I see walk in? Mr. Maserati himself. You know I'm trying to keep my composure, right? Love, that man. Whew! He know he was fine. He stood about six-foot-two and two hundred thirty pounds, with a hint of Hispanic descent. His hair was so pretty, the kind of gray that turned black as it went towards the back of his head. Baby! Be still my culo. Oh, hunni, the culo was smoking by now. You hear me? Smoking!

His salt-and-pepper beard was thick and well-groomed. He had on a salmon pink linen shirt with white shorts a nice pair of Italian loafers. Exactly. CLOCKED'T. As I'm sizing him up, I noticed his watch because it was so pretty and big. In fact, it was that watch from Tiffany's I had been eyeballing. Now, Love, you know damn well I started thinking, *What the hell is he doing in here?* That kind of money is not in this spot. I did a scan of the area and that was NOT the money I saw in none of that square footage. Hell, the girl at the bar had on Payless pumps and what looked like a late-nineties' Baby Phat blouse and CVS lip gloss. No ma'am. Like I said, not in here. Truth be told, I had to step back and look at myself like am I over dressed and why am I even in here?!

So anyway, he saw me looking at him with DEEP LUST in my eyes for all of him. Even the damn watch! I know I am not supposed to lust or covet but, baby! All of him! You hear me? All. Of. Him! Judge your bald head ass granny dayum it.

He made his way over to me to introduce himself.

#Pause BITCH LISTEN! I smelled his scent before he was even near me. You already know. The fragrance smelled like Creed. It was definitely doing WTF it needed to do to me. *#Continue*

As he walked over to me, he greeted me very warmly. "Well, hello there. I saw you outside admiring my vehicle."

"Yes. It's one of my favorites; not to mention you own it in one of my favorite colors." As I give him that sincere innocent flirty look. He extended his hand. "I'm Richard, and you are?" "Well nice to meet you, Richard, I'm Christian. So now tell me, Richard, what are you doing in this lounge on a Friday night?"

"To meet up with some friends for a few and this was the spot they picked."

"Oh, okay. Now that makes more sense."

"What do you mean?"

"Sugga, you drive a $100,000 vehicle, you have on cologne that starts at damn near $400 a bottle and your watch is from Tiffany's, which you had altered. That particular watch doesn't come with a link band, its leather. So, I figure you either own the place or you're in chill mode with friends; and I see I was right." I smirked.

He let out the loudest laugh. "Well, I'll be damned."

"Oh no, don't be. Just be impressed enough to take me for a spin one day and we'll be fine." I winked.

He laughed. "Okay. You got it."

As I texted D to find out where they were, I told Richard I needed to find my buddies.

"That's cool. I'll link up with you later. I mean, if that's cool with you." He smiled.

#Pause HIS SMILE, though! Damn! I was ready to put it all in his hands. Here Daddy! Just take all of my being damn it. His sexy voice, a sexy pretty smile with some great teeth! And I know he has good credit! You know I was OVAH! My inner hoe was SCREAMING. *#Continue*

The fellas informed me that they were upstairs already. As I began to walk up the stairs that lead to the second level, I noticed that they were jamming with the music. So I decided to make my way up. It was cute; a little rooftop action never hurt anybody—a covering with no walls. You already know I'm always ready to dance. I got an Amaretto Sour first, then met back up with the fellas. It was popping upstairs. Multiple bars, sit down areas, accompanied by high bar tabletops. The view was amazing. Love, the deejay started spinning Pooh. Yes, God, for Janet *Thee* Jackson! That was a cue for me to kill it, but still be cute about it. You know "All Night (Don't Stop)" can be a workout, but I am too cute to be sweating, fooling with Pooh. So naturally once I started dancing, the fellas popped up, talking about, "Where the hell did you disappear to?"

"I was downstairs chatting with some of the natives. That's all. Now leave me alone and let me boogie."

That deejay was no joke. He was giving me everything I wanted and needed. And you know it took everything in me *not* to queen out! He was rocking! Yes, I was being cute, swinging my little bit of hair and grooving with the sway. I sure was. With No fucks given.

My throat was a little parched, so I went to the bar to get me a ginger ale, and who do I bump into at the bar? Uh, yes…Mr. Bouncer himself.

Naturally, he saw me dancing and had jokes. Talking about, "I see you, little Janet. Don't give us too much."

Now, you and I both know I was saying to myself, *Oh baby you have no idea. If I really wanted to fuck up that dance floor I could have.* We all know this! I kept it cute, though.

Love, the deejay decided he wanted to play "The Wobble" and you know that's my get down. When I heard that beat drop you know I was 'bout ready to ditch that ginger ale and make that dance floor eat it! Yes! I put my drink down on the table and jumped up. Sye grabbed my arm and asked, "Where are you going?"

"To dance, now let me go!"

He burst out laughing and said, "Gone and kill it then!"

"All the shorty's in the club let me see ya just…"

Come on now! I'm getting amped just thinking about it! The bass and swag of this song just sends me out of here. The song goes off and I'm tired boots! Sye sees me sit down; he comes over and sat next to me. Oh, hunni, he's just cracking up!

"You good now?"

"Of course, I am. That's my song. What can I say?"

"Yes, I see. You got some moves. I ain't mad at cha playa."

"Hey, good music moves me."

"Wassup with you, Christian? How long you here for and what a brother gotta do to get to know you?"

"Well if you go get me another ginger ale or bottled water you can get to know me a lot faster."

"What's wrong with that one?" He nodded at the glass of ginger ale on the table.

"Uh No. I don't want that one, it was sitting there while I was dancing. Matter of fact dump this one. Thanks, boo!"

He surely did go get me another ginger ale and a bottle of water. We sat and chit chatted a little longer, exchange information (yes, heffa, I gave him my number) and then he said he had to go back to his post, and he'd hit me later.

Love! No sooner than he walked away Richard walked up.

Richard sat down. "I saw you dancing and grooving with the smooth."

"I'm sure you did. So, what can I do ya for, poppa? Wassup?"

He smiled. "I like that. Poppa. Hmm. Okay."

Oh, shit, I done started something.

He laughed and then proceeded to tell me how much he would love to get to know me. He liked my personality and my straightforwardness.

"I can only be me, cutie."

He told me he was forty-seven, recently divorced, with three kids and enjoying life.

I sat back, crossed my legs and asked him, "Is there really any other way?"

He smiled. "If it is I don't wanna know or experience it."

"I hear that." I chuckled.

He inched close enough to rub my thigh. As if I really didn't see this coming. He thought he was being slick.

I didn't even realize that we had just talked for an hour and a half. I excused myself to go check on the fellas and to make sure they were good. I know, my maternal instincts. I had to. They had hella jokes too.

"We see you with your pops over there. Ask him what time is check-in? We know he got curfew at the home!"

Jokes for days. Even jokes about his hips, giving me worms... all kinds of stuff.

"Yeah. Okay. All that. Anyways, I was just making sure you all were good. I see you have company. Hello Ladies. I'll let you all continue. Holla at me in a few."

So, as I'm making my way back over to Richard, and before I could sit down next to him again, he got up and grabbed my hand, leaned down and whispered, "Come with me," in my ear and led me downstairs to some empty back room he knew about.

Now, you know damn well I'm always ready to knuckle up if need be. I ain't going out like no chump. LOL. However, I didn't get that "stranger danger" vibe from him. He wasn't forceful or anything, he gently led me to the room. As, I looked around the room "This is very nice."

"Yes. Yes, it is," he said, standing behind me. Bitch! He was being creepy like one of those fine sexy-ass vampires in those Cinemax movies. He was so intoxicating. I think it was the way his body chemistry was mixing with his cologne.

"May I kiss you?"

"Hold up, playa." I grabbed his face and told him, "Open mouth."

He chuckled and said, "Ahhh."

I looked inside his mouth and lips. "Okay. Sure."

"What was that for?"

"Cold sore check, slim."

"I have never ever in my life…"

"Yeah, well, first time for everything."

After his laugh fest, he leaned in and kissed me. Baby! Hunni! Love! This man. This man! That boy could kiss! He began to get a little touchy-feely and I stopped him.

"Um, boo, I don't fuck in clubs. At least not this one. If it had a yacht docking station then that would be another story."

He laughed and said, "Okay, cool. I totally understand. Forgive me."

"It's cool." I pulled his face to me and kissed him again. "Now let's go."

"Ya know, that's a great idea."

"Um, sir, I meant leave the room. I am *not* going home with you!"

"Damn you're fast."

"Yes, dear, I know. It's a part of being cute and in control. Try it on me!" I said as I walked out the door.

He laughed. "You are a trip."

"You have no idea."

As we made our way back upstairs, he said he needed to use the restroom. I knew what that was about. That joker needed to readjust. He was on brick. Those little Speedo skivvies he had on began getting tight in the front. Girl, I was cracking up.

Now, the deejay was playing that good old Mariah Carey, featuring Twister "One and Only, Part 2." You know that's my hip rocker right there. That base and that beat. Rodney know he did THAT! By now I was back on the dance floor, feeling it and slightly queening out. This girl started dancing with me. She was low-key feeling me. She could not take what these hips and body were serving, though. I think she thought I was gone back away. No, ma'am, I love a good challenge. Especially if I can dance with you and vibe off you; I'm good. My favorite verse: *"You got my body lit up like the moon."* You know the fellas loved the fact that I was dancing with fish. They were so hyped. "Get it, Christian! We see you!"

Fish tried to show off and hit a little dip-spin on me. Now this chyle was doing too much, but okay, girl, I see you. Who's watching all of this? That damn Sye! I had dismissed her and was just grooving and bouncing to the music. I was all in the moment. That song always takes me away. It's very euphoric for me. I don't know why, it just is.

The song went off, then he started mixing. It was a nice mix, too. Sye came over and started old school dancing. He was too much. Now if he would have got his big ass on that floor and started break dancing, I was gone leave the floor. Doing entirely too much. I shook my head. He laughed and led me to the bar side.

He whispered in my ear, "I want to taste your sexy-ass lips so bad. They just look so fucking juicy."

You know I was clutching my pearls because I was slightly turned on. Yes! He made me blush and I said, "Maybe one day, if you play your cards right," and winked. "And is that CK1 you have on?"

"Yes. How you know?"

"Oh, sugga, Uncle Calvin is one of my top three favorites when it comes to the fragrance game. He has me on lock!"

"Uncle, huh?"

"Oh, yes, sir! No mistakes."

"Tell ya boys you're going downstairs with me for a few minutes."

"Um, okay. Sure."

I told them and of course, D got in a slick remark, talking about, "Aye, that pussy is on fire! You'd betta be careful before you fuck around and set one of these alarms off in this muh'fucka!"

Shaddup Jerk!

Sye and I go downstairs to the other bar, which is damn near empty. Everybody's upstairs partying and drinking. You know I have a short attention span when music is in the background. As we're chatting, I was still rocking my shoulders and grooving a little bit, when he grabbed my hand and said, "Follow me."

Girl! He was leading me to the same room that Richard took me to!

"Hold fast," I told him. "Let me use the restroom first." I had to do a quick check and reapply lip chap. Made the lips extra juicy. Ow!

I came out of the restroom and glanced over and saw Richard standing outside with his friends talking and laughing. Sye came back and said, "A'ight, let's go."

I followed him into the same room, and we sat down in the booth and continued talking. This time, he's looking directly at my lips. He leaned in and smelled so damn good. That CK1 was doing him right! He kissed my neck, my cheek, and made his way to my lips.

This fool said, "I knew them lips was good! *Yeah, boy!*" He proceeded to tell me how good I smelled as well.

"You say it like you're shocked."

"Well, you were dancing off and on."

"Um, yes, but I was not dancing that hard. I don't do that." He asked me what I had on. "A number of things." I actually had on my Bath & Body Works lotion with my Uncle Ralph cologne. That good old *come her Big Zaddy* essence.

"Nice. Real nice. So, what do the rest of you smell like?" He stood up.

"You'll have to wait and see." I smiled and winked.

So, I stood up because I thought we were getting ready to walk out of the room. Yeah, no. He pulled me into him and started kissing me. Baby! This time I low-key melted. He did it right. He had those thick hands all on the small of my back, and then he moved up my back and started gripping my hair.

Bitch, listen! When I tell you he almost got the drawz, baby. GTD! I had to stop myself before he had my legs in the air with his hands in my hair.

"We can't do this," I told him.

"Oh yes, we can. Ain't nobody gone come in here. I locked the door."

"Oh no, sir, we can't. I don't fuck in clubs unless there is a yacht docking station."

He laughed. "I believe you."

As we were walking out of the room, we ran into D and the fellas. I was a bit flustered. That was all I needed; for those clowns to seeing me looking flustered with Sye's big ass walking behind me, smiling like a damn Cheshire cat. D burst out laughing, followed by the other two. UGH. I just shook my head. By now it's close to three in the morning and we are freaking hungry. As we're walking out, heading towards the door, guess who is still standing outside talking to his buddies? Yup, you guessed it—Richard.

I turned, hugged Sye. "Hit me later when you're free."

"Oh, most def, baby, I got chu."

I backed up a little bit so I didn't seem so obvious when I walked past Richard. I just knew he was going to stop me and say something. *Boom!* He grabbed my hand. "Don't leave yet," he said. "Let me holla at you."

D and the fellas said, "Catch up."

I'm standing there thinking how much of hot box Harlot I am (but way cute) for having scored twice in one night, just seconds apart. Not bad if I do say so myself.

Richard and friends said their goodbyes and we turned and walked away.

"Where do you live?"

"Killeen. I needed to be close to the base since I was new to the area."

"Oh really?"

"Yes, why?"

"One of my offices is in Harker Heights. You know where that is?"

"Yes, my god-sister lives on that side. I'm familiar."

"Cool, I'll let you know when I'm done work tomorrow and you can give me your address and I'll stop by before I go home."

"Sure. No problem." I look up to see the fellas just a few feet ahead of us by the taco truck. We were near the area where Richard had parked, which was by an alleyway near an abandoned building. When I laid eyes on that sexy piece of car candy, my nipples got hard again.

Yes, God! Baby, listen! She was just parked so effortlessly, glowing under the streetlights. He looked at me started cracking up.

"You really like my car, don't you?" He was still laughing. "You are something else."

I burst out laughing. "I know. I really do. I can't help it. They are just so sexy, casual, sleek, and simple with the right touch of elegance. Not to mention this color. Whew, Lord. Come on, somebody! Hmph!" I stomped my foot.

He was just tickled pink at me.

"Unlock, please." He did with the quickness. He opened the passenger side door and sat slightly in the passenger seat so I could fondle the interior. Richard kneeled between my legs and sniffed.

I giggled. "What are you sniffing for?"

"The essence of you."

"Oh no, baby, that's ball spray and other things to keep away orders and sweat. I'm good."

"Yes, you are. My damn."

"I know, right?"

He kissed my forearm and rubbed my inner thigh.

#Pause Now you know damn well I had to stop him, right? The car already had me feeling some type of way. This joker is gone make me "hunch" him in this alley because of what his car is doing to me. I'm such a materialistic tramp. But I'm okay with that! *#Continue*

"Stop it, Richard."

"What?" He flashed his sexy, devious smile, flashing those pretty teeth.

"You are so not slick."

Child, this joker opened my legs some more, pulled me to him and started kissing my neck. "You really don't want me to stop do you?"

#Pause Bitch! What the fuck was going on tonight in Austin, Texas! This culo of mine must give off the scent of fuck Christian the way he likes but in public. Uh, no ma'am, sir!

What the hell is going on here? Yes, bitch! I like it. No, I don't want him to stop. However! You will *not* have my ass all on candid camera in public being a tramp. UM NO! *#Continue*

"I don't, but you have to. We are in public, sir. I don't do that in obvious spaces or places. Besides, this would be so fake. Your car is turning me on and not you. Well, you are, but your car started it. Stop it!"

"Okay. I'll stop for now." He smirked.

"Well, this was fun, but I've gotta go and you've gotta go."

"Oh, so you gone just cut me off, huh?

"Damn Skippy. Now you have a good night. I'm going to find me something to eat, and not from no damn taco truck. Ugh. Call me later."

I hugged and kissed him. As I began to walk away, he said, "I mean, I could eat, too, if that's an invite."

I slightly turn to face him. "It wasn't, but it could be," I smiled. "I have no idea where they want to eat, if anywhere. I think they ate off that taco truck. Let me ask and see."

"Thank you," he said in a flirty way.

Well, they didn't get anything to eat off the taco truck because they didn't have anything they wanted. The cute light skin chubby one (Kirk) suggest we go to The Pancake House. I texted Richard to tell him that they suggested The Pancake House.

So, we got to The Pancake House near our side of town in Harker Heights and Richard pulled up about five minutes after us. They all burst out laughing.

"What are y'all laughing at?"

"Christian! How are you gone just invite these strays to have breakfast with us, though? We don't know him!"

"Boy, shaddup!"

Richard heard D and said, in a much laid-back, low-key voice, "It's my treat. How about that?"

"Aye, welcome to the family, bruh. I'm D. Nice to meet you."

Richard was cracking up and introduced himself to everybody. We sat in the back of the restaurant, talking, laughing, and eating for two hours.

You know I love my military fellas and their mouths. Just rude as hell! No cut cards and straight forward. It tickles them that I can hang with them and be just as sharp and rude as they are. We really had an enjoyable time shooting the shit.

As we were about to leave, I got a text from Sye asking what area I lived in. I told him, and I told him where we were. Low and behold, he lived one complex over from me, so he knew exactly where we were and where I lived. Girl, yes! Only me. All I could do was shake my head and laugh.

Richard offered to take me home and told the fellas they could go on their way. They made sure I was good before they pulled off, which was cool of them. As Richard and I are pulling into my complex and I gave him the gate code, he began to unbutton his shirt. I really didn't think anything of it because it was oddly warm for that time of the morning. He went from buttons to shoes.

I laughed. "Are you hot flashing or what?"

He laughed. "No, just getting comfortable."

I smirked. Yeah, okay...comfortable."

I thanked him for being so cool and bringing me home. He looked at me with the coolest, sexiest look, and said, "You are going to be my one. So be ready."

#Pause BIIIIITTTTCCHHH! Like Really? Now you know I was taken aback by that. Not only what he said, but how he said it. I know that look—that *I'm smitten with you and low-key in love with you* look. Here we go. *#Continue*

"Your one?"

"Yes. My one. Don't worry, we'll talk about it later."

"Hmph, okay. Well, I'm going to get in the shower and crawl in my bed. Thanks again. I truly appreciate it. Can you be so gracious and unlock my door please?"

Well, he unlocked the doors but told me not to move. He got out first, went to his trunk, and came around to my door and opened it.

"Thank you."

"Is this parking space okay?"

"Yes, that's fine. Why?"

"I want to walk you to your door."

"I'm on the second floor, but sure."

We walked to my door, I unlocked it, and he entered. He was telling me how nice the place was and asked if I mind him looking around. I said, "No," as I darted to the bathroom. I think I was in the bathroom all of three minutes. I came out and guess who's laying in my bed ass-naked? Love, I turned right back around and went back into the bathroom. I was not about to play with him. I sat on the toilet and laughed. I turned the water on so he couldn't hear me laughing at him. Like really? Oh, he's a smooth one. He knew I was *not* gone put him out either. I do *not* allow just anybody in my bedroom, let alone my bed. Then on top of that, he didn't even shower before he laid his ass on my sheets. Ugh! That's a big no-no for me. But since I already knew he wasn't funky, I let it ride. I got in the shower anyways, brushed my teeth, pinned my hair up, came out of the bathroom and he was sound asleep.

I'm not gone lie, I straight exhaled. I was *not* in the mood for that. Even though he smelled good, it was still hot outside and I am *not* a fan of musty balls in my face. It's a *no* for me. Look, it is what it is.

That afternoon was very interesting, to say the least. Especially since I was awakened by his phone going off nonstop. He was dead to the bed and didn't hear any of it. I was like, *Dude, really?* I woke him up to give him his phone. I glanced over my shoulder to see Sye's number in his phone. What the fuck was going down right now? My heart dropped.

I'll talk to you later, Love. I gotta go.

Double kisses.

26 FISHER ISLAND

Good morning, Love,

Girl, you know I was coming. I figured I'd give you all the scoop on my Memorial Day weekend exclusive with Chef Mekio and the Speegals all at once. Baby, the way it all went down was no joke. You already know Mr. Speegal called me to facilitate another party. It's no biggie that he wanted me to fly to Florida for this one as well. You know how he does. I get that 911 text followed up by the email and it's on. He plays no games. The bag was packed, the driver was waiting to take me to the airport. Oh, hunni! Sir Speegal is large and in charge! As usual, I was running through the airport until realized I was rushing for no reason. I was flying private charter, so it was no need for me to be busting a sweat, trying to make sure I made it to the gate on time. I know, it never fails. I'm always running through the damn airport. I don't feel right if I'm not.

I get to Miami and check into my suite, which, by the way, was filled with roses and multi-colored tulips. He's so dope and knows the way to my heart. The arrangements were so beautiful. The view from my room was so beautiful, especially at night. I could see the beach, as well as the sun rising and setting. I absolutely loved it.

Once I was settled in, I freshened up a bit and changed my clothes. Then the driver took me to Mr. Spee's home on Fisher's Island. Baby, that was the first time I had learned who, what, when, where and how of Fisher's Island. It was absolutely breathtaking. As we drove through the gates, I gasped at the views and the water surrounding the property. Everything was beautiful. The way the palm trees swayed in the breeze from the ocean, the infinity pool looking like it was merging with the ocean, and the driveway wrapping around the fountain in front of the house. Just absolutely gorgeous. Naturally, I immediately focused on a dinner party and entertaining. As I snapped out of my imagination, I saw Mrs. Spee; just like clockwork, she ran right up to me and hugged me so tightly (as she always does). She could not wait to give me the tour of their new home. And you know what? I was there for it, hunni.

She was teasing me the whole time, knowing I wanted to see the kitchen more than anything. She took me all over the house, saving the kitchen for last. She knew I was going to flip when I saw those beautiful, star bright galaxy granite counter tops accompanied by stainless steel appliances, topped off with a super-fucking-fabulous gas stove. Oh yes, God! She fell out in laughter when I turned around and saw that stove. My face lit up. It just glowed in all its six-eyed glory, with a grill in the middle. Oh, my sweet baby Jesus! Life. Was. Received. I exhaled. We made our way to the patio that was decorated with a beautiful slate stone; where the chef was grilling lunch. They had a very nice outside kitchen area set up. The grill was gas and encased in the slate stone wall with a cute cover. The kitchen had all the bells and whistles. I really wouldn't expect anything less from them.

The chef was cooking his ass off, too. Girl! He was fine as hell! Old thick, sexy self. He had a beard, bald head, some belly and was over six feet. If Tony Soprano and Kevin James had an Italian-Russian love child, it would've been him. I wanted some of him! Whew! Okay, let me focus. I'm back now.

The Spee's and I were discussing the details of the party that was going to happen the following night. I wanted to get a full understanding of what they wanted and the areas where guests were allowed. We talked through everything, signed the contracts and ate that delicious lunch chef prepared. His chocolate mousse was everything. My Lord.

You know I love me a piece of good old sexy ass chocolate

mousse. Let the church say Amen! He put his fat fingers all up and through that thang. Humph! It was damn good. My inner fat boy was totally pleased.

Once we finished with lunch and the quick overview, the driver took me back to my hotel and I hung out for the rest of the night with one of my buddies that lives in Miami. He took me to a couple of the cute little live and hangout spots. Chyle, he had me all up and down those South Beach strips. Wet Willies was lit! I had no idea it was like that. I guess Luda was right in all of his songs where he's mentioned it. HA! Love, I didn't get back to my room until six-thirty the next morning. I'm glad I don't require much sleep. I would have been dead to the bed by the time of the event. Just a hot mess. I'd definitely do it again, though. My alarm went off about five-thirty in the evening, but of course, I was awake well before then. I woke up about two-thirty. I needed to go to the mall to find a cute pair of sneakers. I came back with three bags of shoes and no sneakers. Um yeah, moving on.

By the time I was done prepping and packing, it was time for me to get ready. I hopped in the shower and no sooner than I got out, the driver was calling me to tell me he was downstairs. So now, I had to put a little pep in my step and make sure I was fully packed and ready. I must admit, even though I'm not a fan of all-black, I pulled it off quite well. Of course, I had my boy shorts in my bag, along with my sarong and off-the-shoulder top. I'll tell you about that in a few. I can see your face. So as Johnathan, the driver, was taking me back to the Spee's residence, he and I chatted for a few. He was telling me how long he had been a chauffeur and how much he loved his job. Johnathan had been driving since he was sixteen years old and has loved it ever since.

You know I was not here for that. You know how much I hate to drive. Ugh. The fact that he does it all day every day. No, ma'am, sir.

He laughed when I told him how much I hated driving and bless his heart. He's been driving for many years for quite a few big names in Hollywood and some major VIPs. He was very cool and quite the comedian.

We pulled through the gates of the "Spee Estate" and I swear I think I fell in love with the property all over again. Just so much epicenes in one place. My Lord. The valet, who was a cutie pie, greeted me. Before I got out the car, I had to flip the switch and get into my *young sexy mogul* mid frame. You already know what that means. I did a face check, reapplied the lip, flipped my goddamn hair, adjusted my shades, turned up my glow another notch and pressed my way to the front door.

Even Johnathan said, "Well damn!"

I said, "Exactly," and winked.

I made my way through those huge gorgeous glass doors as the wait staff greeted me with wine in a flawless red wine goblet (the work of Mrs. Spee). As I was walking through the foyer, I heard people laughing and conversing, growing louder and louder as it was accompanied by some old-school jams, i.e. Earth, Wind & Fire. I knew I was in the right place.

Mr. Spee loves his EWF. As I made my way into the lounge area—or what was made into the lounge area of the first floor—everyone had already undressed or was in the process.

Yup! You guessed it, doll. It was a swinger's party. Of course, I knew what it was. That's why they called me. I mean, really.

Mr. Spee came right over to me and introduced me to everyone—as his robe came undone and all his naked ass was out. Not that it phased him one bit. Then here came Mrs. Spee with her naked ass, coming to hug me, too, chyle. I laughed. Apparently, they have mentioned me to the other guest as well. A few faces I remembered, but the others were new to me. I received quite a few "I've heard so much about you" type statements and comments from various guest. It was cool. A little weird considering the environment, but cool, nonetheless.

As I was making my way to the kitchen, Mrs. Spee followed me down the hall and told me there was someone in the kitchen she wanted me to meet officially. Okay, no problem...

"Damn! Who is that? He fine! Whew shit now! Oop. Sorry," I said, covering my moth in shame and embarrassment.

She laughed. "His name is Chef Mekio."

Now you know Mrs. Spee was not going to pick no ugly man to be in her kitchen cooking for her or feeding her hunni. Truth be told, she nailed this one (no pun intended). That man know he was fine. Every bit of six-three, two hundred thirty-five pounds, and all bear. He had a close cut, full beard, tight high butt, thick thighs, some belly and I was ready to hunch! The way I was ready for him to filet my mignon... Baby! Thank God he didn't see me ogling him and lusting for him. He was already cooking and doing his thing.

Mrs. Spee is so damn simple; she closed her robe and walked over to him. "Vlad, darling, this is Christian. This is my sweetheart I was telling you about. He's our facilitator for the night and he's going to be in here with you as well. Make him feel welcomed. I love you both, so I need both of my babies to get along."

Chyle, yes, she was tipsy already. He turned around, looked at me and had the prettiest smile. Why did he have dimples in those adorable cheeks? Yup! That's it. I was ready to be a hot box harlot in the kitchen, on top of the counter and in front of everybody. Again, not one fuck was given.

He responded in a heavy Russian accent. "Well hello, Christian. I've heard a lot about you. Very nice to meet you. Please, whatever it is you need, just say the word and I'll take care of you."

Now why the fuck did his ass have to go and say that shit to me? The way my body warmed up and my eye started twitching.... My response?

"Okay great. Thank you so much. I'm going to hold you to that, Chef Mekio," I said, giving me a flirty smile.

"Please do." He flashed that smile at me again. Baby listen, the way I was ready to...never mind.

"Now that you two have met, I can be on my way. I need another drink. Christian, once you're all settled in, sweetie, come find me. I have the coconut oil you asked for."

Mrs. Spee whispered in my ear how she though Vlad played for my team and how she thought he would be perfect for me. Then she twirled away down the hallway as her robe flew open again. She's too much. I was cracking up. That lady tickles me hunni. And as far as him playing for my team, oh hunni, he was.

I yelled to her as she was walking down the hallway. "Well, we shall see. You know I'm going to find out!"

She laughed and yelled back, "I know you are, my darling, I know you are!" I smirked and shook my head.

As I was setting up my area, Vlad was looking at me. Every time I looked up he was looking at me smiling. So I asked him, "Why do you keep smiling at me? With those adorable dimples."

"I've never met anyone like you before."

"And you still haven't."

"What do you mean?"

"You really don't know me. Then again, I'm not sure what Mrs. Spee has told you."

We both laughed.

"She said you were adorable, cute, smart and you get shit done."

"And she's right."

He proceeded to tell me that there was something about me that he couldn't quite pinpoint.

"Is that a good thing or no?"

"Oh no, Christian, it's definitely a good thing. I just don't know what it is yet."

"Oh, okay. Cool. Well now that I'm all set up, if you'll excuse me, I must go change and get ready to do what I do. I'll be back shortly."

"I'll be right here cooking and waiting."

Love, I smiled and had to walk away from him. I was two minutes from letting him beat my cakes in that damn pantry.

I walked into the lounge area to find Mrs. Spee so I could change my clothes, and baby, she was getting her entire life with her wine in one hand and her robe in the other. Yup, she was ass naked and not one care in the world. She saw me and ran over to me and hugged me again. She told me to go up to her room to change. I was thinking, *Lady, if you don't get your naked ass off me.* I swear she just liked hugging me naked because she knew it slightly freaked me out. I laughed and shook my head.

Her husband was laughing. "Christian, you better not be trying to cop a feel off my wife's rocking ass."

"Boy, gone somewhere. Hell, I need to be more worried about her frisky ass feeling me up."

The room erupted in laughter, hunni.

I made my way up the stairs where there were more people and the essence of sex was stronger in the air. So, being my nosy ass self, I was going to see what was going on in one of the rooms. GIRL! I cracked that door open and that "black bull" was smashing them heffa's off!

I had to back up, though. I didn't want nothing squirting in my eye. He was cute, too. Big old sexy piece of man candy. Had muscles with a killer six-pack, close haircut and a bedroom bully. Ow! So, um yeah. Being nosy didn't last long for me. All that screaming being followed up with "Give me that big black cock!" was just too much for me. Like I just...yeah; nah, I'm good. Then there's the fact that I hate the word "cock," and this one chick just kept saying it repeatedly. That's what my ass gets for being nosy. Ugh.

As I was making my way down the hallway to the owner's suite, a heavenly scent of lavender, vanilla and peppermint was coming from the master suite. I kept walking toward the bedroom, and the aroma was getting stronger. I pushed the door open gently and there was an array of oil burners with essential oils burning on top of them. To the right was a massage table in front of the glass doors leading to the owner's suite balcony, surrounded by candles and very handsome masseuse. I could tell this was the work of Mrs. Spee. He had her name written all over him. His name was Marcus, another five-foot-eleven, two-hundred-pound sexy piece of chocolate man-candy, with a muscled toned body, a beautiful smile and a nice ass! His skin was so beautiful. He reminded me of those super sexy milk chocolate men you see in the "Men of Rundu" calendars. He was a sight to behold. He had a low-cut Caesar with deep waves that was lined up to perfection.

He looked up at me. "Are you my first victim?"

"Victim?"

He smiled. "Well, yes. After I rub you down, you'll be done and out."

"Sure! Let me go change and I'll be right out. Hell, if I'm gone be the first person, then I'm all for it."

I walked into that damn bathroom and I exhaled. It was fit for the gods. I mean, how one could not fall in love with this immaculate space was beyond me. A soaking tub sat beneath a huge window with steps leading up to it from the left side. The floor was covered in white and gray swirled heated Italian marble tiles. The overall look of the bathroom was very spa like. *His and hers* vanities, a separate shower; everything had nickel finishes. Baby, when I tell you my nipples were hard, and my mouth was watering. Then I had the nerve to look up and see there was also a sky light. Damn it! Be still my HGTV Heart. This was definitely a "Luxe master bath".

Once I stopped drooling, I changed into my "candy man" undies (you know, the ones with the sheer siding and back). They were a part of my all-black ensemble anyway so why not. I hopped up on that table so damn fast, he laughed.

Once he covered me with that sheet it was over. Those nice strong hands went right to work. Now I understand why sport players prefer men to be their masseuses. My Lord. His hands, his hands. I made him stop so I could turn on some music. I turned on Ms. Chante Moore. It was too quiet in there for me. I let her sing her face right on off as I was getting the ultimate rubdown. Between his hands, the smell of lavender and vanilla and Chante singing "It's Alright," when I tell you I was in heaven. My body exhaled and I moaned like a busy stay-at-home mom having her pinned up orgasm set free for the first time in six months.

I didn't even realize Mrs. Spee had come into the room to grab something out of the bathroom. I heard her fumbling around in the drawers, so I asked her, "What are you looking for lady?"

"The coconut oil," she yelled out.

"I have it."

"Ah! I knew I wasn't going crazy." Her drunk ass.

Then she proceeded to tell Marcus how he had better save some of those hands for her. I told her she could have him. I didn't even realize that he had been rubbing me down for the last hour. I got up to get dressed, which is where the all-black comes into play. I wear all-black so I can stand out, letting folks know I'm not up for grabs, so to speak. The rule is, anyone dressed in all-black is off limits unless told otherwise. Even though I'm supposed to have on pants, I do what I want, and they know it. Besides, it's still sexy, simple and all-black. I make the rules. So hey, they'll be fine.

I came out the bathroom and Mrs. Spee sat straight up.

"Lady, what is wrong with you?"

"Christian! You look amazing! Oh, my God! I had no idea you had such sexy legs and a nice collar bone!"

"You really need to let your body be free more often, sweetie. I mean, wow! I need the name of your doctor. You look fucking amazing!"

"Unhunh! Hold up! Thank you, Mrs. Spee. This body does pop severely, doesn't it?" I struck a pose. "Mrs. Spee stop it. You know I'm very shy and bashful about my body but thank you.

"Yeah, you do look really nice."

"Aww, thank you, Marcus."

"Okay, Christian get out! I want this chocolate Adonis all to myself. Come on, Daddy, and rub me down!"

"Oh, my God, Mrs. Spee! Goodbye."

As I'm walking down the hallway, I hear her yelling for me to let my hair down. This lady. Yes, ma'am! So anyway, I'm making my way down the hall to that gorgeous staircase and I hear that sexy deep accented voice telling me to "Be careful."

I look up and who is it? None other than Chef Mekio himself. I laughed and said, "Well, if I do fall and hurt myself that means I'll have to spend the whole month here in this beautiful house and I'm okay with that." We both laughed. "What are you doing up here, sir? I thought you were still cooking." He claimed he had to use the other restroom. I knew he was being nosy, too. That room was loud, and they were popping!

As we got to the bottom of the staircase, he caressed the small of my back.

#Pause Now look, we all know what that's the symbol for (if you don't know, pay attention). It's a symbol of familiarity or someone has a sensual interest in you. It's a private area of one's body (or personal space, if you will) and when a guy touches you there, it means he feels intimate or an intimate connection with you. He's showing you he's attracted to you and will usually pull you closer in the process. *#Continue*

The way those big soft hands and thick fingers went down the small of my back; I slightly arched just a little bit. (Oh, I did. I sure did. Judge ya daddy.) So anyway, we walked around the corner and I heard Mr. Spee yell, "Christian! Can I get some assistance please!?" I told Vlad to take my bag and sit it in the corner where my laptop was. I walked my lil cute ass over to the great room where he was, and I looked; this fool was in a sex swing and done got his ass stuck! Like, really sir? Really?! Love, when I tell you he was all tangled the hell up. How he did that I have no damn idea. People were trying to help get him unhooked, but most of them were too busy laughing or too tipsy to even focus. Mind you, this has happened before.

So I politely walked around to the rear of the contraption and pulled the little crank lever thingy and bam! He fell out the swing. He managed not to waste his bourbon and say, "Thank you." I said, "Anytime, sir," and walked back to the kitchen. Girl don't even ask. Last time Mrs. Spee got stuck and I had to do the same thing. He knows his little ass is not supposed to be in it anyways.

#Pause What's so funny about him, he's shaped like a "dum-dum."

Little body with a big old head and waffle bat in between his legs. That's why she's so in love. I ain't mad. It's cute, though. What? Well it is *giggle*. *#Continue*

I'm walking back to the kitchen and decided to get me a drink from the bar first. I asked the cute bartender for a coke with lemon but if he could hold the balls.

I'm not a fan of balls in my glass. Chyle (he had a mean pair of low hangers).

Matter fact, could you make that a Shirly Temple and add some vodka? He did.

So anyways, I walk in the kitchen and Vlad is talking to the deejay. How about I got a slight attitude, though (I know right). I think because of the body language between the two of them. She was cute. Actually, she was fucking hot! I just needed for her to back up out his face, before I punched her in one of her five-thousand-dollar c-cup titty's; because I know those aren't hers. I go over to the area where I was sitting (or my laptop was for that matter) and you know me, I'm sitting cute and perched. So, I crossed my legs and she noticed my sole-less sandal's and decided to bring her Becky ass over to my side of the kitchen. "Oh my gosh! Those are like so cute! Wow. I love those. Where did you get them from?" Now love, you know I'm really not featuring her but I'm going to keep it cute. I smile and say thank you (so fake). A friend of mine made them for me. She makes them for me for special occasions or whenever I just really want a pair. "Oh nice. You think she'll" … no. I don't give out my personal people's info; but thank you, though. Excuse me. I walked away and went to the restroom. Yes, I'm petty. So! I don't need any copycats. Ugh! Chef laughed and shook his head because he caught my shade.

As I'm walking back from the restroom, I heard Mrs. Spee holler, so I ran upstairs to see what's wrong. Mr. Spee's crazy ass was back in the damn sex swing, so I knew he wasn't going up there. I break and I'm running upstairs; I hear Mikeo's big feet ass following me. Chyle! We bust in the room and bam! Her ass in there getting knocked down by Marcus. I'm freaking out trying not to startle them. Chef is standing right behind me in shock as well. I'm just so taken aback by it. I was not expecting that. Oh, my God! But, baby, when I tell you he was giving her all the business! The way his hips were rolling, his stroke game was serious! I had to clench and pray, chyle. You hear me!

"Mrs. Spee, I'm so sorry," I said. "I thought something was wrong. My bad."

Leaving now. She responded with, "Oh, God no! You better fuck me the way my husband doesn't! You chocolate Adonis!"

All I could say was, "Uh-huh! Wait a minute!" But wait! Um Sir. Mekio did you just get hard and grind on me? "Sorry. This shit is hot?!" You know what?! I'm going back downstairs. Bring ya ass! I grabbed Mekio and he's laughing and cracking up all while looking and rooting them on. We're going back downstairs and I'm sure by now you can tell I needs me a real drink. I went back over there and told him to give me a shot of tequila. He laughed and said "oh, shit! Now you're talking Christian!"

I drunk the hell outta that drank and went back to my little area in the kitchen. Mr. Spee's little big head ass was over in the corner getting all his life. Wasn't even paying his wife any attention. He's getting head, his balls licked, and a titty in his mouth, just going ham. I said, "Lord knows, they are paying me more than enough for this, so I will deal!" I got another Shirley Temple and went back to my spot in the kitchen. Mekio came over and sat down in front of me and handed me a water. He could not stop laughing. Like he was really tickled pink by the whole situation. I crossed my legs back and sipped my drink. He grabbed my foot to get a closer look at my feet. "Yes, very nice. Very sexy. You have nice feet. Very soft." Why thank you. That's the work of a good Mai (wink). "What is Mai?" Lol. That's the Korean lady that does my pedicures and manicures. He let out the hardiest laugh. So, I'm guessing you caught that reference huh? Lol. "I did."

He lifted my foot and placed it near his crotch and began to massage my foot. "Christian tell me something about you. Besides how soft your feet are." Lol. Well, what would you like to know chef, and by the way, that feels amazing! He smiled and said good. "Tell me something that I don't already know about you." So, okay, let's see. Like I said before, I have no idea what Mrs. Spee told you already; but I'm just a chill, fun loving person. I enjoy my life and I take nothing for granted. I believe everything happens for a reason. The good and the bad. We live, we learn and if we're blessed enough, we experience love in all its truest forms and fashions. Was that enough? He smiled at me and said he didn't expect me to give a response like that, but he likes it. Well it's my truth. So now, which part of the military were you in? I'm going to guess and say either Navy or Marines. As he switches to my other foot, he laughs and asked how I knew. I said because most of you fellas have that aura about you. My dad was army and I have other family members, who cover all the other branches. You just scream navy to me. "Well listen to those screams because your right. I'm retired navy.

I did 32 years." Oh okay. Nice. You got a good benefits um... package (wink). He smiled and placed my foot right in his crotch and said, "Yes I do."

Baby! The way that sausage was packaged in those trousers. I couldn't do nothing but blush and blink. Now see, you gotta act up. I'm not fooling with you chef. Give me back my foot so I can get up and go make my rounds. As I get up from the table, while walking past him; he kisses my arm and I caressed his face where his dimple is. He got a big ass head, though. Bless his mother's heart if she had him natural. Whew! So, why do I walk into the other room (it's about 11pm) the deejay is kicking up the music and they are jamming ass naked. Everybody. Even the damn masseuse (I just can't). I work my way around the room and make sure everyone is comfortable and doesn't need anything. Yes chyle, even the deejay took her clothes off (well her top). And yes, I made sure she was fine as well (eye roll).

I go back into the kitchen to make sure chef was alright. He began setting out the food at the buffet for them to partake and just do what they do. That spread was beautiful. He had everything from fresh fruit, to fresh seafood, a mixed green salad, dipping sauces (chocolate & caramel) there were Kobe beef sliders, salmon & crab cake sliders. I said yup, the work of Mrs. Spee. I think my favorite part was the sweets table. The options were chocolate, lemon &

vanilla mini Bundt rum cakes, chocolate mousse and fruit tarts he made from scratch. Well actually he made all of it from scratch. I was so turned on when I saw that goodie table. Once we were done setting up the buffet, I made another round and went back into the kitchen. He was sitting down and this time I noticed he had on less clothes. He took off his chef's jacket and changed into his shorts. Oh, hunni Zaddy had guns! He was cut just perfect. Not over done or no muscle neck type bullshit. I sat back down in my chair and he grabbed my foot again.

You really don't have to do that. Although it does feel good; but you don't have to. "I know I don't, but I want, too. I love your soft feet and smooth skin. I'd love to go further if you let me." LOL. No, because I won't be able to focus and just my luck as soon as you get me going, her ass is gone want something. "I think she'll be okay. She won't even notice we're gone. All I need is 5 mins."

Unh-unh wait a minute! What the hell are you doing in 5 mins besides pissing me off?! He let out another hearty laugh and said, "Enough to make you mine for the rest of your life." LOL. I doubt it but okay. I'll be back, I hear her calling me.

I go see what Mrs. Spee wants (nothing as usual), as I'm coming back to the kitchen; Mekio grabs me by the hand and takes me upstairs. I noticed he walks on his tippy toes. It's kind of cute, though. As I'm following him up the stairs, I couldn't help but be somewhat intoxicated by his scent. He smelled so damn good. He guides me into this room that's dimly lit with a few candles. He hoisted me up on the tabletop; and from what I could make out; it was what seemed to be an office. At least that's what it looked like. Again, he placed his hands on the small of my back and pulled me close to him. He asked if he could kiss me. I grabbed his face and said, "Open mouth!" He opened his mouth and said, "No. I don't have any sores or anything but, how's my breath?" I laughed and said fine, we both have chocolate breath. He pulled me close to him and we began to kiss. As I wrapped my left leg around his waist and allowed him to kiss me passionately, I had to snap myself out of it. He made his way down to my neck; just like clockwork he hit that spot and my back arched. That's when I knew it was time to stop. I pulled away from him and told him to stop.

We gotta get back downstairs. They are not paying us to have an orgasm in their office. We both laughed and he said, "Just give me 10 more minutes Christian. I promise you; you won't regret it." As tempting as that sounds sugga, I can't, ten more minutes of you means 10 more minutes of me not keeping an eye on Mr. Spee . Besides, we have time. The night is still young. Now put me down and let's go. Chef leaned in and we kissed again then I jumped down and back downstairs we went.

As we were making our way back downstairs, yet again; I heard the margarita blender going. I knew then, the party was about to go to another level.

Whenever there are margaritas in tow; they get buck wild. I'm not sure what it is extra they add in them but boy oh boy! We got to the bottom of the steps and I heard chef say, "my oh my." I looked up and the lights were off, and they were completely nude getting down with the get down. The essence of sex filled the air and I was slight nauseous. I went back into the kitchen where I was sitting and laughed at chef being somewhat shocked. What's wrong sugga? You weren't ready? Yeah, he wasn't. Poor thing. You should have seen his face. Straight priceless.

As the night went on, they were doing their thing and we were in the kitchen just chilling, talking and getting to know each other. Chef was cool. He has some big feet, too. They were big and pretty.

We were in the kitchen prepping for breakfast (yes, it's an all-night thing) and I decided to change clothes again. I was getting a little cold. They had the air turned on morgue. Ugh. I told chef I'll be right back; I'm going to change. I decided to step in the brunch room slightly off the kitchen to change into a pair of my favorite jeans. I decided to keep on my shirt. You know me, any moment a hot flash hit's me it's over. I turn around and of course Mekio is in the window all smiles watching me. I changed into my butt crack cleeve undies and he seen it all. Lol. *Get your peek a boo ass out the window nosy!* Of course, he laughed again and kissed the window. While I'm walking back into the kitchen the smell of his "French toast creme Brule" was making my knees weak. It smelled so heavenly. I went and stood beside him as he was making the sauce to drizzle over it. He put some on his sexy thick finger and let me taste it. Good gawd! That man can go. I'm not surprised about my attraction to him. He reminds me of my uncle B. A cook that was in the military; was hella cool and mad respected. Yeah, definitely had some similar traits and ways.

As we were setting up the breakfast buffet Mrs. Spee made her way over to me to ask how everything was going between chef and I. I told her all was well and he's a total sweetheart so far. She laughed then responded "See. I knew he played for your team and I knew you'd love him. He's a hot piece of ass and so are you." Then she goosed me and went on her way. I swear I love she! LOL. So, by now it's about 4am and some of the guest are asleep, some are still going at it and the rest are just chilling and drinking. I made my rounds again to clean up and gather the trash etc. Chef was helping me. Of course, he had jokes about Mrs. Spee goosing me. Once we were done with the rounds; we went outside to do a garbage dump. The garbage area was in the rear of the house near the far-right side of the pool. I was immediately stopped in my tracks walking back to the house by the view of the water.

The breeze was so perfect, the way the morning dusk light bounced off the water and just the gentle rushing of the waves. My god, it was so perfect. I stopped to admire all of it. I had to. Mekio stood behind me; "It's peaceful, isn't it? Very calming and soothing." It is. It really is. I even pulled out my phone to take landscape video footage. There was no way I couldn't. As we made our way back into the house, Mekio ask me if he could have a hug. Not that I ever deny anyone a hug, it was just weird. I said sure. I hugged him and he hugged me so tightly. He said he just he wanted a hug and he knew I gave good hugs.

Which was cool because I do, but I don't know. It was just kind of weird. But not weird in a bad way. Actually it wasn't weird at all. I take that back, it was nice. He felt something. Just him seeing that, put something on his heart or reminded him of something, that made him need that hug. Like he had a moment or something. He squeezed me tight, too. Again, he smelled so good! We walked back into the house to finish prepping for breakfast. Mrs. Spee was in the kitchen brewing her coffee (which smelled good) and sitting at the table. She had showered and put on some clothes. Yes, I was shocked too. She usually doesn't do that until much later. Hey lady, how are ya? You alright? "You know what Christian, I'm good. I'm just glad that you were here with me tonight. I thoroughly enjoyed you my darling. As I always do."

Then she proceeded to give me a hug as well. Now, her hugging me didn't bother me so much. She's an affectionate person like me so I'm used to it. Even if she doesn't have any clothes on (oy vey). Of course, she made me sit down to have a cup of coffee with her. Not only did she have the kind of sugar I use, but she also had my favorite kind of "Sweet Cream" creamer. Again, I love she. We chatted for 30 more minutes than she got up and walked down the hallway, then disappeared. Mekio sat back down while the rest of the food was cooking. "Christian, she really likes you I see. She never talks to me that much, let alone is that affectionate toward me." Lol. She's a sweetheart. We've been working together a long time. That's why.

Are you ready to serve breakfast? I'm ready to go back to my room now. "Are you now? Are you tired?" No, I'm just ready to go back to my room and lay in my own bed. Not to mention shower. So, let's move this alone please and thank you. "Aye-yi captain." Oh, that was cute (eye roll smirk). We set up the breakfast buffet and they went in. Old greedy asses cleaned that damn buffet off! Love, it wasn't shit left! I said they asses done worked up a damn appetite, and they hulk smashed that buffet. Baby! We couldn't do nothing but laugh. We had our food separate in the kitchen. I made him put me some of that French toast to the side. Once again, chef Mekio did his thing. Food and pastries as far as the eye can see. He even had another one of my favorites. Bagels with cream cheese and lox. Yes, I would so marry him. The man can go hunni. He threw that meal together so fast. Yessuh!

Everything that I tasted was good. I think everything they tasted was good as well. I mean the buffet was empty. LOL. We were in the kitchen laughing hysterically from listening to Mrs. Spee put people out her house. Some had left already or took their food to go. The rest she was rushing and telling them to hurry up and get out her house. Like for real. She had no cut cards. She made us start cleaning up; which we were already doing. When I tell you mother had spoken, she spoke! "Y'all ain't gotta go home but you gone get the hell up outta here!" Chef and I kept on cleaning and once we were finally done Mr. Spee managed to surface. I have no idea where the hell he came from. I guess she freed him from his contraption. He came in the kitchen with us, had his coffee and ate a little. He then began to retire up to their bedroom but not before hugging me and thanking me as well. Of course; it's always a pleasure working with you all. "Okay Christian my darling. Your driver is here. I hope it's okay that you and Vlad are going to be sharing a car. I got you an SUV. Feel free to use the back seat as much as you like." Oh, my god Mrs. Spee stop it! And thank you, that's fine.

We were packing up our belongings and heading toward the front door when I heard Mr. Spee yell "Christian! My balls are empty and quite satisfied. Thanks kiddo!" All I could do was laugh and say your welcome. Mekio was laughing so hard he turned beat red. Then hit me with the slick remark "I wish you would have emptied my balls." Boy shaddup and let's go! Making our way to the SUV; I look up at the driver and he looks very familiar. I can't quite pinpoint where I've seen him before, but I know I have. You know me love, two things I do not forget; a man's face and his dick. Look, it is what it is. However, that face seemed very familiar.

I spoke and smiled at him (as I always do) as he helped me into the SUV; he introduced himself as Carlos. Mekio was putting our bags in the cargo area, then made his way to sit on the driver's passenger side. While we were pulling off, I couldn't help but to roll down my window and gaze out at that beautiful view one last time. "Christian, are you okay?" Yes chef, I'm fine. I just wanted to get another look. I simply love this. As we were making our way down the driveway and the view was becoming more and more distant, Mekio laid his head down in my lap and said he was about to take a nap. I laughed and said um, okay.

I heard the Carlos smirk and then I looked up and smiled at him as he was glancing at me in the rear-view mirror. I winked at him and put on my shades. No sooner than we were at the ferry to make our way back across the water to the mainland's, this fool was really snoring in my lap. Like really?! Myself and the Carlos were both like damn! I mean the ride from the Spee's residence to the ferry was all of 15-20 mins if even that long. "You guys must have had one hell of a night." LOL. We did. It was very nice, though. We've been up for the last 24 hours, so I think that's maybe why he's so sound asleep. As Carlos drove onto the ferry, he asked me "Christian, you don't remember me, do you?"

Your face looks familiar but I'm drawing a blank. Please forgive me. Where have we crossed paths before? "I drove you to another party in the Hamptons in 2000, and then shortly after that, I drove you to another party in 2007 here in south beach. I see you get around. LOL." Wow! You know all the business and right back at you sir! "I see life has been treating you well. You look good. You lost a little weight I see." Oh please, you don't have to be modest. I was fucking fat and you know it. Hell yeah I lost the weight. I lost a small family of 3! "Christian wow! I am being polite. Lol." It's okay sugga. I know how fat I was. That's why I dropped that shit. Ugh. But thank you for the compliment. Now, forgive me for not recognizing you. I've had so many different drivers over the years. "It's okay. I totally understand. I just remembered you because of your politeness and pleasantries. I see that has not changed." Oh gosh no. That will never change about me. It's deep and it's real. I believe you should treat others as you would like to be treated.

"See. That's why I remember you Christian. I don't come across many clients like you. Most are just rich jackasses who think people are their step-stools." Oh my. However, I'm familiar. I try my best not to be bothered or encounter those kinds of um, "people." Lol. As we pull up to my hotel, I noticed that Mekio is not snoring as hard anymore which means, he was lowkey ear hustling our conversation. Once Carlos gets out to get the bags, I wake Mekio up with a kiss on his forehead. He smiles and says "5 more min's mom." Lol. Yeah okay. I need for you to get your heavy head up off my lap so I can get out. He pops straight up and hops out the door. Carlos opens my door with the biggest smile on his face. Thank you kindly and why are you smiling so hard? "Christian, can I have a hug?" Of course you can!

As I'm hugging Carlos, Mikeo comes around to my side and stops dead in his tracks. Now he's smiling.

#Pause What the hell is going on with these two fools right now?! I tell you what! This will not be another Mexico rendezvous. They better get the hell on somewhere. They are cute, though. I did think about it. *giggle* okay no! #Continue

You good now sugga? "Yes Christian. Thank you so much." Sure anytime. You smell good too! Hmph. Alright now. And wait a minute, and why do you have your bags? Just where are you going? "I was going to go with you and take a nap before my flight." You are so not slick. Are you asking me or telling me? "I'm sorry. Christian, may I please go to your room and take a nap before my flight?" That's better. And yes, you may. You betta glad your handsome and smell good (eye roll). Anyways, thank you so much Carlos. Don't be a stranger. I'll be sure to let you know the next time I'm in town. "Please do. Take my card and keep in touch." I sure will (flirty smile). Now you enjoy the rest of your day and be well (wink). Yes, Mekio I'm ready. Let's go.

As we make our way to my room I couldn't help but to think about the Spee's and how I just love and adore them so much. So free, so happy and not a care in the world; let alone caring about what anyone says or thinks of them. That's the way to live. I just love it. As we entered the room, I dropped my bag and immediately walked over to the balcony. I stood on the balcony and just took it all in. I really love being around people who don't give a shit about what others think. Love you know that already. I could less about the purpose of the party. They were in the comfort of their own home, doing what they wanna do. The way it should have been. To each his own is what I say. If we could only get the rest of this simple ass world to be that way (to an extent anyways). Mekio got in the shower and then came to join me for all of five minutes on the balcony. He just wanted to make sure I was alright. Poor thing was so sleepy he could hardly keep his eyes open. He was literally dozing off while talking to me. I need for you to go'ta bed! He kissed me and then went and laid down. Our flight wasn't scheduled to leave until the next morning. "Mr. Chef" had plenty of time to rest. I wasn't sleepy just yet, so I decided to hop in the shower myself. When I got out the shower, grabbed my Crayola's, my coloring book and went right back to the balcony. Nude and all. The only thing I had on was coconut oil. Sure did. I have an excellent sun kissed glow on my skin.

After about 3 hours of coloring, I decided to climb in the bed beside Mekio (yes, I put some clothes on) and took a little nap myself. Hunni, he was snoring so damn hard he didn't even feel me kick his leg over (SMH).

I think he turned the air up so that I would snuggle up under him on purpose. He was so comfy and snuggly like, too. Just a big old bear and I was loving every bit of it. We woke up about 5 pm and went to dinner. Did a little bar hopping then we linked up with some of my Miami buddies?

We came back to the room had a few more drinks and the rest is a blur. What? I don't... I don't know what you're talking about love (innocent smile). It's a complete blur. We probably just passed out. Yeah. That's it. We just passed out (giggle). You know what though, I actually still keep in touch with him to this very day. We were on the same returning flight. He upgraded his ticket so we could sit next to each other. He flew into Dulles then made his way back to London. He called me as soon as he landed and then again once he was home. Yes, he is. Just a total sweetheart. As usual, the good ones don't live here. I would totally relocate if the love was real and worth it. Definitely. Please are you kidding me?! Ass to the wind and gone. Anyway, that's the story of Chef Mekio and how I met him. Now you can leave me alone. Which I know will not happen.

Hope that satisfied your curiosity about Chef. LOL. Nosy.

Anyways, I've gotta go Love,

TT4N.

-Sweet Kisses.

INITIATING THE BREAKTHROUGH TO THE HGIC

Good morning, Love,

I've been thinking about my story ever since you asked me to tell you about it a few months ago. Then, yesterday, while riding in the car with my parents down Interstate 301 in Maryland, as I was looking out the window, I couldn't help but think about my early childhood days, when everything started. One of the conversations we had was about my "lifestyle choice" and how I went about everything (no, not in a negative way). We were cracking jokes, to be honest. I've been truly blessed to have so many amazing people surrounding me, protecting me and making sure my heart was still intact. I think mainly because of how I am as a person. I lead with love. I've always been that way for as far back as I can remember. It just sucks that so many people think that because you're gay or a person identifies as gay, it must be something wrong with them or you must fit into this box. Well, we both know that's not me. Not now, nor will it ever be. I do what I want, when I want. Period. Nobody defines me or is allowed to define me without my permission.

Anyway, the weather was really nice. We had all the windows rolled down, the sunroof open, I had my shades on and the warm breeze was flowing through the car. It was just really nice. I brought that up because, in just that instance, I drifted off. I was sent into a nostalgic frenzy. My mind took me on a journey that lead me right back to "Nome Street", where my great grandparents' house was located, where I grew up. As I drifted off into this deep trance, I exhaled. Before I knew it, I was standing in the kitchen beside my granddad, watching him cook, smelling what he was cooking (breakfast) and I could see everything clear as day. The sun was shining so brightly through the kitchen windows; as my great grandmother was sitting at the table, drinking her coffee. Grams was cutting up veggies on the island to put into the omelets, and Pop-Pop was at the stove, stirring his grits while smiling and winking at me. It was so blissful. I was in my ten-year-old body again, totally at ease.

All the love in the atmosphere was just amazing. My grandmother and both of my great grands all in one place, doing what they do. Cooking, laughing and talking, all while just enjoying the moment. I was brought out of my trance when my dad turned the music up. I was instantly knocked back into reality. Although I was still in that flash back frame of mind, I went right to what triggered my new "I Don't Give A Fuck" attitude that kicked in around the age of sixteen years old.

If memory serves me correct (and it usually does), it was because of my mother, aunt and cousin who pushed me into that "HNIC" (or in my case Head Gay in Charge) mind frame. They put me through so much shit from the age of ten up until the age of sixteen. It was actually fifteen because once I snapped, they left me alone. Sixteen was the beginning of the new era (that's where B came into play. We'll talk about him later). Even though I knew at a very early age I was "different", they (my grands) were the ones who *always* made me feel *loved* on another level. Whenever I was with them, I knew, that not only was I loved, but I was protected. No matter what. I have not felt that way in a long time. Not to say that my family and friends don't love me or even protect me, but with the grands, it was just different. Remember when I was telling you about the whole blow up between my first older cousin and me? Well, that was the main reason of it.

There were other undertones, but the major reason was that she has always had something negative to say about me. Mainly because I didn't feature her, her constant drama or bullshit she had going on in her life. My cousin and my aunt played major roles in my attitude and the way I handled things in the past, also; the way I handle them now. We were constantly fighting and arguing nonstop. Love, you know that's not even remotely close to being me. Again, she and my aunt were both a part of my growth, so I'm not upset at all. I remember one day I came home, and as I was walking down the hallway to my bedroom, I overheard my cousin, while sitting in my mother's bedroom, say that she didn't like me. My mother asked her why, and her exact words were, "Because he's always so happy. Why does he act like nothing bothers him? We all know he's gay anyway. He needs to just come out the closet already."

My mother responded, "You got your damn nerve. As much shit as you talk and do to people." I had to laugh. She was right for once. She actually came to my defense. I was shocked.

My cousin didn't have anything to say after that but, "Whatever. At least I'm upfront about mine."

Yes, she really did say that out of her mouth. As time went on, my mother and I had a mini battle because she wasn't willing to come to terms with my sexuality. She made it about her. That's when we had our falling out. I could never pinpoint what caused all the drama. Then I figured out she couldn't deal with the truth or reality of it all. I knew what I was at a very early age. The gag is, so did my dad, uncles and grandparents. Ha!

I've always said, that as long as my grandparents and the men in my life were cool with it, I KNEW I was going to be fine. I know their hearts are pure when it comes to things of this nature. There were no undertones or bullshit later on down the line. The one thing my uncles did tell me that rings true to this very day; *"if you're going to be gay, we gone teach you how to fight. You're going to need it. These mother fuckers out here are going to constantly try you."* They told me no lies! I'm not too sure why my mother's opinions didn't matter much, but they didn't and still don't. I'll only ask her if I'm interested. Other than that, nope. I'm good.

I remember one day as I was walking in the house, I came up the steps through the front door and my mother started going off. I had no idea what was going on. She went on for a good five minutes about bullshit. By minute five, I had had enough. Then BOOM! We went at it. It was to the point where we were two minutes from fist fighting. I've never been the type to just let anybody disrespect me. That's the one thing Grams instilled in me. *"You don't kiss ass. If anything, you tell people to kiss your ass. Don't let nobody mistreat you. You never let anybody disrespect you. I don't care who it is. As long as you're right, then you're right."* She told me that when I was ten years old and I have not forgotten that to this day. So, when my mother started going in on me, I snapped the fuck off.

I had just turned seventeen years old and had been through so much. As a matter of fact, I was fresh off the birthday weekend. I remember it was May, because when this happened, I was coming home from a birthday lunch some friends had treated me to. There is nothing worse than having your mood ruined by someone who is just being rude and uncalled for, for no unforeseen reasons. I remember feeling like I was being attacked, yet again, by people who are supposed to love me and care for me.

I remember walking in the house, hearing her fussing at the house (meaning the people in the house already). I asked my brother, "What the hell is she fussing for now?"

"I don't know," he said. "Something about something being dirty."

That's when she turned that bullshit in my direction. I said, "Here we go!"

That's when she came at me full speed ahead. I knew it was either me or her and, *bitch*, it was gone be her. She got in my face and that was it! My brother and older cousin had to pull us apart. I was ready to tag her ass all up and through the first level of that house. Once they pulled us apart, I had to leave.

It was just too much for me. I pulled off in my car and just drove out to Bethesda to my happy place to calm down and talk to God. It helped me a great deal (as usual). When I got back home, Grams was back at the house (remember, she was living with us), sitting at the dining room table. She asked me what happened. I went in the dining room, sat next to her, and I told her what went down. She turned to my mother, who was standing in the other room, and told her to stop her shit. Grams knew I was gay. We just didn't talk about it. That was the thing with that generation; don't ask, don't tell (and that rule went across the board). She and I had an understanding and we were okay with that. She knew everything about me, as she should have. We always talked. There was NOTHING my grams didn't know about me. We were very open and honest with one another. Once everybody was calm and collected, we all sat down to have a talk. They confronted me and asked me questions, which irritated me because they knew the answers to the questions. Well not everybody, just my mother. Again, Grams said nothing. Just listened and sat beside me. I think my mother just wanted me to say it out loud. I would not confirm my sexuality for her. Not that I was afraid or anything, I just felt like it wasn't nobody's damn business who I was loving or sleeping with. I wasn't even sexually active, to be honest.

I'm still the same way to this very day. If you love me for me, then it shouldn't matter. Period. Anyway, so we were sitting down talking and I realized who the root of all of our issues were—my aunt and my cousin. They were saying all kinds of shit about me behind my back. Which, honestly, I wasn't surprised at all. That's what they did. Even now, they are still the same. Nobody in the family is really bothered with either of them or has anything to say to them.

My aunt has gotten a lot better because of her own issues and life experiences. They still talk to each other, but that's expected. Love, you already know how I am and how I can be.

I'm fine until you give me a reason to not like you, trust you or be bothered with you. Then, there's my intuition that naturally kicks in when I need it to as well. I'm always aware of the "what" and "who". Even if I don't say anything, I'm still very much aware.

#Pause What's really funny to me is the way everything came full circle. I'm one of those people that remembers how a person makes me feel and what they did to me to make me feel a certain way towards them. Every negative thing they have done to me or have said about me, I still remember. Don't get me wrong, I also acknowledge all the love and positives as well. It's just with them, their bad outweighs their good. Even though I have forgiven them, I can't forget it because it happened so much and for song long (until I snapped off on them, that is). I greet everyone with open arms and a pure heart, so it really bothers me when I'm treated badly (or well it used to shall I say) *#Continue* Anyway, we were talking, and she wanted to know all my business. I told her I was only going to say but so much.

I went on to tell her whether she likes it or not. "I'm still going to be fine and I'm still going to be gay (yup, I said it out loud). Get over yourself. What I need to know from you is, what the hell has your dumb ass sister and niece been telling you and why haven't you come to me yourself? How simple minded and silly of you to listen to what somebody else has to say about your child. We live together and you see me every day, and yet this is how you treat me. Really?"

Girl, she started to get upset and teary eyed. I passed her a napkin, told her to suck it up and spill it. I don't have time for tears right now. Grams tapped me on my leg and told me to relax and let her speak. My mother began to say how she was listening to my aunt and cousin because I wouldn't talk to her or tell her anything. My response to her was, "How can I talk to you when you're always yelling or arguing? You always turn a good day into a dreadful day, and you seem to know when something good is going on because you ruin it. So now, you tell me why I don't talk to you or tell you anything. Then, to add insult to injury, you listen to those jackasses that feed you more negative information than anything!"

#Pause As you can tell, the Phoenix is rising inside of me. My tone and my attitude with her has now changed. The whole dynamics of our relationship has shifted. I was afraid of this kind of confrontation at first. Now, it's undeniable and I'm ready to rock. *#Continue*

"I need for you to be a mother and act like you know. You know what it is with me and you know what's real. For the sake of *us*, let's not *ever* go through this again."

She agreed with me and apologized. Even my grandmother was impressed with the way I handled things. After we got over that, I made her tell me everything my aunt and cousin told her. Love, why did my mother tell me, my aunt and cousin were going around telling people all kinds of lies about me? Again, not surprised. They have always wanted to know more about me than I would ever let on. From my understanding, they took what they thought they knew, what they wanted me to be, then ran with it. I heard things from I'm coming to Thanksgiving dinner in a leather cat suit (I SWEAR TO YOU) to I was going to jump out the closet during a huge family cookout, I was doing drag, I was having and attending sex parties and orgies. Then, there was the whole thing with drugs and alcohol. I mean, the shit was hilarious. Even my grandmother was like "What the fuck?" It was freaking hilarious.

This is a prime example of how family can treat you. Everybody does not have your best interest at heart. These are people who I would have never thought would hurt me in such a hateful or mean way, then this. Freaking hilarious. I mean me in a leather cat suit. As fat as I was back then; bitch please! I would have had a dayum heat stroke just trying to get the dayum thing on. That would have been one FAT ASS PUSSY. And NOT in a good way either. LOL!

We talked about everything. I told her how I felt, she told me how she felt, and we came to a simple agreement.

"If you want to know anything about me, you just ask. If I want to tell you, then I will. If not, then I won't, and you WILL let it go." After she spilled the tea on those two tacky heffa's, we were good.

Grams and I started cooking dinner. She told me to turn the music on. I knew what that meant. We were getting ready to prepare one hell of a spread for dinner. We did just that. We had everything from baked chicken to green beans, sweet potatoes, corn bread and fresh rolls, cabbage, rice and gravy, macaroni and cheese, smothered pork chops and two cakes (strawberry and Rum) that sat beside a sweet potato pie. Right! We went the fuck in! Usually, when she cooked like that, it was because she was in a great mood or she was thinking. That conversation needed to happen between the two of us. My mother and I were on the same accord now, so all was well. Now I just had to confront those two dry face hussies that thought it was cute to be messy.

So now, cut to the age of eighteen. I graduated from high school, B and I were steady and strong; all was well. I was well into my own, working and life was going great. Everybody was getting along, no real or major arguments of any sorts. The summer was ending, and we were having our yearly cookout. Everybody was at the house, enjoying the festivities and fellowship. Me and B were sitting on the front porch when they pulled up. I'm sure my mother invited them because that's just how she does. When they pulled up, I said, "Oh gawd, here we go."

B asked me, "Are those the troublemakers?" He laughed.

"Of course it is."

They pulled up like all was well and everything was just oh-so peachy keen. Girl, I paid them dust. B and I kept on talking on the front porch while they went into the house. He was asking me about the whole situation and if we ever resolved it. I told him no because It was an ongoing thing. Whenever they show up to an event, the entire vibe of the atmosphere would change. That's never okay. That's only allowed if they were to take it to another level of positivity. Yeah well, they don't.

As time went on, my aunt got better because I had to step to her face-to-face. To the point where we were literally in each other faces, ready to fight at church (Smh. A whole mess).

No fucks on my part was given. She had pissed me off just that bad. You know how I am about respect and respecting God's house. Baby, when I tell you all of that went out the window that day. Whew! After that, she and I were fine. She knew her place and she knew she could no longer do those things to me or be allowed to utter my name in a negative light without consequences. Now, back to this other bitch. So, as B and I were still sitting on the front porch, talking and eating, my cousin decided she wanted to come around to the front and start with the slick-mouth shit. Love, now you and I both know I'm very slow to anger, but this bitch was steady poking at me and trying me.

As B got up to put our plates in the trash, she said out her mouth to him, "Damn! You big as fuck!"

He laughed and said, "Well, yeah, I've been that way for quite some time now. And who are you?" See, he had heard of her but had never met her in person. He knew who she and my aunt were, just never seen them in person. Yes, I did that on purpose. HA!

"I'm his older cousin and who are you? I think I know who you are, though. He doesn't have many male friends."

B laughed, then replied with, "Oh, so you just know everything about him, huh? That's wassup."

This heffa came back with, "I think gay love is cute. Don't you, Christian?"

I didn't even acknowledge her. I kept right on drinking my ginger ale.

#Pause Take a sip. This is where the shit is about to hit the fan. *#Continue*

So, as me and B were getting ready to go to the back with everyone else, I sat down to tie my shoe. He was standing next to me, waiting for me. He cracked a joke about me tying my shoe like a kid. I giggled and said, "Whatever, slim."

THIS BITCH!

"Why don't you just come out the closet already? Bitch, we know you sucking his dick. We know you taking it up the ass. Just come out already."

Love. OOOOHHHHH, LOVE! I was shaking my head. Mind you, she said all of this while standing in the driveway about two feet away from us.

B snapped, *"Aye! Yo, chill! What the fuck is wrong with you?"*

"He knows it's true."

Again, I laughed at her and shook my head. I said, "B, let's go before this bitch make me leap off this front step and kill her."

"You ain't gone do shit!" she said, and *then the bitch spat at me! Baby! Whew, glory!*

#Pause Now spitting is the *ultimate* disrespect you can do to *anybody*. Also, spitting on someone is a second-degree Assault in the state of Maryland. Not that I really gave a damn about pressing charges because now, this *bitch* was about to catch these hands. *#Continue*

It was like I was in the *Matrix* (B's words not mine). I saw it coming at me in slow motion. I swerved and jumped up, but before I knew It, I was on top of her, punching her in the lips and slapping her across the face. I remember dragging her across the lawn while punching her in the face. After that, I blacked out. I don't remember anything after that.

Usually when that happens, it's because I was so mad or angry; that my body's way of dealing with that rush of emotions at once is to shut down. It's like my nerves are in a ball so I pass out. I don't like to fight or have any form of confrontation because of the way it makes me feel during and afterwards. When I came to, I was in the house on the sofa, Grams and B were by me. My godfather was in the kitchen and my cousin was outside with her father. Apparently, I did more damage to her than I cared to remember. As I sat up on the side of the sofa, B was laughing and Grams low-key chuckled. As she closed her bible, she asked me how I was feeling. I told her had a little headache, she passed me some water and an aspirin right away. It was like she knew what I was going to need (not that I'm surprised or anything). Like I said, she knows me.

As I drank the water and took the pills, my godfather came over to me and sat down beside me. He told me to shake it off. Actually, he said, as he put his arm around my neck to pull me close, "Shake that shit off. You did right. You don't never let nobody disrespect you like that. Fuck her!" He kissed my face and walked back outside.

Grams followed up with, "I've told you many times that she wasn't right, and you must watch her. I don't condone you all fighting, but I'm glad you stood up for yourself. That little rude winch makes me so damn sick. Don't you tell her I said this, but good job." Then she got up and walked back into the kitchen area.

This fool, B, sat down beside me on the sofa and was in tears from laughing so hard.

"B, what the hell is so funny?"

"Yo, babe. I didn't even know you had it in you. You moved so got damn fast, I thought I was bugging for a second. Like, it took me a good minute to get myself together to try and pull you off her. You straight punished her! Babe, *you punished her!*"

"Oh, my God! B, please stop," I said, as I grabbed his leg and tried to hold back tears.

He was telling me what happened, and I began to cry. I couldn't believe I had to actually fight her. Not just fight her but fight her the way that I did enough for me to blackout. It was different with my aunt and my mother. It wasn't that bad. This? This was bad. I know, but it just…Yeah. It shook me. B told me to calm down, it was okay because she drove me to the point of no return. It was built up and bound to happen. I got myself together, then I got up to walk outside. As I opened the door, Grams was behind me and B was behind her. I walked out onto the deck and everyone turned, looked at me and burst out laughing.

I wasn't sure what to think of that, so I started smiling. My uncle (her father) came up the steps and told me to sit down. My cousin was behind him. I sat down in the chair, B sat on the right side of me and Grams sat on the left side of me. I looked up and noticed my godfather was standing behind me. He placed his hand on my shoulder as a sign of comfort and telling me chill, I got cha' back. They all knew how extra my uncle could be when it came to us and his simple-ass daughter. My uncle opened his mouth with "Christian! What the fuck happened to my got damn daughter's face, man? What the hell was y'all fighting for?"

"I think you should ask your daughter what happened. The last time I checked, spitting on someone was considered a second-degree assault charge."

He turned and looked at her with the look of shock and awe on his face. This bitch flat-out lied and said, "Daddy, no I didn't!"

My exact response to her was, "Sweetie, you fail to realize I have no reason to lie. Why else would I come at you like that? You see, the thing about me is, they *all know me*. For me to fight you, or anybody else for that matter, I have to be pushed over the edge. You, well you're known for pushing people over the edge. So, when you spit, that was the "over-the-edge" moment for me. I'm not sorry and I don't feel bad," I said, even though I really did. "The next time I'm going to kill you. Now, I'm going to go mingle with the others. Goodbye." I got up and walked my cute ass right on down those deck steps into the yard with everyone else. Apparently, they had all heard what happened. I was out longer than I thought I was. B informed me later that I was out for a full two hours. He or Grams did not move until I woke up.

He said she sat there reading her Bible and talking to him between her scripture readings. My godfather called me up to the deck and told me to meet him in the front. As I proceeded to the front of the house, my bodyguard was on my heels. B would not let me outta his sight, hunni. He said this time he's ready. Yes! He had plenty of *Matrix* and Ninja jokes.

As we made our way to the front of the house, I told him to go sit in his truck.

I didn't mind him listening, just get out of sight. I didn't want my godfather to feel some kind of way. I know how he can be. B did just that; he went and sat in his truck. Actually, he went and wiped his truck down, which was a great idea.

My godfather and I were talking, and he went on to tell me not to worry about her. I did the right thing. That's not what he wanted to know. He wanted to know who B was.

I said, "Oh, shit. We'll talk about that later."

He laughed and said, "Oh, shit!" He was really cool about everything. He just wanted to make sure I was okay. "I called your dad and told him what happened. He just said, "As long as he's all right".

Wow! I guess everyone was okay with the altercation. Like they were all waiting on this day to come. Clearly, everybody in the family had had enough of her shit, too. Even her father (my uncle) got up and walked away once he found out the whole story. He told my cousin she had better be glad I didn't kill her. After my talk with my godfather, I walked down to the driveway to B. I told him what he said, and of course he laughed. I had had enough of them for the day. I hated that she ruined my mood, but it's all good.

I told him I was going to go in to say my goodbyes and then I'd be back out. As I was hugging and kissing people, I could tell they were relieved that I checked her. Just by the little slick remarks and comments they whispered in my ear.

My younger cousin hugged me and said, "I swear I love your ass."

I hugged Grams last on purpose because she was sitting in the house. I had to go back through the house to leave. She hugged me and told me to stay sweet and call her later tonight. She walked me to the door, and she yelled at B that he could have told her goodbye. He jumped out the truck and ran up to the door to hug and kiss his "Big Mama".

As we were leaving the housing development, I put my shades on, looked out the window and just drifted away for a bit. I couldn't help but think of what happened. Why is it that we must go through so much just to live and be left alone? People suck!

B grabbed my leg. "Hey. Where did you go?"

My eyes began to water up again. I reached in his glovebox to grab a tissue. I told him, "I don't like this. I don't like this at all. Why must people be so hateful? Just no rhyme or reason at all. I don't use the word *hate* in a serious manner unless I'm serious. I *hate* that people must fight for their freedom or just to be left THE FUCK alone. Family is supposed to protect you and love you no matter what. I have some family that love me no matter what. They always make sure I'm okay or doing fine and vice versa."

"Babe, you gotta chill. It will be all right. Look, boo, you know everybody is not going to be in your corner. Doesn't matter. Fuck them. I got you, you got me. Between Big Mamma, your dad and godfather and a few others, we got'chu. Shake that simple bitch off and rock the fuck on."

I smiled at him and said, "You are absolutely right."

"Hold Up! Where the fuck was your simple-ass aunt? The one that's always with her co-signing on shit."

"I saw her, she was with my cousin. One thing about my aunt, she's not going to go against everybody all at once. She's too needy for that."

"What you mean?"

"I mean she always has her hand out needing a favor. She's not going to go against my uncle or people who help her with her bills from time to time. She's a jackass, but she ain't no fool. That's how she works. However, she was definitely shook by all of this. I saw her talking to my cousin on the low. I handled her already. She won't cross me again. Then, on top of that; she knows my godfather doesn't like her too much anyways. So she really wasn't going to say anything to me or try me in his presence. The fight this time was the nail in the coffin. They won't fuck with me any further. At least not in my face or in earshot. It will all be said behind my back (where they better stay). Not that I'm going to turn my back on them, because I don't trust them that much. I'm good. Now, can we please go get me some lemon custard? I have a craving for some."

B smiled, leaned over, and kissed me. "Anything for my little Ninja." LOL.

From that day forward, it was a wrap.

I knew, in order for me to survive in this simple-ass yet evil-ass world, I was going to have to fight my way through it. Be it family, friends or just another ol' simple-ass mother fucker in the streets. I just can't be ruled by my emotions. It's okay to have a heart, just protect it at all cost. Change what I can change and except what I can't. Leave the rest in God's hands, allow Him to cover me and press forward. Ever since that day, my attitude adjusted. No, it majorly shifted. The new me was born. I fight tooth and nail for what I believe in. People are going to try you. Fight. Don't give in or budge. Keep your head held high at all times.

Those events are what brought forth the "HBGIC". I now own my destiny. It was a long road and I know I'm not done, and that's alright. No longer will I take to heart what people say or think of me. No longer will I feel sorry for myself or allow others to dump their bullshit on me. I don't give a fuck about what you think. Those same ones that talk shit about you behind your back, will smile in your face with their hands out, looking for you to help them out. Ha! No, sir, ma'am. I know who holds my tomorrow and I know who has my back.

No regrets no apologizes. Life will be lived.

Oh My God, Love! I think I needed that.

Thank you,

I'll talk to you later. Muah!

THE SLITHERING ZIRCONIA

LOVE!

Time for the nitty gritty you were asking about, hunni. Make you a cocktail and let's ROCK! Oh, I made time for you, boo. Are you ready? Good. Let's go.

So, remember you asked me why I fell out with the other group? My ex-best friend (if that's what you want to call her), the one I met freshman year of high school—YUP! Her. Let me give you some background. We met in high school in Home Economics class. We were being plumb fools in class and before I knew it, she and I just connected. Since that day we were pretty much inseparable. I mean, like seriously. It was so bad that we were known as the "Black Will & Grace." She really was my sister (or so at least I thought she was). As time went on, life happened to both of us, but we remained joined at the hip. Whatever she was feeling, I felt it. Whatever she was thinking, I would be thinking it, or I'd just come out and say it. Even finishing each other's sentences. We were so annoyingly cute. I thought she was that last diamond I needed to complete my tennis bracelet.

People loved us. They really did. We even had people assume she and I were married or even dating (right). We were really that close. We had been through so much together, so much I had taught her (yes, even about sex). As time when on, we drifted apart. I would not have thought I would ever see that day, but then again, I always follow my gut instinct. I was feeling like we were going to go our separate ways eventually. Those emotions got stronger within me when I relocated to Kentucky with my job. So, remember when I relocated to Kentucky back in 2007? Well I remember it well because that's when I was having financial issues and I was down and out. I was pretty much at rock bottom. When I got that offer to relocate, I took it. In the meantime, before that, I was working two jobs, hustling and staying with my aunt off "Larchmont", and sleeping on her sofa.

Yeah, it was rough. It made me stronger, though, I'll tell you that. Anyway, I stepped out, no, I JUMPED into Faith's arms and accepted the job offer. I knew it would be the beginning of me getting myself back together. I remember moving to Kentucky and thanking God the whole time for brand new mercies along with new opportunities (whatever they might be). I was ready to receive it all, hunni. I remember her boyfriend was even congratulating me on the come up. He was a little blown I had to leave because I was leaving him with her all by himself (LOL! Poor thing).

He had to deal with her twenty-four-seven now. I was the buffer for him. I was where he would send her when he needed a break from her. Hunni, I laugh when I think about it as well. It's all good, though. We were a little family. Again, so I thought (eye roll). So now, I was in Kentucky, I was working, and everything was going super well. I had myself a new place, I made friends and everything. I mean, I was in a great space in my life again. Everything was working out for me. I noticed as time went on, while I was in Kentucky, she would never come to see me or say anything about visiting. I was the one always going back home to visit and making sure we saw each other. I was the one making sure I kept in touch with her and making sure she was alright. Even the little Facebook post and messages I made would be to reassure her that all was well, and she was still my "BFF." Just cute little things along the way. I noticed I was the one making all the effort to keep us together and our friendship alive (which was the first strike).

I was in my place and decided I wanted to have a little party. I was going to pay for her (and her boyfriend) to come down for the weekend. I just wanted her to be with me and celebrate in my happiness.

#Pause I'll go into detail about her boyfriend later. He was now a part of the family as well. He was there for some major family events along with some mess on my end. He weathered the storm with me. He was for damn sure getting an invite to the party. He really was a class act. I could not be more grateful for him. I thank God for him on a regular basis. I'll go into more detail about how she screwed him over as well. *#Continue*

I had made friends with some fellas on the base. (We'll talk about them later. That's where "Beast" came into play). I was in a very nice, brand new, two-level and three-bedroom townhouse. I had more than enough space. I was excited about flying them down and just spending the weekend with them.

They were going to meet the crew and just enjoy. Love, you know how I am when I'm in "Entertainer" mode. I was going to go all in. I had new furniture, furnished all the bedrooms, brought food and everything. I was ready and super excited. THEN, I got that text: *"Sorry boo. We can't make it. We have another engagement to attend that we RSVP'd for".* My face cracked. My response was *Oh, Okay. I totally understand.* It took me a moment to catch it because I really had to step back and think about it. Why would she wait until one week out to tell me this? I'm glad she told me before I bought the plane tickets, which I was going to do that coming weekend. Well, I went on to planning my party. As I was walking through the grocery store shopping, I was thinking about everything that had happened. It dawned on me that there was some jealousy or resentment on her behalf. This was where strike two came into play. After a week goes by, I didn't mention it again; I didn't even talk to her, to be honest. So, her boyfriend texted me with *"Is everything good for the party? What airport are we leaving out of?"* BAAAYBEEY! My response to him "Now you say what now"? If you could have seen my face. I texted him and told him *"You need to talk to your girlfriend. She said you all were booked already. I moved on and filled your spaces"* (even though that was not true). I was just pissed that she didn't tell him anything or that he was asking me. I was like, who the hell dropped the ball and was that a lie? Yeah, I was pissed. You know damn well I was gone confront her.

I asked her, "What the hell was going on? Why is he texting me, asking me questions about the party, and you all already have plans? What did I miss?"

"We do have plans," she said. "It's with his friends. It's a house-warming party that he RSVP'd for. You need to be fussing at him and not me."

"No, you all need to talk to each other. Once you have it figured out, let me know. I have more things to do. Goodbye."

I hung that got dayum phone up, and I went on with my prepping for my party, making sure everything was in order. By now, I was a couple days out and needed to make sure everything was in its place. All I had to do was be home for the deliveries and set up. Oh, hunni, when I tell you I was ready to rock! Well, apparently, after that back and forth between me and her, I get a text from him that there was no "RSVP" party. He informed me that it wasn't that serious. They could have passed up the opportunity and came to Kentucky for a visit. He was HOET as fish grease about that. I told him he needed to work that out with his significant other. By this time, I was over it. Again, strike two. Now I'm officially giving her the side-eye.

So, cut to my party day; it was a beautiful Saturday, and all was well in Zamunda. LOL! It really was. The sun was shining, the weather was perfect. My house was clean, everything was perfectly in its place. All I had to do was pick up my little cute outfit for the night and welcome my guests. YES! I was ready.

Beast called me to see if I needed help with anything and to see what else he could bring. I just told him to bring whatever alcohol it was that he drank, along with more ice. Now, it's about 5:00 p.m. and I was on my way home from "Lord & Taylors" with my clothes. I got a phone call from "OUR boyfriend" apologizing. I told him all was well. No worries, it is what it is. I could hear the aggravation and disappointment in his voice. I paid it dust. Not today playa. I got plans. I hung up the phone and went to get me a drank at the bar next to the adult movie theater.

#Pause Remind me to tell you about the adult theater and my experience with that. Beast set me UP, child! Whew, Lord! SMH. *#Continue*

I had a drink, then chased it with ginger ale and went home to get dressed. I pulled up to see Beast sitting in his truck. I was curious for a second as to why he was there so early, but he's cool, so I didn't think anything of it. I got out to greet him and see what was up. He brought me a cooler full of ice. He sat it in the garage with a case of sodas and a mixture of alcoholic beverages.

"Okay, I see you, pappi."

He laughed and said, "Yeah. We ain't got time for that be cute shit you be drinking. I don't drink cocktails an' shit. I need some goddamn beer and liquor."

"Whatever. Thank you, though."

#Pause I know what you're thinking, but NO. I didn't. YES, I was attracted to him because of his body build (Black-Bear-Daddy type) and his personality. I think mainly because he reminded me so much of B. As much as I would have liked for it to happen between us, I was content with us being friends. He seemed more like a big brother to me than anything. Like the cool uncle or godfather type. Stay tuned. It may change later *#Continue*

"Thanks," I said, and then told him I needed to go make sure everything was ready and get dressed. "You're welcome to stay and chill, but I won't be much company."

"It's cool," he said, as he came in the house, sat on my sofa, popped him a brewski (his term), turned on the ESPN channel, and was content. I just laughed and shook my head. See, just like a family member.

I gave the lower level a once-over and then made my way upstairs to get dressed. I was getting out of the shower and I noticed my notification light on my phone was blinking constantly. As I leaned down to read my messages, apparently, "Ms. Thing" was cussed out by boyfriend and she was NOT happy about it. *Girl, I do not care! I have a party to get ready for. You deal with that on ya' own time.* She made that decision to go there. So no, I was not about to entertain her foolishness. Yes, I was over her. My instincts were telling me something was on the horizon anyway. I felt it, but I suppressed it in order to focus on my party. I heard Beast saying something as he was walking up the steps. I ran in the bathroom to throw on my bathrobe and to see he wanted. I came out the bathroom about to run to the steps and ran smack dab into him. His body is solid as fuck! It kind of knocked the wind outta me a little bit.

He said, "Damn. Calm down, slim. I was telling you to throw me some towels for the floor and clean up just in case."

#Pause Baby, listen, the way he grabbed me and was smelling so good, I almost dropped that robe and gave it all to him. Whew, Lord! He did smile at me in a way that was very flirty, though. Again, as bad as I wanted to, nope! *#Continue*

"Oh okay, cool, no problem. Thank you so much," I said, and then asked him to go down and set up the music for me. He's very good with that kind of stuff.

"It's already done."

"Wow, thank you."

I gave him the towels and he made his way back downstairs. I got dressed and bounced my little cute ass right on downstairs, too.

My guests were arriving; I greeted everyone, accepted my gifts and the party went off without a hitch. No issues in sight or anything. Good company, good music, great food and some dancing. We had a blast. As the party was winding down, she decided she wanted to text me to death and then call me. Love, you already know what my thoughts were. *Um, no. If you wanted a play-by-play of the party, then you should have had your ass here. PERIOD.*

I don't tend to my phone when I'm entertaining guests in my

home. How tacky. I went upstairs and threw that phone on the bed and went back to the last few guests.

The party ended about 3:00 a.m. As we were cleaning up (myself, Beast and a few of his buddies), I heard my phone ringing. *Okay, it's three in the damn morning, who the hell is this?* I darted upstairs to get the phone. It was my sister calling, telling me to log onto Facebook and read this heffa's post. I'm like, *Really? Now?* It must be serious for my sister to call me and tell me. UGH! I told her I'd check it once my guests were all gone. Of course, she wanted to know what I was doing and why she wasn't invited. Ol' nosey self. LOL. As the last little bit of my guest were leaving, I thanked everyone for coming and celebrating with me. There was no one left but Beast and his best friend. I told them I'd be back. I went upstairs and threw on my sweats.

#Pause YES! The outfit was cute, yet simple! I had on a pair of my favorite fitted jeans with a linen button up that was cut and tailored just for me. Then I changed and put on one of my "Snobby T-Shirts" (they loved it), with a fresh pair of kicks...oh, hunni. You know how much I love cute, simple and clean. I pulled my hair back in a pony, threw on some of my diamonds and things and let them have it. *Snaps* CUTE! *#Continue*

I grabbed my phone and as I was walking back downstairs with Beast and Tony, I was reading this heffa's post and she's talking about loyalty. *I just KNOW this status is NOT about me. It can't be. No way.* Well, you know me, I called her ass.

"Something you want to say to me, hunni?"

"What do you mean?"

"What do I mean? What the hell is your status about?"

"Oh, no that was about something else that happened today."

"Oh, okay I was just making sure. I'll call you later today (it was 3:45 a.m.)."

"Okay. Good. I wanna know all the deets about the party. Goodnight, boo.

"Mmhhmm. Goodnight." I rolled my eyes and hung up.

Beast saw the change in my attitude. "You aiight?"

I told him the whole story. He simply put it, "You may need to cut her loose, lil hommie. Not everybody is going to want to be a part of your come up or success. It's fucked up, but it's real shit. We can't take everybody with us. They may fake like they gone rock with you and be in your corner. They good with you, as long as you all are on the same level. The minute you begin to rise above them, they try and figure out how to fuck up your game. That's not a friend. And from everything you just said, she ain't cha friend, my dude. Feel me?"

Yes, he fucked me up with that one. He told no lies. The funny part, he sounded just like the men in my life. Shaking my head... I was really giving her ass the side-eye now. UGH! I needed to clear this shit up, ASAP.

Naturally, when I needed to clear my head, I cook. Grams taught me it was a great way to entertain my idle hands and not get in trouble. I went in the kitchen and started cooking breakfast.

Beast walked over. "What's good?"

"Oh nothing, just going to cook some breakfast. No, I'm not hungry, but I need to think about some things."

He laughed. "Well shit. What we about to eat then?"

"French toast, eggs, bacon, fried potatoes with onions and I'ma make a cake."

"Yo, Tony! You game or what?"

Tony said, "Hell, yeah! I heard about you!"

"Good. I'll call you when I'm done."

They were sitting over on the sofa, watching ESPN again.

I was cooking and thinking about everything that had happened so far, on top of everything that Beast just said. When I was done, I placed the food on the table and the fellas sat down and ate breakfast. We talked and laughed some more, they thanked me for everything, and left. By this time, it was like 7:00 a.m. Once I secured my house, I retired to my bedroom where I just laid in bed, thinking and replaying everything from past events.

Her responses, her actions were getting worse and worse. I decided to pray on it and take a nap. I woke up to an email from another friend that was in our little circle, who was inviting me to her wedding. I thought, *Okay, cool. It would be nice to see everybody again for a great reason.* What better reason to see your close friends than to celebrate love and unity.

I was excited about going home and seeing everybody. Family, friends and the bestie (TUH!). Too bad when I returned home, I was not greeted the same way by her as I was by everyone else. I got to the wedding where my other babies were (the Queen & the Diva) already. We saw each other and embraced right away. It was so nice. I didn't even realize how much I actually missed them. I held on to them so tightly when we embraced each other. I was almost on the verge of tears. It just felt so good to be home, to feel and to give love to my friends. It was very nice. As the day went on and we were at the reception (and you know I partied down, hunni), I sat back just to observed her interaction with others. It was very interesting to say the least. I noticed she pretty much played me and a few others to left. Yet, she seemed most comfortable with the other girls who we used to talk about all the time because they were so full of drama. Even the bride had her bullshit with her. Mind you, we all grew up together. Some of us met in elementary school and the others were middle school to high school, through college and after. So, we had history and had known each other very well. Some more than others, as you could imagine. Yup, even her boyfriend. I had never met him before they started dating. He said that he knew of me because my mild popularity in middle school and high school (yes, my dancing days).

Anyway, after that event, I stayed for another day and then made my way back to Kentucky. On my way back home, I realized that from now on, things were going to be different. As my success was going to continue to climb, our friendship was going to continue to decline. How and why was my so called "BFF" acting like this? I didn't confront her just yet because I wanted to be one hundred percent sure that, THAT was going to be the case when I cut her off. I needed to have all my ducks in a row before I made the final decision. Once I was back home in Kentucky, I told Beast how the whole ordeal went down.

He said, "See, I told you. You'll cut your grass when you're ready to."

Ya know, he's right. I made the big chop recently. So, let me tell you what happened. So now let's cut to the present day.

#Pause Take a sip of your drink. If you don't have one, go get one. Shit is about to get real, hunni. *#Continue*

My assignment in Kentucky had come to an end, but my position in my field of career choice kept going higher and higher. I went all over the world from Kentucky, Texas, Florida, Korea, Hawaii and even the UAE. Then I finally made my way back home. Of course, she faded further and further to the back. Then, as I'm paying more and more attention, she's getting more involved with those "Drama Filled Chicks" (or as I called them, the "Black Plastics') that we used to talk about so much. The gag, those are the chicks we went to school with and grew up with as well. Yup, they were all a part of our little circle at one point. I just kept them at a distance. I told her frequently, "NO, those are YOUR friends." It seems shady but it's true. I live and I let live. I'm not one of those people to tell my friends who they can and cannot hang out with. I'll tell you either I don't like them, or I don't trust them, etc., but that's about it. If they become an issue for us (like they did), then I'll bring it to your attention and be on my way.

Now, with that being said, I was finally back home in the DC area. I moved to Downtown Silver Spring in a brand new, swanky, high-rise apartment building. It was very nice, and I was doing very well, and I was so proud of myself. I did what I had to do in order to get myself back on track. Once I was all moved in and settled, I wanted them to come see the new place. We needed to catch up. I would either cook or we would go to dinner in the neighborhood. I called, I texted, I sent Facebook messages (yes, I was still trying). In return I got a bunch of nonchalant replies, accompanied by empty promises. Right when I gave up on us, that's when I met the "Black China Doll," my girl "CD".

She introduced herself to me right away and said, "We are going to be friends, so you better get ready." She was NOT lying either. We hit it off right away. I've always said that when God subtracts people from your life, he adds someone or something better. That's exactly what he did with China Doll. She was her perfect replacement and addition to my family. Once CD and I started hanging out, and she was popping up in pictures with me all over "the Gram" and Facebook. Oh, hunni, my phone rang real fast! Text messages were being sent all day and DMs were being sent all night. I said, "Really? This is what we're doing?" Yeah, it was time for her to go. I looked out the window at my lawn, I saw the snake slithering, but I still hadn't cut my grass yet. I just thought *humph, I'll do it later*. She was now officially one of those "other girls."

One day I was outside walking my mother's dog and I received a phone call. Wait, let me back up. Summer was just really beginning. Me and the "Snobby Fam" had been hanging out a lot lately because we were "voted off the island" by the Black Plastics. Yeah, our other so-called friends decided that they didn't wanna be bothered with me and the "Queen" anymore because we were too much for them. I believe the words that was used were "He's too extra and she's too extravagant, fancy & needy." I laughed at the thought of a bunch of low-budget, lonely, dry-faced bitches had a problem with the ones who wanted better for themselves and knew how to enjoy life and have fun. Oh. Okay. Anyway (eye roll), by now it's May, and I was dog sitting for my parents while they were in Las Vegas. I was walking Chef (my mother's dog) when I received a phone call from the Queen. I hadn't talked to her on the phone in a while, so I was glad she called me. We kept in touch via text and Facebook post because of our schedules. Not to mention I was on travel a lot, so time zone differences etc.

I received a phone call from a number that was unfamiliar to me. The caller ID app on my phone told me it was her. I answered with great joy and excitement. Well that was quickly killed by her news.

Once we got past "Hello" and "Hey, heffa, where have you been?" we got right into the nitty gritty. Apparently, she had been deathly ill, and nobody told me. She said that it was weird that she hadn't heard from me during her whole ordeal. Well, I had no idea what was going on. I informed her I was in Texas the time of her health issues, but had I known, I would have taken the first plane back to DC to be with her. She knew that, which was why she was calling to make sure I was okay. Go figure, right? She gave me an earful. What she said, I was NOT expecting to hear. So here goes.

#Pause Take a sip. *#Continue*

The phone call goes exactly like this:

"I was calling to make sure you were alright."

"Yeah, darling, I'm fine. Why? Wassup?"

"Well, I was in the hospital, literally with one foot in the grave, and I didn't hear from you or see you, so I was making sure we were still cool. At least to my knowledge, we didn't have any beef with each other."

"Wait a minute, chyle. What the hell did you just say? You were what? And why didn't anybody call me and tell me? What the fuck?"

"Yup. The sad part is, your so-called BFF knew. I sent her a text message to share with the group about what was going on and why I had been so quiet and not responding to messages, etc."

"Yo, don't play like that. Sweetie, I heard NOTHING. Obviously. You know good damn well I would have been by your side. What the hell happened? And don't leave shit out!"

"Well, I was sick. I was so sick to the point where I had to have a blood transfusion. The color drained from my face so bad I was one shade lighter than pale. I was seriously sick. The doctor called me at home and told me to get to the hospital right away. So, I did. Thank God, I did when he told me. I would not have made it past that night."

"Oh, my God! What the hell? Hell nah, nobody told me about that! What the fuck? Are you okay?"

"Yes, I'm better now. I'm a lot better now. No thanks to our little circle."

"Explain, please."

"Well, I sent your friend a message, explaining to her everything that was going on in full detail. I said this is what's going on, you're going to be my contact and go-to person. If it comes up, you can say this, this and this. That way, everyone will be in the clear and up to date on my issue and the progress.

"Okay, I can understand that. She's the in-between for us and she would have direct access to me."

"Exactly. Well guess what? NOTHING. Nothing from nobody. Not a card, a phone call, text message, not even a damn FB message or post. NOTHING. When I didn't hear anything from you, I knew I had better call you myself."

"And you're right! Thank you. I'm still trying to process this. Like, I promise you, I heard or knew nothing. You know me, family first. I would have taken that L and came right to you babes. Fuck that. Why didn't J (The Diva) call me?"

"Because I told her not to and don't worry about it. I knew your friend was going to do what I asked her to do. We had been talking back and forth for some time now, so I felt like she would execute what we discussed. It was laid out to a tee for her. All she literally had to do was copy, past and hit send."

What the fuck?! Just...Wow! I can't believe this. I'm so sorry this happened, and I was not there for you. Please forgive me. This is just...wow! Like, what the hell?"

"No, you're fine, and calm down. I can hear the pisstivity in your voice." She laughed. "It's okay. I'm fine now. But yeah, I was more so hurt than anything by all of it."

"You damn Skippy! That's fucked up! For real! I mean, thanks for the understanding, but still. This shit ain't right! We are not supposed to be like this towards each other. This is some bullshit. Ever since that little light-skinned bitch linked up with them again, it's been more shade, more bullshit and more drama between us. "The New Aunt Viv" gone make me cuss her dusty ass all the way out!"

"Not "The New Aunt Viv!" I like that! And you're right, I was thinking that all along. You just confirmed what I was thinking and feeling. Ever since she came back on the scene with us, it's been one issue after the next. You are right."

"Man, fuck her. Well, I'll be over to see you this weekend. From now on, you, J or G call me. Fuck everybody else. Clearly, we are all we got now. It's all good. Let them birds fly.

I've been feeling like I needed to cut my grass, but I was procrastinating. Talk about confirmation. So, what else is going on that I missed?"

"I know, and I love you for that. And since you asked, I was gone tell you anyway, but your buddy has been showing her complete ass lately. She's been listing to THEM, about her relationship. She's even decided that she would just disregard us all together unless the OTHERs are by her side. The way she's been letting those girls disrespect her man and talk shit about him is just amazing to me. Especially when she has nothing to bring to the table herself."

"You know what? That sounds about right. I told you from jump, I don't fuck with ol' girl. That's yall's friend. I only spoke to her because when I walk into a room, I speak. I address the room collectively. I ain't like the wench in school and I told y'all that. But I kept it cute. And for her to be acting like that toward him, *really?*"

"Yes, I know. And I thank you. Again, you were right. I'm taking a page out of your book. From now on, I'm following my gut instinct and first mind as well. I was just really taken aback by all this betrayal. Oh no, catch this gag. How about they were all over New Aunt Viv's house, cooking for her and attending to her because? This bitch had a HEAD COLD. A HEAD COLD, Christian! I said, so me being near death was not as important as a head cold. Oh, okay."

"Ay, get the fuck outta here and stop playing with me! You're serious? Wow!"

"Yup. I kid you not. I saw the Facebook post. I even liked the pictures on purpose."

"Wow. I just...Wow! And what the hell kind of advice can those bitches offer? One ain't got a man and the other, she's dating is a GAY ad don't even know it! The other one is NOW married, but if you look at her social media, you can't tell; the other one is going through a divorce, and then this dilly bitch got the piss, but no pot or window. Now what kinda sense does any of this make?!"SMH. "But you know what? Misery does love company, and she's in great company. And what the hell were they saying about him?" I asked her, now I'm beyond pissed.

"Oh, it was a mess. This was the last time I had seen them in person, before I got sick. That's probably when they collectively voted me off the island." She laughed out loud. "They were pretty much dogging him and saying how he needs to grow up and make a decent woman out of her. He's childish and playing too many games. Marry her or let her be on her way. That's when I spoke up and said the exact opposite. He has a great full-time job, good credit and gives her whatever she wants, whenever she wants it.

Yet, she has nothing to bring to the table except a car and bills. Oh, the room got quiet and eyes were rolled. That's when I knew. My time was up."

"I just bet the hell it was. You know shit gets real when folks develop a case of the *"can't takes"*. I'm glad you defended him. You told no lies. I can't believe she's being that tacky. I mean, she and I were having some issues, but I did not think it was to this extent. Now that I think about it, though, it makes perfect sense. From her acting funny since I've been in Kentucky, her dodging me and everything. Yup. That's about right."

"Oh, we know. We would ask if she talked to you and she really didn't have an answer besides, 'Yeah, he's fine.' We were like, wow. That's it? Yeah, something is definitely wrong. Like I said, that's when I said I needed to call and talk to you for myself."

"Well, I'm glad you did speak up on both terms. I appreciate it.

Just. Wow. After all that we have been through, I can't believe that this is the outcome."

#Pause I had to step back for a minute. Replaying all of this over in my mind was pissing me off again. We were a family and this little round-head-pie-faced bitch came in and changed all of it. Then these other low self-esteem bitches allowed her to do it. How weak and simple minded can one be to allow an outsider to come in and fuck up the family? Like who does that? This is the fuck why our community has the issues that we have now (SMH). The amount of damage I wanted to do to them. Whew! I just wanted to make a phone call and have all of them handled. *#Continue*

As our conversation went on, I was informed how my so-called BFF was allowing those raggedy, acid, twat-having wenches' permission to talk about me like a dog behind my back. Not only did my girl (the Queen) step in on my behalf, but she was a true G and told me about it. Then after that, I heard it again from "our boyfriend," and then a few other people. Now it's time to cut the grass. Exactly. Yes, it took me a minute, but like I said, I needed to have all my ducks in a row and be one hundred percent sure. I started thinking to myself; that many people are *NOT* going to lie on you Christian. They all said the same thing. They were outsiders who overheard you and your buddies saying little slick shit out your mouth about me or us.

The one thing I asked her not to be is *exactly* what she turned into. A liar, a fake and a phony-ass, two-faced hoe. She knows many of the battles I went through and what I had to deal with from certain family members. Then she goes and does this.

The funny part is, once I ended our friendship, so many people made the same comment: "It's about time" or "You was too good for that bitch anyway." Again, wow, was my response. I guess I was so busy ignoring her and her issues, I turned the blind eye to all of her bullshit. Well, to an extent anyway.

Then, the worst part is, for her to constantly act that way toward her boyfriend; that shit threw me for a loop. As many times she has cheated on that boy; the nerve of her. I'm surprised her hymen is still intact. Of course, she will *never* admit to any of this or take owner-ship of her faults or bullshit because that's just how she is and what she does. She could be wrong until Judgement Day, but she will *not* own it, hunni. Our friendship was 80/20. I was the 80 and she was the 20. I take blame for part of it. I allowed her to do some of the dumb shit that she did. I was her buffer, the one who schooled her on certain things, the one who told her it was okay to feel guilt-free about certain things, the one who would just make excuses for her. Well, after a while that got old and it dried the fuck up. The older I got, the more mature I got; I changed. I was so used to giving 80 and allowing her to give 20, that after a while, I became immune to it. When I matured and had to grow up, my eyes were opened to a lot of the first-class bullshit she was doing. I saw it, I knew of it, but to think it would be done to me blew me away. My sister told me that's why I should *not* have been shocked by it. The moment I outgrew her, I should have cut her ass off, but because of how I was, I didn't. In the same breath, because of who I became to be, I had to.

The last time I saw her or had any interactions with her, was for her thirty-second birthday dinner. I bought her a pair of high-end earrings as a parting gift. What do I mean? I didn't need to say goodbye to her. Those earrings were my goodbye gift. Those earrings, that was me saying, "These are in remembrance of me." I showed up at her dinner smiling, while acting completely dumb to everything. I took a few pictures, smiled some more, even talked to the "New Aunt Viv" and everything.

Oh, hunni, I was real fake. When she started opening her gifts, I slid her the little blue box, watched her open it, and smirked. See the thing with that was, I was always buying her nice extravagant gifts or "just because" gifts. If I'm walking through the mall or depart-ment store shopping for myself, and I may happen to come across something that I think she would like, I'd buy it for her. Again, I never got that in return. So yeah, this was the end. I was officially bowing out of our so-called friendship. Even boyfriend couldn't believe I brought her those.

He'd never brought her anything like that. Not to take anything from him, but it wasn't expected of him to do such a thing. Me, it was the norm, it *was* expected. He gave me a look like he knew I was up to something. I think he low-key knew, he just wasn't one hundred percent sure (cracking up).

Little did he know I was getting ready to return her to him full-time. No more phone calls, no more text messages, no more emails, stopping by, *nothing!* After that night, I returned to my apartment, never to see her again in person for an entire year.

She would comment on my Facebook post (I'd ignore her). I left her on my friend's list on purpose. We both did (me and the Queen). We wanted them to see everything we were doing. If you want to be petty and uncalled for, oh we can play that game, but you will lose. That's when the "Too Trill Trio" was formed. Me (The Snob), The Queen (and the Mogul, her hubs) and the Diva. We were all we had. We were now our own family. You know what, though, it worked out in our favor. We have no issues amongst us. So much love and support for each other. No worries, no mess, no drama and no fuss. It's "100" across the board! AND I LOVE IT! My girls! Until…we had to deal with "boyfriend." Oh, shit!

#Pause Chyle, take another sip! If you need to refill, then do it because it's about to get even heavier, hunni. SMH. *#Continue*

So, boyfriend sent me a text, wanting to meet so that we could talk. Now you know I gave that MF the side-eye, right? I'm game for meeting up with him. I mean, we're still cool. My beef ain't with him, it's with his other half. TUH! The gag though, he wanted to meet with all three of us.

I sent the message out to my girls and they were like, *Uh, okay.* Everyone was stuck. We wanted to know what the hell he had up his sleeve. We also wanted to make sure that he was *not* trying to set us up with *that chick* on the low. We had nothing to do with her for just a little over a year now. So, as you can imagine, this was going to be quite interesting. We had been keeping in touch with him over the last few months. Especially me because I felt like I at least owed him that much.

I know me, and I know how mean I can be. Like really mean. However, my heart will only let me go but so far. For some reason, my heart would not allow me to be that kind of mean to him. I didn't figure it out until later. It was because he's so genuine and such a good dude. He didn't know how she was. At least not to that extent.

There were a lot of things that she did that he had no clue about. I was to the point where if he wanted to know, I was gone tell him. So, that wonderful Friday night came, and we all met in DC after work, at the bar next to the Verizon Center. We embraced each other (as we always do), sat down and ordered our first round of drinks. As the drinks arrived, The Queen jumped right into it.

"Okay, what do you want and why did you ask us here?"

I said, "Oooooop! Here we go"! Well, he wanted to know why we all stopped talking and what went wrong? We all looked at each other, burst out laughing, and then asked him was he ready for that truth? He said he was, so I asked him what made him ask and what happened between the two of them? We all noticed that, those living their relationship on social media had ceased and the pics had died down…a lot. So, what's good slim?

He took a sip of his drink, then his whole mood changed. He wanted to know from beginning to end about what happened. So, we agreed to collectively tell him, but first, we wanted to know what happened between the two of them. We wanted to know because we were aware of him and his ways, but not the current sit'cho. He began to tell us what happened and… wow! Love, this joker was telling us stuff that we didn't even have a clue about. Baby, when I tell you that bitch is something else! Hunni, she is a trip around the world with no passport and no luggage. Whew!

Apparently, they broke up, but once they broke up, she posted a pic of her and her old boyfriend posted up on the sofa at her mother's house. Mind you, we didn't see this because we are no longer Facebook friends. This was after I made the decision to be completely done with her. I let her watch our antics for a year just so she could feel the burn (and she did). She was liking pics, commenting and everything (yeah, she clowned herself). Anyway, so the pic popped up and he liked it, then she unfriended him. She said that he was being messy. HA! The nerve of her, right? Yeah well.

He went on to ask us what happened and why we "broke up." We told him and the look on his face was priceless. Like, we immediately felt bad for him because we could tell he really didn't have any idea. We were still talking as we ate our dinner and ordered a few more drinks. I was fine until he began to tear up. That's when I got pissed off and I let it rip. I told him about all the times she cheated on him (I ran out of fingers; I was now counting on my toes) and what really happened. How he was looked at as a clown because he was doing things for her that she wouldn't do for him. Then I finished off with how ignorant her mother is as well. She would call and ask him for favors for her, and he would do it because he loved her. Her mother knew this and played on it. His parents didn't know any of this. I know his mother very well and she would have ROCKED THE MOTHERFUCKING HOEUSE! Oh, hunni, his mother does not play when it comes to her baby (as no true mother would).

I told him everything. I left no stones unturned. The more I talked and revealed, the more those tears flowed. Yeah well like I said, he asked, so it is what it is. What's funny is, as I'm talking, they were all in disbelief of the things I knew and information I was sitting on. His mouth was open, and his face was stuck on stupid. Which is why I told him, "Make sure you're ready for the answers to the questions you're going to ask." Once he told me the stunts she was doing, I had to let it out. The nerve of her to call and use him the way she did, then not take ownership of anything she had done. Yes, granted it was his fault for allowing himself to be used by her over and over again, but he was truly in love with her and she knew that. She decided to play with his heart and that pissed me off. It pissed us all off, to be honest.

You know how I am about *love* and that just sent me over. Then, her simple ass mother decided she wanted to get in on it as well. Oh, no sir, ma'am. I nipped that right in the bud. I told him flat out,

"I get that you love her, and she was your first true love, but bruh, you gone have to get over that. There is no reason why you should still be thinking about her when she showed you her true colors. Not only did you all break up, but not even twenty-four hours later, she posted a pic of her and her new, yet old, boo, laid up on the sofa together. REALLY?! This is the chick you still have love for. Are you kidding me?! Not to mention the number of times she's done dirt in your face. I'm just not understanding why you want to put yourself through that mess. You have made some major life changes and accomplishments recently. We are more than proud of you. Why would you let her steal your joy by bringing her and her foolishness back into your life and new home? NO, not acceptable. Now, don't get me wrong, I totally understand love and how it works, but that's not love, sir.

"That's disrespect and a few other things. Hell, it's the opposite of love. I need for you to do better. I need for you to want better for yourself. Yes, it hurts, and it's supposed to. But you allow yourself some waddle time, then you move on. You do *not* look back and you do *not* stop growing.

Everyone was in agreeance with me. He couldn't help but to agree himself. As the evening was ending, we were winding down with dessert and cocktails when he looked at me, then nodded yes. I knew he understood what I was saying. That nod made me happy because it meant he felt what I was saying and knew what he had to do. I made it clear that I understood it was a process for him. Healing takes time; it's not going to happen overnight. Take your time with it, but don't be no fool." We all told him this. He agreed. Time passed on, and he was still in touch with her. He told me flat out that he was still talking to her because he wanted answers. "I can understand that, but if you're talking to her and wanting answers to questions you *know* she's *not* going to answer, then why not move on?"

He didn't want to. I said, "Okay." Then, it got to the point where we would all be out having an enjoyable time, he'd receive a text from her and his whole attitude would change. He would be in a funk or his face would go from happy and smiling to sad and droopy. Yeah, No. I told him, "You need to choose; either you quit her completely, or we gone leave you alone, too. The one thing I'm *not* gone have, is you being a Debbie Downer because that dry-faced hoe done texted you and put you in a funk. So, if you want to be miserable, then you go be miserable alone." I know, Love, that seemed harsh, but it really wasn't. It had been about three months after that dinner; we had been spending time with him, trying to cheer him up and making sure he was alright. So, by the third month I had had enough! Shit or get off the pot. I had to cut him back. When we went to Mexico, he wasn't invited on purpose. When we would have other events, he wasn't invited. It was too much trying to make sure he was okay when he didn't want to be okay.

We are still in touch and I still very much do care for him, but no way in four hell's will I allow him to bring her bullshit into our happy space. Granted, they aren't together anymore, but with him still being in touch with her, she still has that upper hand on him. Yeah well, *not* in my presence or at any of my events, *she will not!* Once he gets it together, then we will go back to inviting him to more stuff. He's been scaled back a bit. At least until he can be his own person again without her. We love him and we want him to be alright. I just pray he gains his strength back, so he can continue on the right path. He has a lovely new townhouse he purchased all by himself. I told him how proud of him I am. I gave him decorating ideas and everything. I told him I was his "gay" now, so he'd better use me wisely. We can't wait for his housewarming party (If we're invited that is. LOL). We all promised him very nice gifts.

We'll even help him plan it if need be. We're just not going to get our hopes up. We are pretty certain that he's going to invite her as well. We forewarned him that if he does invite her, we will not be in attendance. He has wonderful people around him who are all rooting for him just like we are. The funny part it, most of his buddies are glad that they broke up. They didn't like her, too much either.

It's just hilarious how everyone around us (or him) did not like her as much as she thought they did. Didn't even like them together. I think it had more to do with his buddies recognizing how much she made him look like a simpleton more than anything.

One thing I can say about her, she knows how to use people for her advantage. She used all of us at one point and time. Once she was called out on her bullshit, she couldn't take it. So, like I said before, she would deny it or just answer your question with a question.

The heffa is a beautiful liar and an amazing manipulator. I'm not sure who she gets it from, but she's perfected her craft. My hat is off to her. Hopefully as time goes on, she'll grow up and get her shit together. I don't hate her in anyway, I just no longer have love or respect for her. I don't have love or respect for any of them for that matter. None of us do.

I must admit, though, this whole experience was very life changing for not only me, but all of us. It taught us that we can only expect but so much from people. Always listen to your gut instinct and follow your first mind. As much as myself and the Queen saw this coming down the road, we tried to prepare ourselves for it. We just didn't know it was going to be to this extreme. Not only did it make us stronger as individuals, but also stronger in our bond with one another. Everybody is not meant to be in our lives for a lifetime. Only very are meant to stay in our lives through our entire journey. I'm so glad to know that my two babies are with me until the very end. Besides, I already told them they can't quit me. I'll jump out the bushes on both of those heffa's.

Oh, and by the way, I called Beast and told him what happened. Not only did he let out a hearty laugh, but he wanted to make sure I was alright with everything. I told him I was fine. Then I informed him of my exhale moment I had once I cut her off. He told me that was more than enough. That's was what I needed. I agreed then informed him that he was more than welcome to come to DC for a visit. Of course, Beast said he would come to visit us, then he turned right around and offered to have the ex-BFF beat up by his sisters

(LOL). I told him it wasn't necessary. She already lost in more ways than one. Not to mention, she's on a losing streak right now. That's more than enough for us. Every dog has its day and her number has been called. He laughed, then replied with "Okay. Just say the word if you change your mind." SMH. Again, I'll tell you about him later (SMILING).

So, um yeah, Love, that's the story of how the "Trio" was formed. Now you know all the details and don't have to ask about *her* anymore. Oh no, you didn't bother me. I know, like everyone else, you wanted to know as well. It was very obvious, wasn't it? I mean, it went from "US" being in pictures together, to NOTHING. Or me in pictures with the Queen and the Diva only. LOL. We definitely caught it. Funny enough, I still let her off rather easy. I could have went IN and did or said some way harsh things, but nope. She's honestly not even worth it. It takes too much out of me to be evil. However, you and I both know how vindictively evil I can be. Nope! It's all good. We're good. BLESS UP!

Love you much and TTYS,
Eskimo Kisses.

PLAYA HAS MY SECRETS

Hey, Love. Wassup?

You just will *not* let me rest until I tell you about Mexico. LOL! And I know, it's my fault. I totally...I mean, *we* totally enjoyed ourselves. Oh no, I'm good, hunni. I just got back in and I'm wide awake. I got time. I went to hang out with the BFF's at "Mazza Gallery" and did a little shopping (don't judge us). I told you I love them. They totally complete me and all my cute "Snobby" smart ass ways. We just caught up and had dinner after shopping (I know, right). Totally cute. Anyway, make sure you're ready to hear about this. I'm changing into my sweats and slippers, darling, and fixing me a nightcap. Hair is up in a ponytail and I'm ready to spill this tequila with you, doll. It's from the motherland of Mexico, too, so you know it's good. Ow!

So, you wanted to know about our little adventure and my rendezvous in Mexico?

Girl! It all started with Lady E (the Queen). You know how grand she can be. HA! One of the main reasons why I love me some her! She invited me and Ms. J (the Diva) to go with her and her hubs (the Mogul) to Mexico this year and I said, "Oh, *hell yeah!*" After running around getting my passport together, it happened. Oh, baby, when I tell you I shook and booked everything all in one breath. I boarded that plane so damn fast; I made my own head spin. We spent five days and four nights in "Playa Del Carmen". Of course, they were there before me, which made it even better. Check this out, though; you already know the way my hot flashes are set up.

Baby, I got off that damn plane and stepped outside and asked God why He was playing with me like this! Girl! HOT is a damn understatement. I pinned this hair up so fast. If it had been wig, baby I probably would have self-combusted. Whew, Lord! It was instant flashing and sweating for me. I had to step back inside the airport until I could change into something more heat-stroke friendly until my car pulled up. Unh-Unh. Nope.

So, I got in the car and the driver said out his cute mouth (cause, heffa, he was *cute* as hell!), "Is it hot enough for you, sir?"

I laughed and told him he almost made me curse at him. He fell out. "Yes, hot as HELL. UGH!" He laughed then we proceeded to have a little friendly convo. He was cool, though. He made sure he got me to the front door of the resort on time and in one piece.

That damn speed limit was off the hook. I swear it was like every three miles the speed limit went higher and higher. I know I looked up and his dash was reading eighty-five miles per hour. I'm like, *Dude! Really?* He damn sure got me there though.

We pulled up to the valet. I got out and right away and I was greeted with a glass of Champagne (even though I'm not a fan, I drank it anyway just for GP). When someone offers you a glass, you take it. Never know who's watching (wink). So of course, I walked my cute self through those big, beautiful, glass doors. The staff was so sweet and super helpful as I was checking in, which was a major plus for me right away. I was escorted to my suite, which was absolutely beautiful. I dropped my bag's down and I went over to the balcony doors, drew the sheer curtains back, and opened those beautiful double glass sliding doors. I had to let some sunshine in, along with some of that fresh ocean air. It was just beautiful. The way the breeze flowed around the room; those soft, white sheer curtains danced with the breeze, billowing over the sunlight. I looked down and noticed a bottle of Champagne on the table near the balcony doors. It was accompanied by a basket of fresh fruit (YES, I ate an orange and some pineapples immediately. SO DAMN GOOD). I changed my clothes again after a quick wipe down. I had to take what the old folks call a "hoe bath." LOL! That's where you hit all your "hot spots" with some soap and water real quick. I slipped into something more weather appropriate—thin shorts and a thin T-shirt. AND YES, I did put on my "sole'less sandals". You know me so well. I actually had all of them that Shelly made for me. She always comes through for me. I only wear them to the beach or on vacation. I had the black ones on for the first day. So anyways, after changing, I ran out of the room, straight down to the pool area. I looked around a little bit to check out the layout. I love how the pool was the focal point for the outside area of the resort. It sat right in the middle of outdoors along with two bars. One at the top, on land and the other was down in the pool for the guests who wanted to swim up to the bar. If you went a few feet to the near end, you ran right into the beach area. If you went over a little further to the right, where my suite was located, there were little shops and another bar. There was a bridge that crossed over the water of the pool and into the entry of one of the restaurants. Every single detail was immaculate. You know I love that. The sidings of the restaurants were decorated with Mexican Heritage art, Mexican graffiti or Mexican heritage hand-painted tiles. The pool was lined with a very pretty Aqua blue with hints of sea green and jade tile, which sparkled when the water and sunlight hit it the right way. Baby, when they said all-inclusive and everything is at your doorstep, they were not lying.

I kept walking around and BAM! I ran right into J. Oh my God! We embraced and laughed right on sight. It was just too good and juicy for us not to. Oh, darling, it was everything. It's nothing like being able to enjoy an island or a resort getaway with people you love and can truly have fun with. I mean, come on, when they are your BFFs, it can't get any better than that. We went right to the bar and got us a cute little drink, and then we went looking for Lady E. We found her, then we started giggling and laughing like little schoolgirls. Her hubs was cracking up at us and shaking his head.

He already knew it was coming and what was about to go down.

Mainly because we knew the "others" were going to be looking at us from afar via Facebook and other social media apps, in shock and awe. Love, you know I just yucked it up. J, E, and I were having a ball! We enjoyed the pool and the beach for a few hours before going back to the room to change for dinner. You already know I was soaking in that tub for a good hour, too. It felt so good. My butler cleaned it out for me, again, just to appease me and my slight "germ-a-phobe" behavior. Baby! When I tell you it was everything. He had the nerve to add my bubbles and turn on the jets! He did me right! I almost said to hell with them and dinner. HMPH.

We got to dinner and we laughed and toasted and just enjoyed (as we should). Now you know me, and I was wide awake after dinner. I got back to my room, changed clothes and headed back out to the beach for a little while. Why are you laughing? I didn't even say anything yet. So, I changed into my Speedo, a sarong and a tank top. You know how I love to walk on the beach, especially at night. As I'm walking down the sand, starting from the end closest to my room, I heard a voice say, "Why are you out so late and alone?"

I turned around, pushed my hair out of my face, and looked up. It's the same guy who was giving us a show earlier.

So, let me back up and tell you about old boy (I am cracking up). So, remember when I told you how J and I were walking around earlier and getting our drinks? Well, we were walking down the beach earlier as well, and she was showing me what side of the resort her room was on. Which happened to be the side where the shops and stands were. We're walking down the beach, enjoying the water and the sights when I looked up to see a couple on their balcony sunbathing in the nude. I'm so glad I had my shades on because I was looking (with my looking ass), trying to see what I could see. Catch this, though; as soon as I thought I was being slick, my shades slid off my face from me sweating like a hog (chyle, it was HOT BOOTS!) and right into the water. I picked them up, shook the water off, then began to wipe them off on my t-shirt. I just so happen look up and the guy was looking right at me. I put my shades back on (of course).

He then stood up and began toweling off. J was *not* ready for that. Her facial expression was priceless, and I was just cracking up. Oh, baby, I enjoyed that full body view! Kat Daddy had body and was hella sexy. Yes, God! Frontal and back views. Whew! He and I locked eyes while he was toweling off. I glanced over and looked at his wife, she was HOT, too. Wifey had a great set of titt's on her. You know I love me a good set of titty's and some kick-ass cleavage. HMPH! She was rocking! Anyway, J and I got to her room. I looked around her room and it's pretty much the same layout as mine. She's just a little closer to the water than I was. While she's changing her bathing suit, I stepped out into the hallway to use my phone for a few. Guess who walked out of the room directly across from hers? YUP! "Mr. Body" himself. He smiled and said, "Are you lost?"

#Pause Now you know damn well that was a corny flirt line, but only because he's fine as frog's hair, I'm going to let him have this one. *#Continue*

I smiled at him and said, "No, I'm not lost. She's changing; I'm using the phone. I mean, if that's okay with you."

He smiled back and said, "Sure, that's fine."

I noticed he had a heavy accent, yet a sexy voice. "Where are you from?"

He smirked. "I'm from Turkey. And you?"

"I'm from DC."

"Washington?"

"Yes, Washington, DC. I gather you've heard of it?"

"Yes. I'm familiar."

I just bet you are, I thought to myself.

"Is she your wife or girlfriend?" He was referring to J, of course.

"No, she's one half of my best friend circle."

"Oh, Okay. I understand. She's *hot.*"

"Well, thank you. I'll be sure to tell her what you said."

"Please do. She's very *hot!*"

Then it clicked. "*Oh! Okay!*"

J comes out the room with that *what the hell* look on her face.

"Enjoy the rest of your day," I told him as we walked away.

We walk out the door, down the steps and I looked back. He was in the window, watching us walk away. I locked arms with J and whispered to her in my best Loretta Divine voice from *Waiting to Exhale*, "He's watching us walk *away*."

She squealed and said, "Oh my God, what have you gotten me into?"

I burst out laughing as we scurried around the corner like two little Geisha girls. We met up with the others by the pool and then the beach fun happened. Now, cut back to that night with him standing in front me half-naked and smelling so good. I couldn't help but size him up again. For some reason, he seemed taller to me. I'm aware that six-foot-two is taller than me, he just seemed taller and sexier. Could have been the alcohol in my system that had me a little off, or it could have just been the moonlight and the night air (*Or* that shot of Tequila I had). I have no clue, but baby, I was there for it. BLOOP!

As the night breeze from the ocean blew my hair and sarong ever so gently, I responded with "Well, it's a nice night and I'm wide awake so I figured why not. It helps me to clear my head. Is that okay with you?" He laughed and said, "Sure. I agree. It's a very nice night and the view from where I'm standing isn't, too bad either."

#Pause REALLY?! Did he just try it with that one?! Boy, gone. So, let's indulge and see where this goes. Sure, I'll bite. *#Continue*

"Yes, it is a pleasant view, isn't it?" Chyle, insert flirty smile here. "So now, tell me; why are you out so late? And where is your wife? I know you didn't leave her all, alone did you. Wait. Hold up, slick, I didn't catch your name."

He laughed and said, "She's not alone. She's off with her friends drinking and dancing. My name is Asil." "I know that's right. Now she knows how to have fun. I love it. Nice to meet you, Asil. I'm Christian. Walk with me. Let's chat for a bit." As we're walking down the beach, I moved closer to the water so I could feel the water wash over my feet.

He began to tell me about why he's in Mexico and the purpose for their trip. He and his friends go various places every year just to get away and reconnect. I think that's dope. It's a great idea; a fantastic way to keep in touch with each other and just catch up.

"That's cool. Where have you all been so far, if you don't mind me asking?"

He went on to tell me, however, I noticed we had some vacation spots in common. Everywhere from Africa to Monaco, which happens to be one of my favorite places. Girl, I looked up and in the middle of our walk, I see more couples in the water and on the beach. I'm like, *oh, okay. So, this is what you all do at this hour. I'm here for it.* The older couple I met earlier when I first came in were out there as well. They were so cute together. Enjoying the beach at night together, *ass naked*, and everything. I Love it. I mean, it is an all adult resort so do you, boo-boo's. If y'all love it, I like it.

We continued to walk to the other end toward his room, still talking. He's a real cool fella. We turned around to walk back toward my end where my room was and naturally the water made the sand super soft and my clumsy ass fell and dipped into the water. (Yes, I did.) The funny part was he caught me and we both laughed. It was so doggone fast. There was no way I could avoid that one. The bottom of my sarong was soaked; I was wringing it out and laughing at the same time. Catch this, he said, "Let me help you with that." Baby, he snatched my goddamn sarong off so fast and rung it out for me, I thought I was having a moment. Like, *Sir! Really?* I was standing there in my Speedo and tank top, blushing and laughing. I mean, I was really cracking up. The other couples were laughing as well. The waiter was even laughing. He was *fine as hell, too!* You know me, I said to hell with it. I tied my tank top on the side and continued to walk my little cute, thick ass right on down the rest of the way. We got to the cabana beds and had a seat. You know how I sit on my legs, Indian style, with one under me? He was sitting the same way. I had no idea he had even taken off his shorts. So now he's sitting in his Speedos as well, facing me. Baby, that bulge was *serious*. I was so glad it was dark. He couldn't really see my eyes because they were surely looking. We chatted a little longer and then I got up to hang my sarong on the fence so it would dry properly.

#Pause. Sip your drink, it's about to get real, boo. You know I slightly set him up for this bait; he damn sure bit. Hook, line, and sinker. *#Continue*

When I turned around, guess who's laying down stretched out on the cabana bed? He sure was. The gag, this joker took off his Speedo. Yup! Old boy was *butt-ass naked*. I acted like I wasn't taken aback by it. Not to mention the waiter was only a few feet away. He was close enough for him to see him lying there in all his glory.

"Do you feel better?" I asked him.

"Yes," he said, "less restricted."

#Pause I'm thinking, *speaking of boa constrictors*. Love, the way he let that snake loose, and it was straight up on chill mode. It was pretty, too. What? Oh, please. It does not matter how dark it was, I saw it. *All of it.* Even the vein that was on the left side and the birth-mark on his inner thigh. *Try it on me. Tuh!* Ta hell with a 20/20, I got that Dickey-Dickey vision. I don't miss *nothing!* (Hi-five). *#Continue*

"Oh, Okay cool. I feel you."

"Well, lay down beside me," he proceeded to say, "So you can feel me."

I giggled and replied with a flirty, "Maybe. But for now, I prefer to sit up. So, what else do you want to talk about?"

No sooner than I said that, he snatched off my tank top and said, "I want to see you."

I was like, *Damn!* "Can you chill with all the clothes snatching? You do that way too fast and you're way too comfortable with it, and I'm not sure how you gone see me and it's dark out here." Oh, I know. He pulled a *me* on me.

He said "Oh, I can see you just fine with the moonlight. You have a very sexy collarbone I'd love to kiss place soft kisses on it, non-stop." I'm thinking "Well Shit! Alrighty then, sir.

I continued to make small talk and tried to fight the urge I had to mount him and just ride until I got seasick. I know, child. I know.

He sat back up and told me to lay down. He actually forced me down. I'm like geeze. This joker like it's rough. I'm with the shit though. LOL. I lay down and he climbed on my back and began to procced giving me a back massage. He told me I just needed to relax. You know damn well I will *not* pass up a massage offer, hunni. I still had on my Speedos, though. As the late-night breeze was blowing, while gently caressing my body (it felt so good), he was rubbing my shoulders and then made his way to my lower back. I'm not gone lie, it felt so good. I was in a brief state of euphoria. The breeze was perfect, my eyes were closed, and he was rubbing me down. I noticed he was getting a little too "excited." I mean he did have his dick right on my butt, rocking back and forth. I opened my eyes, looked up and who did I see? The waiter was looking at us with a smile on his face and a gleam in his eye. He was into it. I could tell he wanted a piece of whatever was getting ready to happen. Girl, yes! He was all into it. He was cute, too. He inched closer to us, too.

As Asil moved to the small of my back, I felt him when he leaned down toward me. He gently moved my hair out of the way and began to kiss my neck. I giggled and told him to stop it before he started what he couldn't finish. He whispered in my ear that he was already started and that he'd wanted some of me since he saw me earlier, which I could tell by his behavior. Then he kissed behind my ear and made his way back to my shoulders.

I rolled over and asked him, "So, what about your wife? Does she not have a say so?"

"It's okay. We swing. As long as we play safe, it's cool."

#Pause Now you know damn well I knew this shit already. I could tell by the way he was looking at us earlier and he was too interested in J, which means his wife is probably on this resort with another man (or woman) that's done already caught her eye. *#Continue*

"Hmm, okay."

"Now that we have that out of the way, the ball is in your court, Christian."

"Well, no, there are two of them sitting on my belly button right now, but okay."

The laugh he let out was a cute, manly giggle. I rolled back over and told him to keep massaging my back. Mind you, the waiter was still standing there, looking and listening to all of this. While he massages my back, he slightly pulled down my Speedos and began kissing my back. He started between my shoulder blades and went all the way down to the small of my back. He could multitask very well. His hands never stopped moving while he was kissing my back. It felt so damn good. I opened my eyes and BAM! The waiter was standing closer to us with a BONER. Girl, I cracked ALL the way UP! Like, REALLY?! But hey, the shit was HOT. I'm not mad at him.

I told Asil, "You must stop now," and he told me he didn't want to stop, and he knew I was enjoying it because I arched my back and let out a soft moan. Yes, he was telling the truth, but I was not gone say it out loud. *#Pause* Okay, boo, take another sip and guard your nipples. I'm about to go *in*. It's about to get *real*. *#Continue*

"How about we take this back to my room then?" I'm sure as you can tell Love, he was more than ready to do so. "Hey, cutie, what's your name?"

"Louise."

Well, Louise, can you be so kind and pass me my sarong, please? He passed it to me, and I gave him a flirty "Thank you." As I was putting on my sarong, Louise (the waiter) asked if he could go. You know I burst out laughing. Like, really?! Bich, did he just? Um…wow!

He smiled and flashed those pretty white teeth. He was cute, too. He was about five-foot-eleven (same height as me), two hundred thirty pounds, black hair, olive sun-kissed skin tone, nice shaped up beard, little belly, thick, cute tight butt and some sexy legs. He even smelled good. Yes, I was shocked as well about the smell good part, too. It was hot as fuck outside and ain't no telling how long he had been outside. Hence the reason for my being shocked. I turned to look at Asil who was smiling as well. I was like, *what the fuck is really about to pop off in Mexico?*

"Are you game for one more?" I asked Asil.

"Definitely."

"Well let's go then."

Chyle, Louise jumped over that dayum fence so fast. Slow down, papa, I got you. We're walking back to my side of the resort and Louise could not keep his hands off me. Like, really?

I was walking, trying not to laugh because he was on me! I mean, like hands all on my back, all on my nips, trying to walk and kiss my neck. *Boy, relax!*

Asil was laughing as well. He told Louise, "You are excited, no?" I said, "*Yes!*"

We come to my room door, so I tell them to wait here and I'd let them in through the balcony door.

#Pause Hell NO, they were NOT walking in through the front door. You know people be watching. Besides, it may get a little loud in my room and I don't need the neighbors knowing who was in there with me. LMAO! *#Continue*

Catch this tea, I go in the room and Louise had jumped over the balcony already and was in the room. I cracked ALL the way up. *Wait! How the fuck?! Ooohhh.* I forgot I left the door open and just had the screen door closed. I'm so glad a rodent didn't get into my room. I would have freaked. Their wildlife was NOT a game. Those lemurs were bold as fuck and were ready to mingle. Even the lizards were bold (ask J. LOL). Anyway, once I finally stopped laughing at Louise, I turned up my iPod. Asil was standing there naked already. Mind you, all he had on were his Speedos. He did not put his swim trunks back on. So, um yeah, he was ready. Louise went and jumped in the shower. Which was fine with me. *You betta go on and wash them salty balls off and make'em fresh. Respect, son.*

So, back to my iPod and why it was playing my Latin Lounge Jazz & Samba playlist. Not that I was complaining. It was perfect timing. As I was cleaning off my bed, Asil came up behind me and took my tank top off, pulled my sarong off and proceeded to pull down my Speedos with his teeth. I'm just like, *Oh, Okay!* When I tell you he was so smooth with it. Baby! *Yes!* So noooow you wanna be smooth, but yet outside you was a full-on bully. Yeah, okay. He pushed me on the bed on my back, and then climbed on top of me. He started kissing my face and lips then made his way down my chest while paying close attention to what made me moan or swoon. He continued to kiss and lick my upper body. He made his way down to my belly button, then put in work when he got to that "V." Baby! He made me arch my back and everything. Oh, he got me. That joker got me. *He definitely got me!* Oh, but wait, he was not done. He threw my leg up and went into overtime. I said, "Well, DAMN! DO YOU, BOO-BOO! DO YOU"!

I heard the water cut off in the shower but didn't really pay it any attention. Not even ten seconds before I realized that Louise was out the bathroom, BAM! He slapped his dick on my forehead. Nah sis, I wasn't ready (smh).

#Pause WAIT A MINUTE! Where the hell did *that* come from? His little thick cute ass had that HAMMA! Girl, it made that "THUMP" sound on my forehead. BITCH! I was OVA! Oh, I had a slight case of the can't takes. I was like, *you know what? Y'all not gone wear me out tonight and me not be ready for it. Yeah right. #Continue*

I told Asil to hold up, let me up. Of course, he thought something was wrong. "No, you're fine. I need to put my hair up. Hold fast, champ." I went to the bathroom to get me a hair tie and my scarf. Came back, him and Louise were going at it. He had Louise gripping the fuck out of my sheets and his toes throwing up gang signs (damn). Well, since Asil was pleasing Louise, I slid under him (Asil) and started giving him head. You know I was on get-back, right? I could *not* have him making me moan and squirm like that and not get his ass back.

I used that trick jaw, dropped my throat and I made his ass say, "Oh, shit!" real loud. GOT THAT ASS! I was working him, too. I worked him so good he stopped working on Louise. Louise got up to get behind me and DAMN! He had that tornado tongue. The way he ate the cakes. Yes, God! He was eating the groceries like it was his last supper. I politely let him, too. Old boy put in work. He knew exactly what he was doing. He made me stop working Asil over. I couldn't even focus on him. He had my legs shaking and knuckles popping.

I was damn near close to running. Whew! So, naturally, in my mind, I was thinking about the get-back for him as well. I wouldn't get him with oral, I'd get him another way. Asil was laying back just enjoying himself. He was in a zone. Who, Asil? *Yes*, his dick was very pretty. He had a nice set of low hangers as well. You know I love a good set of low hangers. He loved for them to be licked and sucked. It's one of his hot spots, I noticed.

As I went back to licking and sucking on Asil, he was playing in my hair and Louise was playing with my...well, everything. They both were very hands on. I couldn't help but to love it. Asil pulled me up to him and we started kissing with some slight roughness. *Damn he could kiss!* Louise began making his way up behind me, kissing and licking all over my back. As I mounted Asil, Louise stood up in front of me so I could keep sucking on him. As soon as I deep throated him, his knees buckled, and he plopped right down on Asil.

#Pause When I tell you this jawbone work is *not* for chumps (YEESSS! Hi-five). You good, boo? You hanging in there with me so far? I told you the shit was HOT. Take a sip. Or take a shot. Whichever you prefer because I'm not done yet. Oop. *#Continue*

So, after a few minutes of this soft sex shit, I was over it. I hopped up off Asil and turned on my "freak the fuck out" playlist on my iPod. I was ready to move this shit along. Enough with this *be cute* shit. Who came on the play list first, you ask? None other than the epicenes of Mutha "Lil Kim" herself. That good ol "Big Mama Thang" set me off right. The GAG was, Louise knew *exactly* what song it was. He was *in it!* I said AW, SHIT NOW! Yo! Louise was ready to ROCK! Asil didn't know about it, but his head was rocking to the beat, though. He was with it.

"Now!" I said. "We are going to do things my way and I'm about to drive. Let's do this, fellas." I climbed back on top of Asil and I was riding him reverse cowgirl to the beat of the track. He loved it. I made Louise stand up in front me. I didn't deep-throat him this time. I needed him to focus. I looked down and noticed that Asil's toes were curling and throwing up those good old gang signs. I made Asil smack my ass to revert his attention, so he doesn't cum, too fast. I was enjoying him. I pulled back from Louise and told him to lay down. He gladly followed my instructions. He wanted me to kiss him, so I did. While I was kissing him, I mounted him and began to ride him as well. He wanted me to slam him harder and a little faster (he liked it a little rough). I'm good with that.

While I was riding Louise, Asil kneeled down on top of Louise and got some head from him. The shit was HOT. As the songs kept getting freakier and freakier, so did we! So, as the moment went on, I noticed Louise was becoming more and more in touch with his body, with my body and with the moment. He really didn't feature Asil too much. It's all good though, I didn't mind being the even medium. As Louise and I were getting more intense and heated, Asil pulled my hair and grabbed me by the throat.

#Pause Now you know damn well I was getting ready to dig in his ass, but not like that. You know I don't play with that hair shit. I had a moment, for a brief second, but I remembered where I was and what I was doing. He didn't know and clearly it was one of his "things," but bitch! Yeah. *#Continue*

Asil whispered in my ear, "I'm going to make you mine."

I low-key rolled my eyes and chuckled. Mind you, I was still grinding on Louise. He (Louise) sat up, pulled me closer to him and went to work on my nipples! Yes!

The boy can GO! He made LOOOOVE to the TITTIES! Yes God! He had my body quivering. His mouth game was dead-damn-serious! I told him to stop before he made me cum faster than I wanted to. He laughed and said, "Okay." I felt Asil getting a little uneasy because I was giving Louise so much attention. I got up and turned around to face Asil. He laid me down on my back and threw my legs up in the air. He made sure my ankles were by my ears. I felt every bit of his girth as soon as he slid right between the cheeks. Even though he wanted me to understand where his stroke game was coming from, and I did, that shit was hella uncomfortable.

"Hold up, pa, we gone have to switch this up." I rolled over and got on top while leaning forward. That was much better. I saw Louise out the corner of my eye; he was just laying back, enjoying the show. Since my body was enjoying Louise more, I made the decision to get Asil out the way . Since I noticed he liked it better when I was riding him with the twist motion (Lynn Spin much) that's exactly what I went back to. Two whole minutes of that and I saw the blood rush through his body. About another minute and he was yelling something in another language followed by a loud, "FUCK YOU! RIDE IT ALL OUT, BABY, YEAAHHH!" Chyle, then he started growling really loud and hard. You know exactly where my mind went, right? YUP! "Gur? Gur? Oh, now I'm a keeper at the damn zoo" (#Savannah).

I heard Louise laughing and egging him on. I went to get up and he pulled me back down and said not to move yet. Now you know I'm a smart ass. I began to grind on him slowly and he was still cuming. The more I moved the more he growled. The shit was freak'n hilarious! He loosened the grip on my waist, so I assumed it was okay for me to release and move. I giggled and asked him, "Are you cool? Do you need anything else?"

He had the biggest smile on his face and said, "No, Christian. You don't need to give me anything else. This is bliss."

#Pause BISH, LISSEN! The way he was set up and chilling all up and through my man-gina parts. If I could get pregnant, fuck around it would be his and *not* Louise's. I mean, dayum! You know when men are aggressive and do all the work, that's how you end up with boys. *#Continue*

As, Asil got up and went into the bathroom, Louise made his way over to me, still laughing and started kissing me. I mean really passionately kissing me, too. It was one of those kisses where you grab your significant other by the face with open hands while gently grabbing his head and hair. Even the way we laid back on the bed was like our bodies became one. It was more of a passionate type moment more than anything. Asil came out the bathroom, still ass naked, came over and interrupted us by rubbing his dick on my lips and then kissed me (I know, right?), and thanked me for the fun.

He said, "See you for breakfast."

This joker jumped back over the balcony, still naked and went on his merry little way. I just laughed and shook my head. Louise and I laughed and continued to kiss. Louise stopped kissing me, looked at me right in my eyes and said, "Thank you for this. I'm enjoying myself and you so much. *Me gustaría poder estar contigo para siempre.*"

"I caught the first part. You wish what?"

"I wish I could be with you forever."

"Oh, wow. Well, thank you. Why do you feel that way?"

He went on to tell me how he said when I first came in (he saw me, he was sweeping), he liked the way I smiled, smelled and looked. He also liked the way I was polite and greeted everybody with a smile and a warm hello. I told him I couldn't help it. That's just who I am. We both laughed and then he kissed me again. Now, as you can tell, this session has gone from X-rated to the Soap Opera (sex wise that is. LOL). We kissed a little longer and then we just got straight into it. The funny part is, neither one of us even realized what time it was. It was five in the morning and the sun was beginning to peek over the water. Not that it bothered him any. Once we both reached our climax point, he laid right beside me and went to sleep. Naturally, I wasn't sleepy. I think I was still in shock and awe to have him to say that to me and yet he's still here like he had no other plans.

No, I wasn't bothered by it. You know me. I prefer some kind of connection before sex happens. When it's this kind, a sensual connection, it's even better. I just laid there and played on my phone.

He snuggled up under me and threw his arm over me and would not let me move. I said, "Okay player." He really was feeling me and feeling some kind of way. I whispered what time did he need to be up and out. He told me to wake him in two hours. I set the clock and then dozed off for a few.

Love, you know I didn't even sleep that long. I slept for forty-five minutes and it felt like I had a full eight hours. I was trying to get up and get in the shower, but Louise would not let me move. He was knocked out, but had his arm locked on me.

I'm just like, *Wow*. This dude was not playing any games. It was cute for a few mins, but you know damn well I am not the cuddle kind. I'm either going to get hot or aggravated because I can't position myself the way I want in order for me to get comfortable. So, I decided to be nice and lay there for another forty-five minutes until right before the clock went off. I eased myself out the bed from under him as soon has he exhaled and went to turn over. I got in the shower and it was feeling so good. As I'm washing my face, I feel two hands slide around my waist, then on my stomach. I jumped and was ready to swing and he laughed.

"No need to be startled, it's just me."

"You walk light I see. That or I was just way too engulfed into this shower." "Oh you were engulfed in the shower". He said, as he moved my hair and kissed my neck. I told him not to even start his engine. He had things to do and I was going to meet my fam for breakfast. He said he still had ten mins. No sooner then he said that, we were both good and soapy and, in the shower, and rocking again! The way he threw my leg up, slid inside of me, and had me pressed up against that wall was something else! Whew! I felt, um, "so excited." We both nutted, showered off, got dressed and left (as he jumped back over the balcony).

I went and met my fam for breakfast, and he went and checked in at his workstation for the day. I walked into this beautiful restaurant with soaring ceilings, sultry decorated walls that gleamed and beamed with sunlight from all the floor to ceiling windows. It was absolutely beautiful. I walked around the side, where it opened up to the seating area; all for me to look up and see J flagging me down to where they were seated. I sat down and crossed my legs like the proper young lady that I was raised to be. LOL. I sat right across from J. I took my shades off and looked up. She's right in my face. I think she knew I did something the night before, but she wasn't sure. I could tell by the way she was looking at me.

#Pause I'm one who has the "tell" after I've had some pretty amazing sex. I have that after-sex glow. I didn't realize it until ex-hubs told me. You know that joker knew me inside and out. Literally. I think that's why we used to go at it the way we did so he could see me glow afterwards. I know, a whole jerk! LOL. *#Continue*

Anyway, we were sitting at breakfast and J. was looking at me with this grin on her face. It's so freaking funny. I was trying not to look at her, but I couldn't help but laugh. She burst me all out and said, "I know you did something. I just need to figure out with whom." I was cracking up and I asked her what she was talking about. That's when "E" looked up and said, "She's right. I can tell. You're glowing and not from the damn sun."

Chyle, I fell out laughing again! "Oh, my God, y'all don't know my life! It's the fresh air and the Sun. I'm glowing darlings. Let me glow." They fell out laughing. I got up to go to the buffet to get me an omelet made with avocado, tomatoes and onions and guess who I saw behind the omelet station? Yes, Mr. Louise with his chef's jacket on, looking too cute.

He looked kind of sexy, to be honest. He smiled and asked me what I would like.

So, I told him what I wanted. Now you know my attention span is short. I left the line, waiting for my omelet, to go look at the rest of the beautiful restaurant. There was food, beverages and desserts as far as my little eyes could see. The display and presentation alone had me floored (you know I live for a good presentation). Listen, why did I forget all about the omelet when I saw the brownies, cookies, fruit and tarts on display? I made us a plate of goodies and went back to my seat. J asked where my omelet was. No sooner than she said that, Louise walked up and sat my omelet down in front me. I laughed and said, "I'm so sorry. I forgot all about it. Thank you so much."

"Anything for you, Christian. Enjoy."

WHY did he have to say that? You know damn well J took it and ran with it. Little did she know, he really was the reason for all the glowing? HA! I mean, she just had all the jokes. It was even funnier because she was right, but I didn't unseal my lips. I let her joke on and on. Once breakfast was over, I went back to my room. I needed a nap.

That mini morning workout and shower had my body relaxed. I got back to my room to see that room service had cleaned up everything already. I took my clothes off, opened the sliding glass door, laid on my bed, turned my music on low and passed out. That breeze felt so good. I slept until about two o'clock that afternoon. I was sleeping so well until I was awakened by kisses on my thighs and on my neck.

I laughed, stretched and asked him, "What are you doing and where did you come from?" Mind you, my eyes were still closed. I assumed it was Louise. Nope, wrong! It was Asil. I jumped up.

"Boy! Stop it. Asil, where the hell did you come from?" He was laughing. Talking about he jumped over the balcony. "Where is your wife and crew? And put your dick away please and thank you. Wait, let me look again. Okay put it away! So wassup? What are you all up today?" I got up and went to the bathroom. "And talk loud so I can hear you. I gotta pee!"

"Need some help?"

"Um no, I don't need any help. I've been peeing all on my own for a while now. Thank you. So, what's on the scroll for today, sir?"

He told me they were leaving on the evening flight. So, we chatted a little more and he told me how much he enjoyed me, and he wanted us to keep in touch, blah-blah-blah. Girl, I gave him my email address and called it a day. I think it was obvious I wanted to get back to my little Spanish pappi more than anything. I don't know what it was about Louise, but I was so feeling him. I think it was our connection during and after sex.

#PauseClairityMoment This is a prime example of how we need to be careful when it comes to sex. We need to be cautious about who and what we let inside of us. We all share a certain kind of energy, that when we have intimate or passionate sex with someone, some of their residual energy stays behind within us. Sounds crazy, but it's true. Many don't understand it until it's too late. If they ever do. Well, with this one, I definitely caught it. When we are in tune with ourselves, we notice things like this right away. Asil was obviously just sex. Nothing more. I could tell by the way I was playing him to the left and had no kinds of emotional attachment to him whatsoever. Not that damn Louise, though. We swapped energies. The funny part is, he was well aware of it just like I was. He would NOT leave me alone. The way I would catch him gazing at me, then he would smile. He was just so CUTE! He was smitten, as I was with him. I just knew it couldn't go beyond Mexico. Would have been nice, though. *#Continue*

I put my clothes back on as we were talking, and Asil and I made our way back to the pool area. I needed a drink. The sun was shining, and it was that cool late afternoon early breeze happening. Just so beautiful. We went over to the bar and I ordered another "Shady Lady". It was so freaking good. It was like a tropical fruit punch with alcohol in it. Exactly. It hit all my spots. WHEW! I began to walk away with my drink as I hear Asil yell my name. I turn to respond, and his wife was standing next to him. Now I immediately began to smile and size her up. She was just damn flawless. Her swimsuit was the business. It was black with the side's cutout and she had on a gold body chain that went from around her neck, down her stomach and around her waist. She had on gold bangles with D&G shades and an animal print wrap to match, while rocking a sunhat with a sick brim. Oh, the heffa was serving "New Hollywood Glam Girl" money. I was present for what she was serving. He called me over to meet her. As I made my way back over to the bar, I couldn't help but think, *what the hell did he tell her, if anything, and what the hell is she about to say out of her mouth? What the fuck do I need to meet your wife for? I'm sure you didn't meet all the dudes she was banging while she was here, but okay. I'll keep it cute and casual for now.*

"Nice to meet you."

"You as well," she said, extending her hand for me to kiss it. Girl, bye. I shook her hand and swooped my hair outta my face. TUH! So, she said, "He talked about you over breakfast this morning. You must have made some impression on him."

I smirked and replied, "What can I say? I tend to do that to people I meet."

"So, I see. I'm Anastasia, Christian. If we were not leaving in a couple of hours, I'd like to get to know you. I have a feeling you are something else."

"Oh, I definitely am; and right back at cha mama. By the way, nice titt's and I love what you're serving right now."

She laughed and thanked me.

Then Asil said, "I told you."

"You're welcome. So now, what can I do you for?"

"Oh, nothing, darling. I just wanted to meet the person who had my husband's undivided attention. That's all."

"Okay, I see. Well, nice to meet you. You all enjoy the rest of your day and I wish you traveling mercies."

"Why thank you, Christian. If you're ever in Turkey, please look us up. I was told you have his contact information."

"I do and thank you."

#Pause Now you know damn well her ass was low-key trying to read me and test me. I was NOT about to give her ass the time or day. YES, I fucked your hubs; get over it. She seemed a little irritated, to be honest. Was it because I'm cute, thick and black or she just got a case of the cant takes? Either way I really don't give a fuck. Girl, bye. However, I DO believe in giving props when props are due. She was on one hundred (looks wise), but the way I was reading her energy, she was on negative one hundred. *#Continue*

"Well you all have a good one and take care."

I shook her hand again, then I went to shake Asil's hand, but he grabbed me and hugged me. He kissed my cheek while whispering in my ear, "Don't let this be the last time I see you, please."

I laughed and said, "Uh, okay. You've gotta let me go now. I must get back to my family." He let me go and as I made my way over to the beach where the fam was, I looked back on the slick tip to notice that both were watching me walk away. Well, you know me, I turned up my walk and pumped right on to the beach.

The fam was over on the beach, chilling in the cabana that Lady E had gotten for us. Little did they know the night before I was laying on the one right next to it getting all my life. So, we linked up and we were just having a grand old time, hunni. We were laughing, dancing, having drinks, ordered a little lunch and then who walked up and brought us our drinks? YUP! Louise. I loved that he was so incognito about it all. He kept us with drinks and everything. He made sure we didn't run out or needed anything. Again, they had no idea. I laughed when J said, "DAMN! How many jobs he got? That man is working!"

"Ain't nothing wrong with a hardworking man hunni. Okay?" (Hi-five)! Again, I did not unseal my lips. The whole thing was quite comical.

As our trip was ending, I took some time to walk the beach alone the next morning. I went out to watch the sun rise over the water one last time. It was a 4:45am when I decided to go sit on the beach. I was sitting on the same cabana bed we were sitting on earlier, when I heard Louise say, "I'm going to miss you." He scared me at first. I told him stop that boogieman creep shit. He laughed then apologized. He sat next to me and took my hand. "You know, Christian, I've never experience anyone this fast before in my life. We connected right away, and you seem to be a very rare soul."

I laughed and said, "So I've been told," and thanked him for the compliment. As I watched the sun rise over the horizon, I felt him looking at me. I looked at him, "Why are you looking at me and smiling so hard? Put some of those teeth back in your head." I leaned in and kissed him.

"See, that's what I'm talking about. You're sweet, funny, nice and you treat people like people, not to mention you're very lovable."

"Thank you, and I was taught to treat people how you want to be treated. The rest is all me."

"Christian, please stay with me for another couple of days. We can figure something out."

"Thank you, sugar, but I can't. I must get back home to my family and work. How about this; we will stay in touch and check on each other often? When I get ready to come back, I'll give you a head's up. Also, if you ever come to DC to visit, just let me know and we can hang out."

"I would like that very much. Now, let's go back to your room. I have something for you."

"Oh, unh-unh! I am not falling for that again." We both laughed. He told me to go back to my room and he'll bring it to me. By now, the sun was up, and my soul was totally satisfied. It was so beautiful. I felt amazing. I definitely needed that. I said to Louise "You know what, I wanna dance. I wanna dance right now. I feel amazing". So I turned on Rock Da Boat" by my baby Aaliyah, and I let have. Right there. I didn't care who was watching me. Funny enough nobody was out there but the two of us. He sat back and watched me do my thing. And I rocked it right there on beach. My eyes were closed, and I was completely in the moment. Once the song went off, I was back, and I was good. I opened my eyes and he was smiling, then gave me a standing O. LOL. "Christian I didn't know you were so light on your feet. Very nice". "Thank you" I said. I kissed his face then told him I was ready to go back to my room now.

I went back to my room to take a nap before our flight. I was sleep for about an hour when I awakened by kisses on the back of my knees then up my legs.

I thought, *Lord, if this is that damn Asil again, I'ma lose it!* No, it was Louise. I giggled and told him to stop it. He kissed me all the way up to my lips then he kneeled in front of me as I sat up on the side of bed.

"Wassup, poppa?"

He smiled at me and said, "This is what I have for you." The first gift was a bottle of champagne for my friends and I to drink at home on the anniversary of our trip. Then he took my hand and placed the second gift in it. It was a box that had a pretty bow on it. Like, for real. I didn't know who tied it, but *wow!* He told me not to open it until I got home. So, I shook it. He laughed and said, "*Oh no!* Don't do that! You're going to break it."

"Oops. My bad. Okay. I'll open it at the airport. That's about as long as I can hold out. I'm telling you now." We both laughed. I thanked him and we kissed again.

It was time for me to check out and he walked with me to the front desk. Talk about being passionate. We kissed once we got in the hallway, we kissed again on the elevator, then we kissed once we got off the elevator. We just couldn't get enough. As I was sitting at the checkout desk, talking to the attendant about my stay, I glanced over. Louise was smiling at me again. This time it just seemed different. I didn't say anything, but it just felt different. I guess I was crushing on him harder than I thought. Once I was done, I walked over to those beautiful glass doors to make my exit. I walked outside and quickly made a U-turn. HOT AS A BITCH! Whew! I stepped back in the foyer. He laughed at me as he handed me a water.

My driver pulled up and opened my door. As I began to make my way to the car, Louise asked if he could sit with me for a second.

"Sure," I said, but now I was getting slightly irritated, so I asked, "What's wrong?"

"Nothing," he said. He just wanted to kiss me one last time. So, we did, only this time he whispered he was in love with me in my ear. Even though I low-key saw that coming, it still shocked me a little bit. I told him that was sweet, but I didn't do long distance. If it's meant to be it will be, regardless of what happens. He agreed with me. We kissed one last time and then I slipped him something in his shirt pocket. I told him not to pull it out until he was securely by himself. He laughed and said okay. We kissed again and then he got out the car.

As my driver pulled off and I put on my shades, I must admit; this trip was better than what I had totally expected. My BFFs, a nice little fling, surrounded by beautiful blue water and nonstop drinks. Now that kind of fun never hurt anyone. Baby, I was present for all of it. BLOOP!

Yes, we came home and laughed about everything. We have some wonderful pictures and great memories. I can't wait until next year. No, they don't know about Louise or Asil. I think I'll tell them one day. What did I slip him? Well, now, darling, I can't tell you that. It was just for him. It was something for him to remember every bit of me (innocent smile).

Okay, Love,

I'm off to bed. You have a great night, hunni, and I'll talk to you later.

Love you 4 Life.

BLACK WALLS & VIDEO BOOTHS

Love!

Girl! Let me tell you what Beast did to me last night. Go get you some popcorn and a drank. Oh, you are going to just *love* this one. So, okay… Remember a couple weeks ago when Beast and the fellas were at the house hanging out and everything? Right. Well, in the mist of our convo's I brought up the adult movie store up the street from my house. I wanted to know what the hell "peepers, and video booths" were. I mean, I know what a video booth is, but what the hell is a "peeper?" Now you know in DC we don't have stores like this (well not anymore). The ones we had are closed or have been closed since before I was even old enough to go. Leave it to me to come to Kentucky to see a few on one strip. Let alone up the street from my house.

Okay, so cut to this past Thursday night. Beast texted me to see if they could come back over on Friday night and shoot the shit again. So, I'm like, "Yeah cool, no biggie. I'll cook; you all bring your liquor (as usual)." Friday came, I was off work, so I decided to go to the grocery store early to pick up a few things. I didn't mind cooking because you know I don't play cards anyway. It would give me something to do and to keep me busy. I could talk shit from the kitchen while cooking. I decided to make finger foods—fry up some chicken, make some mini sandwiches, meatballs, macaroni salad and some green beans. A nice little spread for them. I mean, I ain't gotta go all in. It's just cards and shit talking. I'm sure they were going to turn the TV on ESPN, and then the radio eventually. So yeah, nothing heavy. Blah.

I went to the store, got what I needed and was back home and prepping by 2:00 p.m. As I was coming back home, I rode past that damn adult video store again. This time I said, "I'm going to ask Beast's ass about it again. I know him and his friends done been in there. Since all their asses is coming to the house tonight, I'm gone ask!" I even set a reminder in my phone for me to ask so I wouldn't forget again. YES, I WAS PRESSED! LOL!

So anyway, I was cooking and everything, he texted me and told me they would be to the house about 7:00 p.m. I was like, *Perfect*. I would be done cooking and ready to rock. No sooner than I was fresh out of the shower, he texted me to tell me he was five minutes away. I told him the front door was open and to come on in (like he normally does).

I was putting on my shirt when I heard my alarm beep and I heard him yell, "Hunni, I'm home!"

I replied, "Rent due!" I heard him burst out laughing, then like clockwork, turn on the TV (right). I finally came bouncing down the steps ten minutes later to him smiling at me. Yes, I still have a slight crush on him, so I just winked at him and made my way to the kitchen. I know, I kept it cute. But trust me, he *knows* I'll give him the business. I gave him a foot massage last week and he loved every bit of it. If I wanted him, I could have him. That's the fun of it, though. Anyway, the rest of the fellas started to roll in about 730; which was fine, because by then I was officially done cooking. They were all sitting at the dining room table enjoying themselves. Talking more shit then the law allows. LOL.

I was in the midst of prepping my cake to go in the oven (it was about 8:45 p.m.) and my phone reminder went off. I turned it off and burst out laughing. Of course, Beast's nosy ass wanted to know who I was talking to.

His buddy jumped in and said, "You act like you jealous or something."

He responded with, "Never that."

I laughed and said, "If you must know, it was a reminder for me to ask you all something. And since I have your attention…"

They collectively said, "Aw shit! Here we go!"

"Whatever. So, I wanna know about the peepers and booth place up the street."

They all burst out laughing at the same time then looked at Beast.

"Christian, what the fuck do you wanna know?" Beast asked, smiling.

"I wanna know what it is and why is that little ass store always packed on Friday and Saturday nights?"

They laughed again.

"Christian. You really wanna know?"

"YES! Tell me."

"Well, what do you think it is?"

Well, obviously, it's an adult video store, but why are all those cars always up there. What the hell y'all be in there doing?" They laughed. "What the hell is so funny? I'm serious. I wanna know."

"Okay. If you wanna know, we gone show you. We were going up there tonight when we left here anyway."

"Unh-Unh! And do what?"

"You'll see." As they laughed.

"See? Now y'all got me nervous."

So anyways, they were done eating and I was putting the glaze on the rum cake when Beast came over to me in the kitchen. He leaned back on the counter with his arms crossed.

"If you gone hang tonight, you need to change your clothes, kiddo."

I laughed. "What? Why?"

"Trust me, you're way too overdressed to go in there."

"I have on jeans and a T-shirt."

"Nah, slim. I know you. You need to put on some sweatpants and chill shit.

"I don't think I own sweatpants. I have to look."

Beast laughed. "I can see right now; this is going to be a long night."

"Eeek! I'm excited. Thank you!

He laughed and shook his head.

"Let me clean up and I'll be ready. You all can eat the rum cake. It's ready." I sat it on the table.

I went upstairs to see if I could find me some sweatpants. Ironically, I had *one pair*. I know, right? Go figure! I put those on with my dark blue sweatshirt, my black and gray hat (that I could use to cover my eyes, if need be) and my old sneakers that I wear to do stuff outside. Oh no, hunni, I took that hint and put on all old stuff. I came bouncing back downstairs full of excitement because I was about to see and learn something new. I was way too excited. LOL. They were all laughing at me. Beast told me I needed to calm my little ass down. They ate more than half of the cake and was feeling quite nice. I made the rum cake a little strong by accident. They were ready to go for real now. I gave myself a once over and then locked up my place. Beast told me that I was going to ride with him and to only bring my I.D.

Once I locked up my house, I jumped in the truck with Beast and we were on our way. His buddies had pulled off already and by the time we pulled up, they were already parked. Before we got out, he told me to leave my phone in his truck (which I was already going to do anyways). We get out and head for the door. Naturally, I'm following them. Beast was in front of me, telling me to stay close to him. I didn't think anything of it and said, "Okay."

We walk in, and the store is cute. It was bright, full of adult entertainment and "other things." I was looking around, didn't even realize that I had walked away from them.

Beast was on my ass when I turned around, though. I kept hearing a door open and close behind me, but I didn't pay it any attention. I made my way back over to the other side where the cashier was, and he spoke to Beast. They laughed it up and everything.

I was like, *Um, frequent here much?* The cashier asked for my I.D. I gave it to him.

"DC, huh?" the cashier said. "Let me guess, you're military, too, right?

"Yes sir, I sure am."

"Well, welcome. Hope you have a great night. Stick close to your buddy, he can give you the in's and the outs. Enjoy."

"I just bet he can. Thank you."

So, Beast asked me if I had any cash and I told him I didn't.

"No problem. You gone give me back my money, chump."

"Wait, what I need money for?"

"I'm about to show you. Take this and put it in the money slot." He hands me a ten-dollar bill.

"Uh, okay."

I put the money in the slot, and it made a click sound, then the door unlocked and opened. I was like, *What the hell? Chyle!* I walked through the door and Beast was behind me, then the door slammed shut and locked. Now that freaked me out and made me jump. He and his buddies laughed and told me to relax. I nervously laughed it off and said, "Whatever." As I stepped further into the room, I was PUNCHED in the NOSE by this horrible smell. It smelled like bleach, sperm, sex and dirty panties. YUCK! Girl, I'm not lying. I needed a new set of nostrils. Whew! All the walls were painted black. When you first walk in the door, the restroom was right in front of you. If you looked to the left, there was a doorway that led to two other private rooms. If you looked to the right, you saw a long hallway filled with about eight video viewing booths (four on each side), with a soda machine at the end of the hallway.

The other fellas had disappeared. It was just me and Beast standing there. He told me to follow him. Of course, I did, and I was HELLA NERVOUS! That damn SMELL! Like I just *GAGGING* couldn't. I told him to hold on. I went into the rest room and put some soap under my nostrils and on my mustache. You're laughing, but that shit was GROSS! Like for real. I can even smell it when I think about it. GAG! He laughed at me and told me I'd get used to it. I told him I didn't want to.

Now I'm back to following him down the hallway. He opened the first door to show me the first booth. He put a dollar in the machine and chose a video. He clicked on the first one that popped up, touched the screen and the video clip played. He explained to me how people who want to view the videos before they purchase them, they can view them in privacy in the booth. I just said, "Okay."

We left that one and went across to the other booth. He told me he was about to show me what a "peeper" was. I was starting to relax, but when he said that, I kind of tensed up again. He opened the booth door; the video clip was already playing.

"Look at the wall. You see that?"

"No. what?"

"Look down."

"Uuummmm. That little hole?"

"Yes. Look in it."

"What the fuck? NO!"

He laughed. "Just look in it, man!'

"Um, okay."

So, I leaned down to look in the little hole. There was a man in the next booth, watching a video and um, touching himself. He had DICK, TOO! LOL! I popped up so dayum fast! I wasn't expecting that. Actually, I don't know what I was expecting. Just not that. He laughed at me and told me to come on. I followed him to the next booth.

#Pause Now listen (SMH). HMPH. Take a sip, boo. #Continue

He opened the door; a video clip was playing already. I looked at the wall automatically, then, like a big dummy, I leaned down to look in the hole. No sooner than I leaned down to look in the hole, Beast snatched me up FAST AS HELL! Oh, my God! Thank goodness he did! No sooner than he snatched me up, a big old White dick came through that hole!

Me being me, "I said, "Unh-unh!" and I smacked it!

"Oh, yeah," said the guy in the booth next door. "Smack that cock, baby. He groaned.

"UNH-UNH! What the hell? But did he just GROAN at me, though?"

Beast started cracking up. "Man, you don't put your damn eye down there! That's a glory hole."

"What the hell is that? Oooooohhhhh! Ewwwww!"

"Yeah! If dude in the booth want his dick sucked, he puts it through that hole and makes it happen."

"Oh my God! I almost got a black eye! Via White dick and glory hole realness. Oh, my God!"

"You simple as hell. How the hell somebody like you don't know about this?"

"Because I never really thought about it! Let alone paid it any attention. I mean…eeewww. However, I'm slightly turned on by the idea of anonymous sex, though. Hhhmm. Interesting."

Beast shook his head. "Let's go. The tours not over just yet."

"OH, GAWD!"

We walked back down the hallway toward the main door. We were headed to the other side to two other rooms. Remember I said if you go to the left through the door, there were two other rooms? Well, we went to the left. We walked straight to the room right off the left, but to the right. It was a little room about the size of a bedroom. That was the "gay friendly" playroom. Beast signaled me to come look. I peeped around the corner to see a flat screen television mounted on the wall with gay porn playing, a sofa and three chairs. The light was very dim. The fellas were engaging in some sexual activity, when I noticed one of Beast's homeboys were getting some head from one of the dudes and the other one was watching. Yeah, I wasn't expecting that either. Although I DID LOOK! OOP! I said well alright now. Beast laughed and told me to come on, unless I wanted to stay in there with them. I told him, "No, I'm good." Again, I was turned on by their openness.

Beast took me back out by the main entrance before we made our way to the last room.

"Now okay listen to me. This last room I'm about to take you to, you stick by me. You don't move unless I move, I got you."

"Okay now you're making me nervous again."

"Nah, you good. I got chu."

"Okay, I'm ready." I shook my head.

This time, Beast was in front me, but he had me by my hand. My heart was REALLY racing now. I was like, *Lawd, what did I get my nosy ass into now? UGH!*

So, we walked down this long hallway. It was dark with very dim lighting. We came to the corner, turn to the right and BAM! The room opened up. It's this BIG ASS TV screen in the middle that sat up on a platform. I looked to the right and the room had a bunch of recliners, chairs and sofas that lined the back wall. Let's just say, I now see where the rest of his buddies went. That room was FULL of men. I was like, *Wait a minute. Wait a minute.* It was straight porn playing on the screen. Some of the fellas were watching while beating their meat, others were just chilling, a few others were giving and getting head, then I saw two females. Beast told me to stay right where I was, he was going to get us a chair. BIIITTCCHHH! Now listen. When I tell you I was NOT ready for that or that SMELL. I gagged again. Then when I saw "fish", I definitely gagged. Not because they were females, but because of how they looked. UNH-UNH! GIRL, NO! NO MAYUM SIS! NAH!

Beast came back with chairs for us. We sat down along the wall by the hallway we came down to enter the room. I leaned over to ask him, "Where the fuck did those girls come from?" and he said, "Just watch." I was like, *Will I watch without throwing up?* Ugh. Let me describe these heffa's to you. The bigger one, she had pigtails in her hair, these thick-ass eyeglasses on, a SUPER too small black dress, no panties (barf, I know) and knee-high black boots. The other one was super skinny, looked like she was on meth (again, vomit) with a black dress that was a mess (literally, #MonicaLewinsky), hair pulled back in a ponytail, black knee-high boots and, hunni, they was working the room.

Beast and I were sitting there just watching all of this go down. I was trying to keep my food down. Beast leaned over to me and whispered, "Watch this." The chubby one was getting smashed off by some dude, then once he was done, another dude went in raw right behind him, then once he was done, another dude came and stuck his face in her cooch. YEAH! I was a full-on resident of "I'm About to Throw the Fuck Up Lane." Love...Sis...NO, MAYUM! Now we both know I am no stranger to the swinger lifestyle (at all). It's just neither one of them looked sanitary, or even cute for that matter. Beast was just cracking up at me and my facial expressions. You know whatever I'm thinking shows up on my face. I couldn't hide my disdain at all.

Girl, I stopped looking at them and focused on the rest of the room. They were in there getting it in. Before I knew it, I was leaned over on Beast's lap, looking at the sights.

He laughed. "Check you out. You all into it."

"OH! My bad. I'm sorry, sugar. Just, wow! And I see your friends are really enjoying themselves. So, this is what you all do on the weekends?"

"Yup. Well some of us. I only come in here when I can't get no company or super fucking horny."

"Hhhmmm. Okay. And from what I can tell, you're having a moment now." I looked down at his crotch.

"Oh, shit. My Bad. But yeah. You can help me with that later."

"You, betta gone. You know I will. Ow!"

"We gone see," he said, smiling.

"Okay you are going to have to stop with the jokes. This is NOT the atmosphere for those kinds of jokes, sir."

"Who said I was joking? You think I don't see the way you look at me? I know what you want, and I might just give it to you tonight."

Girl, all I could do was laugh and blush. He had me slight fucked up. LOL. Now, I was turned ON! I was ready to leave and then WHHHHYYYYY did the chubby one bring her ass over there to us? Now, Love. Love. My LOVE. SMH. So, Miss. Thang walked over to us and she started rubbing Beast's shoulder. I moved her hand and told her, "No, thank you!" This dizzy bitch thought that meant for her to come and touch me.

"Oh, so you want some of my attention, baby?"

"Miss Thang! If you don't carry your ass on from over here, YOU BETTER!"

"You're feisty. I like that."

"If you want to keep your fingers and limbs, I suggest you "like" somebody else away from me," I said through clenched teeth, "OUTTA MY SPACE! NOW!"

"Okay. I can take a hint."

"Apparently not. Now gone and carry your ass on. And tell your friend don't brang her frail ass over here either."

Beast was just yucking it up. He just thought it was so funny that I was being harassed by her. He told her to go 'head, we were fine. Of course, he was calmer about it then I was. I was NOT here for the foolishness. It was about 3:00 a.m. when I finally looked down at my watch. Time flew by. I guess because I was so engulfed in what was going on, I didn't even pay the time any attention. I leaned over and told Beast that I noticed some familiar faces in here. He told me, on the regular basis. I told him I was ready to go now. I had seen enough. He said he was ready as well.

We went to go tell his buddies in the other room we were getting ready to leave. We bust that corner and, baby! They were getting it IN! They were sucking, fucking and everything. I said, "OOOOOOP! Alright now." Then I looked again and saw one of the Colonel's I was cool with.

He saw me looking at him, winked at me, and kept right on going. I winked back at him and went back into the hallway. Beast laughed.

"I knew you could handle this. I've been watching you long enough. Hell, I've been around you long enough to know you by now."

"Well, I don't need to blow his spot up. Shit, he ain't bothering me none. Let them do them."

"That's what I mean. You don't give a fuck. That's why they like you so much. Come on, we'll talk about it more outside."

"Okay."

We came out the exit and the cashier told me to have a good-night (while smiling, of course). Beast and I jumped in his truck to head back to my place. We laughed about the "Black Dress Skeezer's." He pulled in my driveway, then said he was coming in. I'm thinking to myself, "*Let me not get too excited. He was probably just talking shit anyway*". I told him that's cool. We were still in the garage when I undressed and threw my clothes on the ground. I told him to stay put, I'd be right back. I ran upstairs to wash my hands and slide on my robe. I came back down, and I started putting the rest of the food away, when I heard him come out the bathroom. He washed his hands then went and got a beer. He then asked me if it was cool if he spent the night.

BITCH! My knees buckled. Girl, I fell all in the fridge (LOL). I gathered myself and managed to peek from behind the door. I told him, "Sure. The guest room is already made up, so knock ya'self out."

"Fuck a guest room. I'm sleeping beside you."

"What?! No, you're not!"

"Yes, the fuck I AM. And I'm not gone stand here and keep talking about it."

"Oh, shit! You betta watch it. I like that aggressive shit."

He laughed and said he was going to get in the shower. I told him, "Good. And do NOT sit on my bed with those clothes on. I'd have to burn my whole bed with the sheets on it."

He laughed while walking upstairs. I was done putting away the food and sat in the chair for like five minutes, trying to mentally digest what just happened. Everything from the adult store action to this joker upstairs in my shower. I just shook my head and laughed. I cut us a piece of cake and took it upstairs.

As I walked into the room, he was coming out the shower with my other bathrobe on. Baby! ZADDY had BAWDY! I had to back up and look again. I've always known he had body up under those

BDUs, but GOOD GAWD! I told him I put some cake on the night-stand for him and NOT to eat mine. I took my clothes off and got in the shower. I had to wash the stank of that place off me (ECK). Anyway, I got in the shower and for some reason, it felt extra good.

Even though I had a slight feeling nothing was going to happen between us, I showered with my "Hey Zaddy" body wash. I mean, just in case! So, being slick, I dried off and put on my night clothes in the bathroom. When I came out, he was already in the bed with the TV on and eating his cake.

I must admit, though, he was a sight to behold; this big sexy man lying in my bed, with his upper body expose, slightly under the comforter, with one leg hanging out, looking all sexy, eating cake like a true fat boy. HA! I never really realized how hairy he was. Just all kinds of MANLY SEXYNESS! Whew, Lord! Be still my culo. HMPH. I climbed in the bed, ate some cake, then got irked because I had to jump back up and brush my teeth again. I brushed my teeth then climbed back in the bed again. I turned the light off because he was finished; then I scooted down on my pillow. While I was checking my text messages. He leaned over and took my phone from me and placed it on the nightstand.

"Um, 'scuze you, rudeness!"

He laughed. "We about to have us some pillow talk. You be aiight."

"I guess!"

"Nah, I'm for real. I want you to hear me."

"Okay. Go."

"You know tonight, the fellas was testing you, right?"

"Continue."

"They wanted to see how you would react to seeing shit live and in your face. I knew you'd pass with no problem."

"Of course. I don't care what they do. As long as it doesn't hurt anybody or them, or me for that matter. I mean, I'll admit I was taken aback by the sex room action, but shit, I've seen way more than that. It's just usually in a private controlled environment."

"What do you mean?" He moved in closer to me.

"It's usually at someone's home. A very private party...so you just gone lay in my bed naked, though?"

"Sure am. You feel that monster, don't you? You feel it?"

You know what? Matter of fact..." I turned on the bedside lamp again. "Let me see it!"

"Aiight." He snatched the blanket back.

"Oh. Oh my. Oh, my word. Nice. Very nice. Hmph. Okay, thank you."

"You good now? You can touch it! Go 'head!"

"I'm good. Thank you." I turned the light back off.

He laughed. "Aiight. Cool."

I laid back down and we continued to talk, as he snuggled up under me. I told him, "I don't have time or room to judge people. Just don't hurt nobody. Live your life and do what you do. I just wasn't expecting THAT to be going on in there." We both laughed out loud.

"That's why they fuck with you."

"Yes, I'm used to that response. That, and you all are aware that I don't go around telling people's business. I respect you all and your positions. Not everyone will be as accepting as me. Besides, I'm no fool. I know some of the snobbiest people who get down with the get down and are some of the BIGGEST freaks walking this earth. People don't shock me that much. Notice I said that much."

He agreed with everything I said. He also told me that he was glad he met me. He knew from day one I was going to be hell on wheels, but in a good way (if that's even possible but okay). He then told me that he was attracted to my confidence and my slight fem qualities (which I already knew). He laughed then threw his big ass leg across my whole body. I burst out laughing because I pretty much disappeared. He rolled over, climbed on top of me and began to kiss me. I knew he could kiss! His lips were too damn full and juicy for him not to be able to kiss. I would have been so disappointed if he couldn't kiss. Whew, baby! He kissed me down! But

I had to push his big ass up off me, though. He was crushing my windpipes. LOL!

Big Daddy is SOLID, hunni. All Beef. Anyway, I rolled on top of him and sat up. The light from the TV shadowed my body on the wall. It was kind of cute. Anyway, I straddled him, looking at him.

He smiled. "What?"

"What is this? NO, I'm not reading anything into this. I just need to know. I don't want no shit outta you later on, sir."

"Never. I might walk past you and push you into a wall or something, but we good."

"You betta don't! Fucking with your strong ass, you'd push me THROUGH that bitch!"

"Fuck you, Christian!"

"I'm just saying. I'm low-key frail. You high-key strong as fuck!"

He laughed. "You got all the jokes, I see. We need to go to sleep."

"Um, I do what I want."

"I can put you to sleep. I'm just saying."

"You will do no such thing. Thank you."

I climbed off him and went to get back under the comforter. He jumped up so fast he scared me.

"What are you doing?"

"Why you always playing with me, Christian? You know damn well you want it." Now, he was back on top of me.

"I do, but I also follow my gut instincts. And right now, it's telling me *no*."

"What the fuck? Why?"

"I don't know, but if you don't mind, I need for you to get from in between my legs."

"No. I'll move when I'm ready. Right now, I'm not ready. Now grab my face again."

I grabbed his face and we kissed again. Clearly, he liked it like that. I could tell that he liked the intimate side of things. I picked up on it a few months back. He would always touch me on the small of my back, find little ways to touch me or rub my shoulders. Even while at work he would find ways to intimately touch me. Then, while we were laying there kissing, as soon as I started rubbing his head and caressing his back, I felt him um...GROW.

Oh, me...oh, my! Then he started kissing my spot, and baby! Whew! All that kissing and licking on my neck he was doing, was the business. He pushed my hands over my head and went to work with those lips. That man can GO! Mouth work boo. MOUTH. WORK!

I told him he had to stop, though. As good as it felt and as much as I was enjoying myself, I made him stop.

"I'll respect your wishes. I like you too much to fuck it up."

"Why thank you."

"But um, what am I supposed to do with this?"

He pulled back the comforter and well, let's just say, all the blood had rushed to his groin area.

"Go pee."

"That's fucked up! You know damn well I ain't gotta pee!"

"You might."

"Christian, stop playing. Come on. Hook me up. Give a brother some bop."

"LOL! Nope. But I'll fix it for you."

I reached over in my nightstand and grabbed the coconut oil. First, I oiled down my hands, then I scooped some out for him.

"What are you doing?"

"You're not allergic to coconut oil, are you?"

"No."

"Well good. I said I got you, so chill."

I scooped that oil out and rubbed down his stomach, thighs, then made my way to his balls, then his dick. He was loving every bit of it.

"Shit, Christian! This feels good as fuck! Oh, my God!"

"I know it does. Just relax. You see, people don't realize the power of coconut oil. I love it because it won't chafe you, it softens your skin and keeps your skin hydrated. I'm sure as you can tell, how soft my hands are right now. Right?" I was working his shaft.

"Oh my God Yes! Fuck!" He covered his eyes.

"And you can see how much you are enjoying the pleasures of my soft hands, right?" I said, working his shaft and caressing the head.

Girl, he was grunting and groaning.

"Exactly. This is why I don't mind giving you the pleasure of experiencing my hands. Now, just imagine if this was my mouth."

"YOU GONE MAKE ME NUT!"

"If you're ready, I can make you explode." I kissed the head.

I was working the HELL outta that sausage, hunni. He could not take the twist and turns of these hands. He was in heaven. Baby, his toes were popping, throwing up gang signs and everything. I had that ass on LOCK! I was twisting and turning these hands in an upwards and downwards motion, then I hit his ass with that "Kung Fu" grip...girl, he was over! Beast nutted so damn hard and loud; I just knew he was gone wake up my neighbors. He was just THAT loud. All that damn noise.

However, I am good at what I do, though. *Hair flip.*

"Don't move, I'll be right back."

"Don't worry I can't. SHIT!" He was still shaking and growling.

"No worries. I got chu, boo."

"Christian! SHIT! Oh my God! I gotta get me some damn coconut oil. FUCK!"

We both laughed. I cleaned him up and made sure he was good. He said he had NEVER had a hand job like that before. I told him, in my African accent, "It's the oils of the coconut."

He burst out laughing and said, "Now I can go to sleep."

Hunni, he did just that, too. He rolled over, I turned off the TV, kissed me again and then he was snoring within like five minutes. I'm like well dayum. LOL. I went back to checking my messages before I dozed off.

It was about 5:30 a.m. when we went to sleep, and I had the nerve to wake up at 9:38 a.m. (of course, he was snoring down when I woke up). I did my morning ritual and went downstairs to cook breakfast.

I wasn't sure if he was going to stay for breakfast or not, I just made enough just in case. He woke up about a quarter to eleven. I looked at the microwave clock when I heard him go into the bathroom. That's when I turned on the coffee pot. He came downstairs while I was finishing up the eggs and walked right up behind me, pressed up against me and started kissing my neck.

He then said, "Good morning," in that sexy-ass deep voice of his, which made me swoon. He turned me around so that he could kiss me. But first he hoisted me up on top of the counter. Whew LAWD! That shit was HOT! Hmph. He was back in my bathrobe and ready to eat. He went right into the cabinet, got him a coffee cup, poured him some coffee and sat down at the table with the morning paper. I'm looking at him like, this muthafuck'a is REAL comfortable right now. But, Love, catch this; I was okay with it and him. That shit slight turned me on (SMH). He's so damn manly and bully-like. Whew. Anyway, he went upstairs after breakfast and got dressed. I was cleaning up the kitchen when he came back down, grabbed his car keys, turned me around and told me he'd be back later on tonight.

"Are you asking me or telling me?"

"I'm definitely telling you. You will see me later on tonight."

I smiled. "Yeah okay. Well I'm going shopping in a few, so I'll hit you when I'm on my way back home."

"You asking me or you telling me?"

"Oh no, sugga, I'm definitely telling you!"

"Grab my face for me."

I grabbed his face the way he liked, then kissed him very passionately. The way that I liked. He told me I play too much. I was trying to make him fuck me in the kitchen, kissing him like that. He told me to follow him to the door.

"Um, sir, I don't have any clothes on."

"You only coming to the garage door."

"Ugh! Okay."

So as we're walking to the door, I stopped, and he went to turn on his truck. I got a slight chill. It was chilly out because its fall, so

I ran back in to grab my throw blanket off the sofa, then came back. He's walking back to me, laughing. He handed me my hat and slid me a couple bills.

"What is this for? I believe I owe you ten dollars. Remember?"

"You do, but you more than made up for it. Besides, you said you're going shopping. And since you cooked for all of us last night, you good."

"Beast! Y'all did *not* eat three hundred dollars' worth of food."

"Don't worry about it. You good. I got chu."

"That's fine. You don't have to convince me. Thank you. I'll make sure I pick up something for you." I winked.

"Now you're catching on."

I laughed. "Whatever."

He gave me another kiss and hopped in his truck and pulled off. I couldn't help but to laugh at all of this. This dude went from giving me all kinds of side-eyes at work to being one of my best friends in life *ever*. His personality reminds me of my buddy, Mason. Don't ask don't tell, very macho, don't ever talk about or mention nothing that we do (not that I would ever), gives off bi-sexual vibes and somewhat mysterious. He and Mason could be damn twins. Not to mention he's super private like I am, and you know I love that.

I got dressed and went to the Jeffersontown Mall. They have all the good department stores on that end. I knew what Beast wanted, so I went into one of my favorite little stores and brought me some sexy underwear. I heard him when he looked in my underwear draw the last time he was there. I brought some cute lace ones just for him. The rest of the money he gave me went toward my jeans and sneakers. Love, you know what though, as I was driving back home. I thought, all in all, Beast is a good dude. I love his personality and his company. I texted him when I was closer to my house. I didn't realize I had pretty much spent all day at the mall.

He met me back at my house like he said he was. This time he had an overnight bag. I was like, *Oh, okay*. He pulled up when I was taking the last of my bags in the house. He walked in the door and saw all my bags and shook his head.

"What? I told you I was going to the mall. I need more fall clothes."

"Yeah, but damn. Did you leave anything in the store?"

"Look. It is what it is."

I handed him the bag that had my underwear in it.

"What's this?" He smiled.

"Opening it and see." I walked away.

"Oh, shit! That's what I'm talking about!"

"You wearing these tonight?"

"No, baby, those are for you."

"Bullshit! My nuts won't even fit in these."

"Yes, I know. Pick out a color and I'll put them on later on."

"See? That's that shit I like! Hmph! You gone get that Hamma!"

"Yeah okay. Anyway, did you eat, or you good?"

"I'ma go get something. You good?"

"Yeah, I had a salmon & pecan salad.

"Cool. I'll be back in a few.

"Okay. Well, take the key or the garage door opener. I'll be up-stairs putting my stuff away."

"Oh Shit! I get a key?"

"Boy, just take one."

Needless to say, we had some great sex that night. He really did put that "Hamma" down on me. I think those lace undies sent him over. It was a very nice weekend with him. We went to breakfast Sunday morning and met his buddies at the pancake house. They were funny! Apparently, they all knew that he stayed over my house two nights in a row. They had all kinds of jokes, too. Jokes about him smiling, floating, being nice and covering my breakfast bill and everything. It was nice, though. I felt like I was out with my big brothers. Even after we were finished breakfast we just sat, laughed and chilled a little while longer. Since it was Sunday, I didn't stay too long, though. I needed to get home and decide what I was going to cook for dinner. Beast dropped me back off at home and told me he'd be back later for dinner, which I figured when he kept asking me if I knew what I was going to cook yet.

I really did and do enjoy his company. All of them, to be honest. They turned into my family away from home. They seemed to occupy my after-work time a lot! Which, I didn't mind though. And just to think, we bonded over glory holes, video booths and sex-lines. Go figure! I never went back there again, but the fellas did. Beast told me he hasn't been back since he'd been dealing with me, which was cool with me, to be honest. I mean he made sure I kept his balls empty. HA! Even though we didn't always have sex or fool around. We just enjoyed each other's company. I think he was more lonely than anything, to be perfectly honest. That's the vibe I got from him in the beginning. I was showing him some affection, attention and giving him some QT, so he was content. And honestly, so was I. He was filling my void (no pun). LOL!

So yeah, that's the story of me almost getting a black eye via a glory hole and a "Big White COCK!" Ugh. I hate that word. COCK. Yuck.

Anyways, this was fun, Love.

I'm glad I could make you laugh.

I'm going to bed now. Yes, alone. LOL.

Goodnight, my dear.

Love you much.

Eskimo kisses.

"DON'T F*!K WITH THE QWING DOM"

Love!

Hey, boo. You know what's funny? I was talking to B earlier and he was talking about that time we had to fight those "goons" in the movie theater parking lot. Oh, my God! Girl, yes! I was telling my sister about it last week. It's funny, he would bring that up after so many years. I remember that shit like it was yesterday. I have never been in that kind of situation. But hey, my man needed me, so I came through.

I remember we had been in and out all day, off and on, just doing some stuff around the house and getting the house together. Just cosmetic stuff and cleaning up. All while having fun playing with Bella in between and all that good old homey stuff. We decided since it was our date night, we would go to the movies and see *Collateral*, starring Tom Cruise and Jamie Fox. We made sure all was well before we left. We chose an evening movie because it would be cooler outside, and I prefer it that way. He was good with it so hey. We pulled up to the theater and I happened to look up, it was those same goons that I was going to fight at school before (right! A whole three years later). I let out a giggle, B asked what I was laughing at; I told him. He looked up, laughed and said, "Yeah well". Another words, he ain't give a shit, but I know how immature they still were, so I made sure I kept my eye on them. I had seen them every once in a while around the area, and the sad part, they were still acting like we were in high school. The shit was pretty fucking pathetic to be honest (SMH).

Anyway, we parked on the far side of the parking lot closer to the main street but made sure we were in the streetlights. Not because of them, but mainly safety reasons. We finally made our way into the movie theater, but I had my senses open and eyes open. "Collateral" was a pretty good movie. We sat in the movie and chatted for a few, waiting for everyone to exit (like we usually do). We decided that we would do dinner next door at the Greek restaurant since Greek is my favorite and we were so close. Not to mention hungry as hell, so hey, why not. As we were walking out the theater, B said he had to use the restroom. I said, "Cool, I'll check my messages one last time." I was on my phone when I looked up and saw the goons walk in the restroom behind him. I'm like where the fuck did they come from?! Oh nah! So in my regular fashion, you know my ass went right in there as well. I just faked like I was fixing my hair, then washed my hands. If some shit would have popped off, I had my man's back. Fuck that!

B came to the sink to wash his hands and saw me. He laughed and said, "Come on." As we were leaving out the restroom, I heard the ugly, big-lipped one say, "Yo, wasn't that dude from school? Lil faggie, cuz'?"

Me and B laughed and kept on walking. I said, "Yeah, I told you they hadn't changed."

"Yeah, I see. Clown-ass dudes."

We went into the restaurant and was seated right away. We ordered our drinks and was just laughing, having a grand old time with the staff. We were even laughing with the other guests. They had a live band and everything. It was really nice. Now, naturally, I eat and enjoy my Greek food (you know I go HAM when I get the chance). Especially since I don't eat it that often. I ate my salad and nibbled on some lamb and chicken. B asked me was I alright? I told him I was. Even though I really wasn't. You see Love, I knew those jackasses were going to try something. I felt it in my gut. When they saw B, then saw me, I could tell by the way he looked at me in the bathroom, memories were jogged.

B knew two of the dudes from around his way. He told me they never really talked or anything, but dude always stayed in trouble. So, all of that played a part in my mind. B has never lied to me and I knew he never would. Didn't have reason to (not without a very plausible reason). Anyway, yeah, I didn't eat a lot on purpose. I actually took most of my order to go. We sat in the restaurant for about two and a half hours before we left. It was about 11:00 p.m. when we decided to call it quits. I went to the restroom before we left because my nerves had me ready to pee like a racehorse. That and all that tea I drank.

B cashed us out and we made our way toward the exit. Low and behold, who was coming out of the movie exit as we were coming out of the restaurant the same time we were? Right, what a coincidence (side eye). I made sure B was aware, and he said he saw them. Then he started laughing at me.

"Babe, you gotta chill," said B. "Besides, they fuck boys. If some shit pop off I got chu.

"No, we got *us*. Fuck that."

"Aiight, babe. We got us. You ready now?"

"Yup!"

We left out the door and started back towards the truck. We heard them behind us a few feet away, giggling like a bunch of little bitches (as usual). Because that's what fuck boys do. They act extremely childish and do childish shit. *#Pause* It's just so funny to me how I can recall this. I know why, though. You'll see why in a few. *#Continue*

As we made our way around the corner into the parking lot, B was close enough to unlock his truck, so he hit the alarm button to unlock it. By this time my stomach was in knots because my nerves were alerting me of what was getting ready to come. I could tell that some shit was about to pop off. We kept on walking, talking and laughing. I could tell B knew I was antsy. He was saying stupid stuff to make me laugh. He would crack jokes and say things that my uncle Bias would say, because he knew I would laugh instantly.

So, as I was laughing at B, I heard, "Shut the fuck up, faggot," come from behind me, followed by them laughing collectively. That's when I heard their leader say, "Y'all gotta chill!" That made me laugh even harder. Then I heard the big-lipped ugly one, with the thick ass "Mr. Magoo" glasses, say "YO! Is this nigga laughing at us, though? What the fuck?"

B told me to chill and get in the truck. I walked around to the passenger side door, when I heard their "leader" say "Aye cuz! Let me holla at you for a second." I turned around to throw my food in the back seat, and B pushed me in the truck and shut the door. He then leaned on my door so I couldn't open it. He knew I was getting ready to get back out. LOL!

It was four of them and two of us. I knew they were going to try my husband and I was not about to be that bitch that was gone let them. Oh I think The FUCK NOT! I knew when I heard him say, "Let me holla at you," then his body language told me the rest of what I needed to know. After he said that, he wouldn't look B in his eyes or face, then he tilted his head to the left while looking at the ground. By now, I was sitting on my knees, ready to pounce outta that damn truck! I knew he was going to swing on him or at least try to.

I yelled at him, "B! He's about to swing on you!"

No sooner than I said that, that dusty ass jerk swung on him.

B moved his head to left and the boy punched the truck. That's when B lost it. RIGHT! I was like, *this jackass swung on you and because he hit your truck you SNAPPED?* REALLY B? UGH! Anyway, by this time, B had punched dude with one punched and stretched him out.

#Pause This is another reason why I don't like for him to fight. Once he gets mad, it's a wash. When my Big Bulldozer sees RED, its lights out, hunni. Ugh! *#Continue*

So, as this joker is laid out on the ground, his boy bucked bad and attacked B. B moved away from the truck and I began to open the door, the ugly big-lipped one slammed my door shut. He almost got me in the door. B was fighting the other two at the same time, while one was on his back and the other one was in front of him. I saw the leader of the bunch looking like he was waking up. I said, "Oh, hell no!" I was I looking out the window and yelling at B to be careful. I was quickly frozen in fear when the dummy who was holding my door shut, looked me straight in the eye and said, "If you get out, I'm fucking you up." When I heard B yell, it snapped me out of it.

Baby, listen! My baby yelled, and it was on! Like I said, his yelling snapped me out of it. It was more like an "AAHHH!" I said, "Oh fuck this!" I jumped over the divider into the back seat, jumped into the cargo area, grabbed the tire iron (you know I fight dirty), jumped back over the seats, then I jumped clean out the driver's side passenger door. I came around the back of that truck SWINGING! I tore his Big Lip ass THE FUCK UP! Oh baby I bust his shit all up! Then I felt bad when he stumbled. LOL! He said I chipped his tooth. I said "FUCK YO TOOTH BITCH!" I quickly snapped outta that convo when I looked over and saw them on top of B. I ran over there and started swinging again! I crack the skinny one right upside his head, then stomped on his chest. The other one moved when he saw me. B jumped up and punched the skinny one and knocked his ass out.

The leader of the pack was back up, but he was still stumbling, so I went over and drop-kicked him in the back and B punched him again. He was out (smirk). We were tag teaming the shit outta those jackasses. They started it and damn it, we finished it. We looked up and they were all down. The big-lipped one that started all of this, even in high school; it was the same thing. His ugly ass running his mouth. Anyway, I was leaning up against B's truck and I hit him on the side of his knee with the tire iron. I ain't cripple him, but I damn sure hurt him. When he buckled over, I kicked him square in is ass. B told me to get in, so we can go. I jumped in and threw the tire iron back in the back and we pulled off.

By the time we were pulling off out of the parking lot to where the traffic light was, the police was speeding into the parking lot. We passed them right on by and burst out laughing. That was something else I was thinking about. What would have happened if the police pulled up or if we would have gotten caught? We had an all-out mini brawl in that damn parking lot. I knew somebody was gone call the police. All those big, black men fighting in the parking lot. Girl please. I knew it was coming.

I'm just glad they didn't come until we were gone already (as usual). B and I were making our way up Maryland Route 301 when we both burst out laughing again. I told him I needed something to drink. He agreed and we pulled into the first 7-Eleven we saw. We got out the truck looking a HOT MESS! My baby's shirt was all tore up, he had a slight bruise on his forehead, my shirt was ripped and so were my jeans (but I actually looked kind'a cute though. LOL. I know, only me). We looked at each other and laughed again. We went in and got us some water and chips. Once we got back in, we sat in there in silence for like two minutes, looked at a few folks go in and out of the store, then looked at each other and yup, burst out laughing again.

You know what Love, I'm not gone even lie, it felt good to give those jackasses what they deserved. We pulled off and began to make our way back home. When we jumped back on Route 301, we weren't too far from the house. On the rest of ride home, he asked me was I alright? I told him I was, and I think I needed that. He laughed.

"Babe, I'm so glad you had my back. I just knew I was gone have to fight by myself." He laughed.

"WHAT!? Why would you think that!?"

"Babe come on. You're NOT a fighter. That's why I pushed you in the truck."

"Yes, that's true, but I will fight IF AND WHEN I have to. I was NOT gone let them jump my man while I sit in the truck and scream like a white woman in distress. NOT ON MY WATCH."

"Well yeah that much I remember. I'm still trying to figure out how you leaped off those steps and on top of your cousin like that."

"Exactly! Don't doubt me. Besides, you know I got cha'back. Ain't nobody finna fuck with you, or us for that matter. Besides, they had it coming."

"Yeah, I know. I just wanted to make sure you good. You know I got chu. Besides, your uncle and godfather would fuck my shit up if they knew I had you out here in these streets fighting and shit."

"No, they wouldn't. Not when its self-defense."

As we pulled up to the house and into the driveway, I told him, "Don't worry about it. We good. I got'chu and you got me. Now, turn your truck off so we don't wake up the house."

His truck pipes are loud, and they are extra loud when it's quiet outside. I began to take off my sneakers, then my jeans.

He asked me, "What the fuck are you doing?"

I climbed across that middle console, mounted him and slobb'ed him down. I needed for him to relax and to know that we we're good. I mean I'm sure he did, but still. So, I mounted him, pulled that dick out and went to work! Baaybeey! That was some of the best sex we ever had in that truck. (Nah, that wasn't the first time. LOL). We bounced the hell outta those struts and shocks.

After we were done, he laughed, then said, "I swear I love your crazy ass."

"I know you do. Now let's go in the house. I might be ready again in a few minutes."

"Oh, shit! Yeah, let's go!"

As I was getting out the truck from the driver's side, I had to put my underwear back on before I went in the house. I wasn't sure if anybody was awake or not. Can't be caught assed out (*Literally*). Of course, as we're making our way in the house, my nosy ass grandmother was awake, talking about she wanted to make sure we got in alright. Girl! Any other time her ass would be sleep. *Now* she's woke. Then again, I know her spirit of discernment, so ain't no telling what she was really feeling. She probably felt that something was wrong with me. I'm glad it was dark, and she couldn't see how bruised up B was. She would've really gone off. That's her baby (eye roll). We managed to make our way upstairs without her paying too much attention to us, which was a good thing.

We got in the shower and then crawled in bed. We laughed again, had sex again, then laughed some more. The shit was just Hella funny to us and quite sexy to me. I loved that we could fight together. LOL. It wasn't just the fighting part for me, it was more of a respect thing for me (if that makes sense to you). I don't care about anyone's orientation or race, just respect people. All those hate slurs he was throwing at me, then behind my back; Nah, we not doing that. Then on top of that, you threatened us, then attacked us.

Yeah no, that wasn't cool at all. I don't bother anybody or attack folks, and I'm not going to allow that shit to happen to me or mine.

B went to sleep after a little pillow talk, telling me how much he loved me (as if I didn't know). He just wanted to make sure I really knew it. *Boy, okay, already!* He knows I love him, and he'll always be my baby. That's never up for discussion.

I couldn't help but to lay there and think about what had happened. It's funny how just when I thought it was over, it wasn't. Hopefully now it is. So, I had thought. Right! Catch this GAG.

One of my play aunts was getting married and she invited us to the wedding. I was glad she thought enough of me to invite me, let alone him, too. You know some people are funny acting about stuff like that. TUH! Anyway, cut to 2 months later, and we are on our way to the wedding reception. Chyle! Guess who was the groom's nephew? YUP! The leader of the goons himself. Me and B cackled when we walked in and he saw our faces. I made sure he saw us hugging her and talking to her. Then when his uncle spoke to me and hugged me, he was OVER! Baby! The pleasure of the GAG was all MINE. You already know I flipped my hair and was extra friendly with his uncle. HA!

When it was time for us to leave, we made our rounds again, then made our way out to the car. Mr. "Let me holla at you..." Girl! He followed us out to the car and wanted to talk to us. Before he could say anything, B said, "Aiight! Now look! I ain't in the mood for this shit again today!"

Goon Leader replied, "Nah! Chill! I just wanted to apologize. Straight up off the no bullshit. If my uncle and new aunt fuck with you, then I do, too. No hard feelings. Truce?"

B said, "Nah, homie. I'm good," then went to open my door.

"What the fuck? *Really?*" he said to B.

Before I got in the truck, I replied with "Let me explain something to you. What you just displayed was disrespectful. You basically said that, had it not been for you seeing our interaction between your uncle and my aunt, you would not have extended this so-called olive branch. That's why he declined your apology,"

"Oh, shit,"

"Yeah. But thank you. You have a good evening."

I got in the truck, B closed my door, walked around got in, then we pulled off. He wasn't too pleased with me explaining to him what the issue was. B told me I should have let him figure it out. My response to him was, "What if he never did? What if this would have kept going? Then I would have had to include other people in this. Then, my uncle and godfather would not have been happy. Not to mention, if it's always an eye for an eye, wouldn't the entire world be blind? Yeah, let's nip it in the bud now."

B looked at me, then leaned over and kissed me. "That's why I keep you around."

We got home, took our clothes off, had sex, I cooked dinner we ate, and chilled. BLAH! All in a day. That fight episode put quite a few things in perspective for me, too. Even the aftermath of it all was an eye-opener for me as well. B was used to fighting and going about his business. That night resonated with my soul for quite some time. I had to develop tougher skin, deal with it personally, then I could release it. I never told B it bothered me for as long as it did. I know he wouldn't get it (which was fine), but I just needed some time to deal. I was so glad I could release it when I did, though. Another weight was lifted.

So yeah, that fight was funny as fuck. It was like "AAAHHHH! Y'all got that ass OWNED by a FAG! No pun intended but hey. LOL. Whew! I know, "Petty Pete" I was. It is what it is. Needless to say, things were made alright in the world that weekend. A lesson was learned by all parties involved. And if it wasn't, then hey, I'm always ready.

Anyways Love, I gotta go cook dinner now.

I'll talk to you later,

Double Kisses!

MY 6-FOOT-8 FRESHMAN LOVER

Well, good evening, doll. How are ya?

I am in a great mood. Just got back home from shopping and hanging out with my loves, The Queen and The Diva. Of course, we had a wonderful time. We always do. We went to the movies and then to dinner. I was thinking about you the whole time. You asked me about how Bear and I met, and you wanted to know the whole story. So, go get you a cocktail and buckle up, doll. I'm about to give you all the deets. ALL OF THEM. I mean, you DID ask. No, I'm kidding. Well, MOST of what you want to know. I can't be telling you all me and my baby's business (smiling).

So okay, let me see if I remember this correctly, and I usually do. The year was 1998 and I was a freshman in high school. I remember I would see him walking around the hallways from time to time, because he was so BIG & TALL. The very first time I saw him, I could not take my eyes off him. He was this big ol' chocolate teddy bear that I wanted to hug. Because I was so locked in on him walking down the hallway, he gave me that "wassup" head nod and I immediately became flustered, then filled with emotions. Then, as I was walking down the hallway to my class, I looked back and he looked back and smiled. After that, I darted into the bathroom to get myself together. I was SHOOK, hunni (I swear I was). He had me like, *Wow!* I had flirted with boys before, but with him it was different. Later on, whenever we would talk about this, he would say

I was flirting but I didn't think I was. This big old handsome bear of a man just mesmerized me.

So anyway, later that morning, I decided to go ahead and stick to my plan of leaving early. It was about quarter-to-twelve when I decided I had had enough. I walked out the front doors because the back doors and gate were locked. As I was making my way across the neighboring community college's parking lot, walking toward the football field, I heard a horn blowing. I didn't pay it any attention and just kept on waking. As soon as I got to the football field's first goal post, I heard a whistle followed up by, "Christian, you just gone ignore me huh?" I burst out laughing and turned around. All I could see was a green Chevy Tahoe because of the glare from the sun blinding me. Using my hand as a cover, so I could try to make out who the person was, it was him. He yelled, "Meet me halfway!" Although I didn't realize it was him, I started walking back toward him. I don't know why, but I did. He met me halfway, too. The conversation was interesting. There were a lot of smiling and eye flirting between us. Mainly because he got out of his truck looking too damn delicious. He had on his tank top (wife beater), gray sweatpants and timb's (which were loosely tied). Baby listen! Love, when I tell you I had to keep my composure. He was so BIG and BEARY. I was turned the fuck on! Whew! Arms all big, chest all broad and hairy. Just sexy as fuck! My culo was JOOK'N! Anyway! And NO, that is NOT what he had on when I first saw him in the hallway at school.

"Um, where are you on your way to? We still have about," B looked at his watch, "three hours left, sir." He smiled.

"Wait a minute. How do you know my name? And none of your business. My parents are at work, thank you." I smiled. "That's a nice watch." I grabbed his arm to look at his big face watch."

"Thank you." He smiled. "And yes, I know your name. I better. Your brother is one of my best friends and has been for the last few years. You didn't know that?"

"Obviously not. Which brother are you referring to? You do know that I have many, right?"

He laughed out loud. "Yes, I know and I'm talking about Knuckles."

"Oh, gawd! I should have known. Keith! Let me guess, you're a jock as well, right?"

"Yeah. So! I mean, why I can't just be a football player? And since you don't know me, my name is Tony. Nice to finally meet you, Christian." He smiled.

"Yeah, Tony, nice to finally meet you as well." I laughed. "I'm not sure how I missed you, though. I mean, it's not like you're small enough to blend in. NO HATE!"

He burst out laughing. "Lil man got big jokes! Okay. Yeah, no hate. It's all good. I'm either at work or at practice. That's why. I mean, if you ever come out the kitchen long enough, you'd know I've been to your house quite a few times."

"OOP! And now you're a creep. Okay, it was nice talking to you. I've gotta go now. Bye." As I started walking away, he burst out laughing.

"Aye stop playing with me Moe! I ain't no damn creep. Well, I'll be over later on this evening. How about you make yourself notice-able and I'll make sure I speak?"

"Hmph. Okay," I said, walking away, "well, I'll be in the kitchen cooking with my grams. I'll see you if you happen to walk past the kitchen."

"So you gon' be cooking again, hunh? Yeah okay. I got chu. You want a ride?"

All I could think was, *Boy, you have no idea how bad I wanna ride those shoulders and straddle those strong thighs.* GOOD GAWD!

I just said "Oh, no, I'm fine. Thanks, though. You have a good one." I walked away.

"A'ight. I'll see you later."

I turned around to see if he was watching me walk away, and he was. BOOM! I smiled at him again and he gave me that "smirk head nod" thing that boys do. I kept right on walking. He jumped back into his truck and pulled off. I finally made my way across that big ass football field back home. Nobody was home yet, but my mother left me a note saying that Grams would be to the house about 2:30 to cook. I had about two hours before she showed up. I went right upstairs, hopped in the shower, then took a nap. Why does it seem like that mid-day nap is ALWAYS the BEST? I remember because that was the first time I woke up at the foot end of my bed. Chyle, I don't know how I did it, but baby, I was SLEEP! When my alarm clock went off, I woke looking all lost and disheveled. Like, what the hell kind of sleep was I doing? I jumped up, washed my face, made myself slight cute and then bounced on down the steps. No sooner than I was done prepping the set-up space for Grams to cook, she was walking through the door. She's my little breath of fresh air. She always glowed whenever I saw her (*smiling*). My doll. Naturally, I jumped right into her arms and greeted her with our usual hug and kissy face.

As she was unpacking, she was giving me the rundown. She was telling me how she just wanted me to help her prep for a party and then help her pack it away. Other than that, that was it. That's just fine by me. The easier the better. I just didn't realize how much we had to prep, though. She low-key set me up. LOL.

We were prepping away when she told me to turn on her music. I knew what that meant. Turn on her gospel and let her cook on the good foot. I did just that. As she was singing and cooking, I was sitting at the island making the vegetable, cheese and meat platters.

We had a nice little system going for us. It was just so cute. So, as she was running out of stuff, she was making her a list. I called my uncle B to tell him she needed a store run. Of course, he had jokes. You already know how he is. When he pulled up, I was prepping the salmon and getting ready to start the dessert. She ran out the door, then I heard him honking the horn. I'm like, *What the hell?* I go over and look out the window. Its Keith and Tony. I heard Uncle B when he said, *"Goddamn! You's a big motherfucka! You play ball, boy, or you knock planes outta the sky?"* Everybody burst out laughing, and Grams telling him to shut his mouth and leave them alone.

She said, "I'll be back, babies. It's food in the kitchen. Tell Christian if you need something."

They were so funny as they responded with "Yes, ma'am" like little school kids. *(Laughing out loud.)*

I turned my music on since I knew she was gon' be gone for at least forty-five minutes to an hour. Yup! I turned Pooh on. The "Velvet Rope" was still fresh and new, so I figured why not? I mean, I was still cooking, but now I was dancing around the kitchen, too. And you KNOW I was partying down. I heard Keith when he came in through the garage, but still hadn't paid him any attention. My focus was on trying to get as much done before she came back, so she wouldn't have to double back on anything. The funny part was, I was already in the process of making Keith a sandwich. We already know his daily routine after practice. He wants a cold cut, bottle water with an apple or some type of fruit. Mind you, I'm still dancing off Pooh while making his snack. I go to turn around and BAM! Tony was standing there, watching me, grinning.

I jumped back and said, "See? Creep!"

He burst out laughing. "I mean, you was partying. I ain't wanna bother you. We know how you are about Janet. Shit."

"What do you want?"

"Why we gotta always go through this, though?"

"'Cause you a creep! What chu' want?"

"I'm NOT. I was letting you do your thang. Can a brother get a sammich?"

"Really? Okay fine. Only because I was raised properly, and I heard Grams when she told y'all to ask me."

"I'm saying, though. You heard Big Mama. So hook me up!"

"You are *really* trying it. But okay. Whatever. What do you want?"

"Oh, I want everything on it, no crust and melt the cheese. Thanks."

"BOY! Get cho ass outta here. I'll call you when I'm done. BYE!"

He walked off laughing.

So, I made him a sandwich, and I made it just like he asked for it, too (on purpose). I was gon' be a smart ass and do the opposite, but I played nice. When I went to give him his food in the basement, he had the look of shock and awe on his face. I knew what I was doing.

Keith's greedy ass wanted another one, but he wanted his like that. UGH! I made him come get his, though. I needed to finish my cakes (yes, I was being slight petty). Anyway, I was finishing up the salmon and my cakes were in the oven. Grams and Uncle B wasn't back from the store yet and they had been gone for about two hours now.

She was with Bias (Uncle B), so ain't no telling where he had her at. That's just how he does. His old mama's boy ass. Anyway, I'm still cooking and jam'n when B decided he was going to bring the dishes back upstairs. This time, I was facing the door, so I saw his shadow as he was coming around corner. I was covering the salmons with foil and looking at the door. He walked in the kitchen smiling.

"What are you smiling for now?" Him smiling made me smile.

"Baby, that damn sandwich was so damn good, I could kiss you."

I laughed while blushing then responded with, "Why thank you. Glad you enjoyed it."

"Oh, I definitely did." He pulled out the barstool at sat down at the island. "So wassup wit'chu?"

"Well, right now I'm cooking, but for the most part; what you see is what you get (smiling).

"Yeah, so I see. So how come I don't see you that much when I come over here?

Because you probably come by during the hours I'm not available. I may be a freshman but I'ma busy person. I work with my family's business or I'm just out and about. I'm not a home body. Or at least I try not to be. I have my moments, though.

"Oh ok, cool. I mean your brother did say you are the Social Butterfly of the family. I see it's true. I've been over here a few times and never really saw you.

Really? Keith said that? Wow. He's right, though. Hmph. Go figure.

"Was he wrong or something? You seemed surprised."

No, he's not wrong. I just would not have expected him to use the term "Social Butterfly." That's all.

"Oh Okay. So now back to my question. Wassup wit'chu? Who you rocking with or you single? Or that's not where you at right now?

You are so funny. And yes, I'm single. Why?

"I was just asking. I mean you cute and shit. A brother feel'n you. Or at least I'm try'na feel you. If you let me.

Oh, that was cute. You are just on fire today. And thank you. You're not, too bad yourself *wink*. Now can you please move over out of my way so I can finish my desserts.

"Oh, My Bad! LOL. *moves over*

Thank you. So now the question is, wassup with you? Now that I know where you stand.

"What chu mean?

Well, clearly your cool and hella handsome... but you're also DL. No, I wouldn't out you, nor would I blast you. Just know that I am NOT in the closet and I don't be bothered with bullshit. From NOBODY.

"Hold Up! You think I'm handsome *leans in closer*

Now see! That's all you heard. LOL.

"LOL. Yeah, you're right. I mean only super close friends and fam know about me, but that's about it. Is that a problem for you?

Nope. You just need to make sure it's NOT a problem for you. I'm used to this battle and all the tricks to the trade that come along with it. I'm very careful and cautious. That's all.

"That's wassup. I'm here for that. Besides, ain't nobody fucking with me."

"So, I see! Well, it was nice talking to you and actually seeing you Tony. But, I've gotta finish helping my grams. Hell, if she ever comes back. What the hell?!"

"Sooooo, is that your way of asking me to leave you alone?"

"Yes. Politely anyways. You're distracting me and I really need to finish. Besides, I can't focus on Pooh and her music while talking to you."

"Oh, GAWD! You and that woman! It's all good, though. I'll go back downstairs and let you finish. It was nice talking to you as well, Christian. Don't be a stranger."

"I can't be, I'm in *my house.*" I smiled.

"True. Well, I won't be a stranger then." He smiled.

"Mmmhhmm, enjoy."

As he walked away and made his way back downstairs with my brother and some of the other fellas from the football team, I couldn't help but to smile. Actually, I was smiling and blushing. My smile was one of those cheesy giddy smiles, too. Like, I couldn't believe I was talking to him, let alone he was standing in my house, in my kitchen and actually flirting with me. Like, I just saw this dude walking around the hallways at school and now he's in my house, downstairs chilling with my brother. Whew! CHYYLLEEE. HMPH (SMH).

Once I got myself together, I continued to cook. Grams and Uncle Bias came back (finally). He had her all up on "Ebony End" (DC) and everything (Lord knows I miss him, too, with his crazy ass). Anyways, so as the evening went on and we finished cooking, she went on home and I made my way back up to my room. (Yes, this was before she moved in with us). I was in the process of cleaning up my room and looking for something to wear to school the next day. I heard the door when it opened and closed because some of Keith's buddies were leaving. Then I heard Bella when she came upstairs because of her collar (that little jingle noise it makes). As usual, she laid outside my door while I was cleaning and going through stuff. I was going through my closet when I heard her bark with that slight grunt tone. I know her bark, so it wasn't anything serious. When I said, "Girl, stop making all that noise," Tony peeked his big head ass in the room and gon' say, "Don't fuss at her. She's guarding you. I could have been a stranger."

I laughed and said, "Or a creep!" He burst out laughing.

"Here you go. Is that my name now? Creep?"

Well, you did just creep up the stairs and poke your big head ass in my room. You just weren't expecting for my doggie daughter to snitch on you. Speaking of which. Bella! What the hell?"

"What?" He laughed.

"You must come over here more than you let on. She doesn't fool with a lot of people and she's very protective of me. Now that I think about it, she didn't even flinch when you were downstairs or in the kitchen. So yeah. Just how often have you been here? Hmph."

He burst out laughing. "Eh, you fast as shit! I didn't even catch that."

"Yeah, yeah, and why are up here anyways?"

"Because they said you were up here, and I wanted to see what you were doing. May I come in?"

"You a creep and you're nosey. But sure, you can come in. Sit in the chair and *not* on my bed."

"Oh, I can't sit on the bed?"

"No, you cannot. I don't allow just anybody in my room and when I do, the only reason you should sit on my bed is if you're going to get in it. I don't allow people on my bed, especially in their outside or street clothes. That's gross and quite unsanitary."

"Oh, I can take my clothes off and get in the bed if you want me to!"

That cracked me up! "That was cute. Anyway! I'm looking for something to wear for tomorrow. Ugh. I might just call it a day. It's going to be Friday; all my work is done anyways. I might just skip tomorrow."

He laughed. "You can't blame a brother for trying! And you gon' skip because you don't feel like going? It must be nice."

"It *is*! I have the grades to do so and my parents trust me. Now those other ones you hang out with, not so much!" I laughed.

"Yeah, all of us be in study hall 24/7." He laughed out loud. "That's wassup. Can I come by tomorrow and chill with you for a few?"

I smiled at him. "That's a good question. Anything is possible. Let me think about it. I'll let you know before you leave.

He smiled, too. "A'ight. That's wassup."

He sat there with me the entire time I was cleaning up my room and straightening my closet. Of course, Bella was laying there as well. She wasn't gon' move anyway, she never does. As the night went on, it was about 9:00 p.m. now and we were just chatting away. Oddly enough, Keith or any of the other fellas didn't come to look for him. I don't know what he told them, but nope. Not a phone call, nobody came upstairs, nothing. The night was moving right along. About a quarter to ten, I was a little hungry. We both went back downstairs to the kitchen... mind you, he had taken off his shoes by now. Hunni, he was REAL comfortable. Not to mention, I slid into my PJ's. on purpose (giggle). I had on my gray night shirt and my super short jersey shorts (you know I had those stilts out on purpose). YUP! He was loving the view, too. I caught him sizing my legs up a few times while I was standing in the closet.

Anyway, we were downstairs in the kitchen, nibbling on the extra meat and cheese tray I made earlier for Grams; still talking and laughing. This time it was a little more intimate. He just had on his T-shirt and sweatpants. We were sitting closer to one another. Close enough for me to place my leg on top of his as he would rub my thigh from time to time.

I was really enjoying his company. We just laughed and talked in the kitchen for about another hour and thirty minutes. I took a few things from the tray back up to my room along with some water and sodas. I just did *not* want him to leave. Then, I thought about it as we were going back upstairs, nobody was home except for Keith, and his room was in the basement. Daddy was still on travel in another country, and my mother was cross country on travel. Hunni, I took full advantage, too. OH NO! Not like that! NO! LOL! Stop it! I mean of the opportunity to get to know him and do what I wanted. The sex part didn't come until later. Well, somewhat (giggle).

We were back upstairs in my room, Bella was asleep in my bathroom on the floor while he and I were talking, laughing and listening to music. I was shocked; he enjoyed the slow jams just as much as I did. It was nice. Now, it's about 11:30 p.m. and I wanted to be polite so I told him, "Don't let me keep you, if you must go home." He thanked me but said he was fine. And then it happened...

"I'm good. I mean, it is getting late and I'd hate to have to drive all the way back to DC this time of night. Alone. All by myself. All alone. Just so alone." He laughed.

"REALLY? All of that! And it's not that late. It's only 11:30. My grams is still woke. If she's even home for that matter. But okay."

"Come on. I'll behave. You can trust me. I prom-promise."

I burst out laughing because I said that a lot as well. He had no clue.

"UGH. If you stay, what are you going to sleep in? Obviously, I have NOHTING you can fit. Daddy might, though. MIGHT!"

"I'm good. I have a bag in my truck."

"Wait a minute! What?"

"Nah, it's not like that. I keep a bag in my truck because I never know what I might end up doing or going. I just always have me something fresh on standby. I can also tell just by this little bit of time we've spent together, you do as well."

"You're trying to make me fall in love with you sir (SMILING). I do keep a fresh bag in my trunk as well. I have one at school in my locker, too."

"See, I could tell. Hell, you washed your hands like a hundred times in thirty minutes. While you were cooking. LOL.

Oh sugga no, I do NOT get my hands dirty unless I want, too. We can talk about that later. Go get your bag so I can turn on the alarm. I know Keith is asleep. He's, too quiet.

"A'ight bet.

He bounced his big body ass right on down those steps and outside to his truck. I swear I think he was happier then I was. Which was fine because I was totally feeling him anyway. In all honesty, I was falling in love with him. Love, I know (SMH). You know me, I'm all things love.

I never fight my feelings or hold back what I'm feeling. As far as love goes anyway. I just felt it. The more I talked to him, the more I was falling for him. Also, the way we were interacting with each other; it was like he KNEW exactly what to say, how to touch me and how to swerve. Bella went with him outside while he went to his truck. That was another GREEN LIGHT for me. Bella was very smitten with him. I was watching their interaction from the kitchen window.

He sat in the truck and waited for her to finish using the bathroom, then she went right over to him and jumped her big ass in his lap, as he proceeded to rub her and talk to her. She was loving it. I'm just like oh shit, my daughter likes you right away. Oh, OKAY. Hell, Bella didn't even like daddy right away and he was the one that brought her ass home. LOL. So, yeah, he was making his way into my heart very fast.

As they came back into the house, I was locking the door and turning on the alarm; I heard Bella's food bark. I went and stood next to the kitchen's entry way just to watch the two of them interact. He was asking her what she wanted. She was next to the counter where I kept her treats. *She's telling you she wants a treat.* He looked up, smiled at me and said, "Oh Ok." The treats are in the 3rd container from the left. He gave her a treat and of course she was just, too excited. After that she was content. We made our way back upstairs to my bedroom, where Bella went back into the bathroom to lay on the floor.

"You mind if I take a shower?"

I sure do not. Hold on.

Bell's, SHOWER.

She knew that meant I was getting ready to get in the shower, so she needed to exit the bathroom. His reaction to it was cute. The look on his face like what the hell? I said yes, she understands me very well. We have that connection (wink).

He showered and came out with his shorts on. Yup. Just his shorts. YUP! Nothing but shorts. Yeah. YEAH!...BAAAYBEEY! He knew exactly what he was doing. By now it's about midnight or a little past midnight and I walked downstairs to check on Keith. You know I always check on him before I turn in for the night. He was out. SNORING and sucking in the walls in chyle. LOL. As Bella and

I made our way back upstairs, I heard B telling his mother he was staying over Keith's house again and he'll see her tomorrow. Which made me think, DAMN! I really need to start paying attention more. LOL. How have I NOT seen him before. This joker has been to my house multiple times and every time he's been here I have not seen him or been home. I guess this time, it was just meant to be. How did one day of he and I locking eyes in the damn hallway turn into this? You know I always say that things happen when they are supposed to. Yeah well, it damn sure did this time.

Anyway, we came back in the bedroom, Bell's goes back into the bathroom and he's sitting in the chair looking at TV. The ESPEN channel no less.

Are you alright?"

"Yeah, I'm cool. Where did you go?"

We went to walk the house one last time and I went to check on Keith. He's knocked out and snoring as usual. Why wassup?"

"You do that every night?"

Yes. Well, when it's just two of us in the house or me by myself. Why?"

"No reason. That's wassup. Just curious. So how is this sleeping thing going to work?"

Where do you normally sleep when you're here?"

"C'on man! You gon' make me go downstairs and sleep on the Sofa in the basement? Come on now. I'm saying, though. You got this bed all up here by yourself and shit. Let me get a pillow and some mattress.

He started cracking up. "You on fire tonight I see. Now let me ask you this first. What are you going to say when he comes upstairs and see's you lying beside me in the bed? He's NOT ready for that and neither are you."

"DAMN! You are good. I didn't even think about that. So, what we gon' do?"

We, ain't gon' do shit. Now if you want, you can go next door and sleep in the guest room. I don't mind. Or...

"OR WHAT?!"

Calm down. LOL. Or you can lay beside me, and I'll set my alarm. I know what time he gets up. Then you can go hop in the other bed.

"OOH! I Love You! OOP. You know what I mean!

Aaaww you love me! LOL.

"Aye go head. But anything is possible. *smiling*

HMPH! Say so now.

So, he stayed up until about a quarter to 1 looking at the ESPEN highlights then he climbed into bed. I had actually dozed off just that fast. LOL. He woke me up when he got in the bed. Not that he disturbed or anything. I just didn't realize I had fell asleep. When he climbed in bed, he snuggled right up under me. He was close enough for me to feel his heartbeat. His heart was beating so fast. I grabbed his arm and wrapped it around me, then began to caress it slowly. I could feel his heart beat slow down, then he dozed off. Baby listen, the way this BIG MUTHA-FUCKA STARTED SNORING! Oh my God! He snores JUST LIKE DADDY! Bella jumped up and came out the bathroom and looked at him like what the fuck?! I was cracking up. She was legit annoyed. Daddy snores but she doesn't sleep in the room with him. I snore but NOT like that. And I only snore when I'm tired. GOOD GAWD! I remember my mother would tell daddy to turn over off his back when he got outta control, I made him turn over. He laid on his stomach, he didn't snore as bad that way. I can see right now; I need to fall asleep first fooling with him. LOL. I do daddy the same way or close my door all the way. I let Bella out the room and she laid in the hallway. My baby said oh hell no!

My alarm went off, but he was slightly woke already (well kind of). His snoring was NOT as loud or heavy so I could tell that he wasn't sleeping that hard. I turned over to face him and he began smiling at me. I softly said good morning then kissed his face. He smiled hard then, told me to "stop playing,

Morning Wood is REAL and it's happening NOW." I laughed because, um yeah, I'll stop playing. Anyway, you need to go get in the other bed. I'm sure when he notices your truck is still here, he's going to come look for you.

"Yeah, you're right. I'm not going to class today. I'ma chill right here with you all day. I mean if that's cool with you. Unless you have other plans.

LOL. That's fine. Let me clear the air first then I'll give you the green light.

So, he got up and went into the guest room and laid back down. Bella came back in my room and I swear I think she rolled her eyes! LOL. She went back to sleep in the bathroom. I went downstairs to make sure Keith was woke. He has the tendency of turning off the alarm clock and going back to sleep. He was actually woke and getting dressed. I was slightly shocked.

Hey, Tony is upstairs asleep in the guest room.

Keith: Oh shit! I thought he was gone. My bad, I straight went to sleep on my mans.

Um yeah you did. But it's cool. He kept me and Bell's company while I was finishing up with Grams. He's cool, you can snatch something out the fridge for breakfast. I'm staying home today and I'm gonna cook dinner tonight, too. I'll probably grill as well. I'll text you later. Have a good day. Hit me if you need something.

Keith: A'ight cool. Tell T I'll hit him later.

He's gonna be here for dinner I'm sure. Grams likes him. LOL.

Keith: LOL. A'ight cool.

As Keith was leaving, I called Bells downstairs so she could use the bathroom. Ironically enough she was already coming down the steps. I went in the house to drink my water and start breakfast. I waited about five minutes before I texted Keith to make sure he was at school. I had to think fast, so what I did was; I asked Keith to look in my locker and bring my English book home with him today. Of course, I didn't really need it, I just wanted to make sure he was actually at school. You know, just in case I decided I want to give B a little slap and tickle action. Oh I'm quick with it hunni. Ow! LOL. Even, though I knew I wasn't going to. Just to be on the safe side.

Anyway, I went back upstairs while Bell's was eating, and made my way into the guest room. He was knocked out. On his back, on top of the cover's, just looking all kinds of bearishly sexy. Love, I wanted to mount him so BAD! LOL. I was standing in the doorway (like a creep) watching him sleep until Bella came upstairs. I went into my room to get in the shower. As I was undressing and turning the water on, I heard the door open, I just didn't pay it any attention. I just figured it was Bell's. I turned on my music, pinned my hair up and hopped in the shower. So, um yeah you can imagine what happened next. He came in the bathroom and got in the shower with me. YES, he scared the shit outta me. He kissed my neck and said good morning. After me damn near drowning myself, I turned to him and said Good Morning.

And what makes your slick ass think I want to share my shower with you?"

"I mean it's kind of, too late now, though. You're good and soapy, plus I'm already in here and wet.

You just have all the answers huh? Yeah okay.

He leaned in closer. "Can I get some good-morning sugar?"

So, I did. I kissed him; it was cute. It was funny to me, though because he had to lean down in order to kiss me. Thank God, I had one of those hand-held shower heads. Yeah, he definitely needed it. LOL. I got out the shower before he did. I was sitting on my bed oiling down my legs and feet when I heard "DON'T GET DRESSED YET!" My heart dropped and I was about to run!! I was like uh NO. I am NOT experienced in that sir. I've done other things but certainly NOT that. LOL. So, I said I'll play along for a little bit. I sat on the side of my bed in my robe looking at a little TV until he came out the bathroom. He finally came out of the bathroom. Then he proceeded to walk over to me, made me stand up in front of him, took my robe off:

"I just want to look at you in all your little chubby fat boy glory."

*I peer up at him with the "wow" look on my face. *

Um, Okay. What will this do?"

"I just wanna see you. All of you. I want you to see me for me and all of me as well. I LOVE what I see in you, on you and around you. I just wanted to see you completely naked to see if you matched. That's all.

WELL SHIT! You keep talking like this you gon' fuck around and end up a baby daddy!

". I'm just being real with you. I wanted you to know how I feel. So, if you game, I wanna rock with you. Straight no chaser.

Hmph. Okay. We'll talk about it more. Not right now, though. I'm still feeling you out. I'll let you know within a matter of moments.

"Okay. I can respect that. Besides, I know about you. I hear Big Mama talk about you enough to know how you are and what's good with you.

What I tell you about being a creep?"

"Aye go head.

We kissed and rolled around on the bed for a few minutes. Thank God Bella broke us up. Ain't no telling what would have happened if she didn't. Whew. She wanted to go downstairs, so she was barking for me to let her out the room. LOL. My girl! It was getting hot and heavy too hunni. Just kissing him was turning me ON! Like, how is this dude doing everything right? Yeah okay. The day went on and we were just laying around the house talking, kissing, playing with Bell's and just enjoying each other's company. About 2 pm he said he had to get dressed and make a few runs. Which was cool because I need to get dressed and figure out dinner. I told him I was going to cook dinner and he can come back later. He said cool, he'd see me later. He wanted to talk more about us being a "US." Love, my heart was getting ready to jump outta my chest. Like what the hell is happening?! IS THIS REALLY HAPPENING? I NEVER ever doubt myself or my emotions. Especially when it's matter of the heart. This time around, it was definitely screaming to me loud and clear. Something's your heart and soul will NOT let you ignore. I remember changing my mind on the whole grilling thing because of the thunderstorm. I decided to cook a regular dinner. I decided to make a Chicken Lasagna with garlic rolls and a salad. I knew that would soften the blow on Keith. He's very smart and intuitive but he doesn't say a lot. If I know him the way that I do, and I DO; he's going to catch it sooner or later. More so sooner than later. You laugh but I know him, and it will come right out the blue. I made a quick trip to the store for everything I needed. I texted Keith to tell him what was on the menu, he was more than excited. It meant he'd have leftovers the next day.

I was back home beginning to cook when my phone rang. It was B telling me he was on his way and he wanted to know if I needed anything. He also wanted to know if Keith was home yet. I told him he wasn't, then I informed him of what was on the menu. That's when I got that "Oh, shit! You gon' make me marry you." I laughed then hung up. Whole time I'm thinking, um yeah; that's the goal slim.

I was finishing up the last touches on dinner, when I heard car doors closing. I peeped out the window, they both pulled up at the same time. Bear walks in first and yell's "Hunni I'm home!" I laughed then I snuck him a kiss. Keith was walking through the garage as he always does so he didn't see us (I know right). The table was set and all I had to do was pull their choice of beverage out the fridge. B went upstairs to change his clothes and Keith went downstairs to change his clothes. Bella and I was sitting in the kitchen when they both came through the door at the same time, they sat down, and their eyes got so BIG AND BRIGHT. I really did have to laugh.

They looked like kids in a candy store. They BOTH can EAT. Keith is used to me cooking like this, B was being introduced to my skills. I gave them the spatulas and let them dig in. I went to let Bell's play in the backyard for a few minutes while we were eating and talking. It was just really nice.

Keith: CHRISTIAN! Oh my God! Are you baking a lemon cake? YES GREEDY!

Keith: LITTLE BROTHER YOU THE MOTHER FUCKING MAN! I LOVE YOU MAN!

I know and you're welcome.

"DAMN! And you baked a cake? I LOVE YOU TOO! If it's as good as this lasagna, shit! I'm here for it!

"Thank you as well. I'll call you when it's done, Keith."

"YOU BETTER!"

As Keith was getting up from the table, he went to let Bella in for me, then he made his way downstairs to play his video game. I was cleaning up and loading the dish washer when B came over and set at the island. He thanked me for dinner.

"You know Christian; that was really nice. I haven't sat down to a home cooked meal in a while.

"Don't you live with your mother? I know she cooks."

"Yeah but Ma is a quick cook, or she barely cooks. If, she cooks."

"Oh okay. I see. Well, I'm glad you enjoyed it. It's something we do around here on the regular basis. I was gonna grill, but because of the storm, those plans changed quickly."

"That's wassup. See, that's what I'm talking about. You keep your family together and you make sure everybody is taken care of. You make everyone feel loved and welcomed. I can guarantee you; they appreciate that shit.

"That's how I was raised. Thank you for saying that out loud and you're welcome."

As I finished loading the dish washer, he asked me sit down beside him. I knew what was coming. I felt the shift in the atmosphere. He was getting ready to completely expose his heart and soul to me. Now, he was getting ready to be naked in front of me. I can always tell when that's about to happen. I took the cake out so it could cool then I sat beside him.

"Okay, my Sugar Bear, wassup?"

He chuckled. "Sugar Bear? I like that."

"Yeah, that's my name for you. "Bear" or "B." *Only I can call you that, too!* Don't get a bitch smacked!"

"A'IGHT! You got it. I like that, though. I'll be your Bear. Speaking of which—"

"Yup. Go ahead I'm listening."

"Hunh? You act like you know what I'm about to say or something."

"I do but go ahead."

"What am I going to say?"

"You're about to expose yourself to me. Like the naked convo we had earlier. Now talk."

"Oh my God you are a trip. You're right, though. I want you to listen to me.

"Go 'head, sugga."

"Thank you for not judging me and making me feel any less than what I am. I really want us to rock. Like straight up off the no bullshit, I'm digging you. I know you digging me, too, but it's all good. If you feel otherwise or the shit is too much for you right now, just let me know and I'll fall the fuck back."

I smiled. "You're just so cute. I need for you to breathe and relax. You're so tense right now. Relax, I'm here and I hear what you're saying. Continue."

"...and why are you smiling at me? Shit."

"Because you're cute," I said, still smiling. "Now finish."

"I want you to rock with me Christian. Be my number 1. Let me be your number 1. I mean you can say no, but I'll creep on your ass until you say yes…

And you know what? I believe you!

"As long you know I'm serious. But on the real, just within the last twenty-four hours of being with you and around you, I've fallen in love with you. And I—"

"STOP. Just stop and listen to me." I stood up beside him and gently grabbed his face. "B, you don't have to explain anything to me, sugga. I already know. If you've been paying attention to me, as much as you claim you have, then you know I feel the same way."

As usual, he was cheesing hard.

"Stop smiling and let me finish."

He laughed.

"If you really want to do this," I continued, "we can. Like I told you before, I don't take no bullshit. You see how they are about me. Don't make me call my father then follow up with my godfather, because you hurt me or decided you wanted to be a first-class jackass and got beside yourself. And I mean it."

"I would *never* do anything to hurt you. If we can be upfront with each other and keep it one hundred, we gon' be fine."

"Okay. I'm here for it then."

We kissed again, but this time it felt different. I could feel the passion radiating from him. It was definitely "OFFICAL" now. I went over to finish the cake. No sooner than I was done adding the icing, Keith was coming back upstairs. He cut three pieces of cake, grabbed him a glass of milk, hugged me, thanked me, said his goodnights and went right back downstairs to his game. B laughed and was like, "REALLY?"

"YUP! That's his norm," I said, laughing.

I noticed Bell was quiet; she was downstairs with him chill'n. She came up after he went back down. She laid down as B and I continued to talk. I told him, "Keith is not stupid. He probably already figured it out or just figured it out. He's going to ask very soon. Mark my words."

B didn't think so, but I know my brother very well. It was coming more so sooner than later. What do you mean *how do I figure?* Even though you're right, because I know where you're going with this, they never assume that just because I have male friends that the person I'm with is gay. I broke them out of that habit a long time ago. Even still, at that time, it was the same. They never assumed. They would ask questions, but that was because they were already questioning whoever the dude was anyways. With B, they never asked or really paid him any attention. Remember, him and Keith were friends, on top of him being a jock. So, they didn't put two and two together and we never said anything. So, they didn't catch it until I was a senior in high school. Even then, they only caught on because *we allowed* them to.

B was enjoying the cake. I added a little whipped cream for him on the side and a little fresh fruit...oh, hunni, he was in heaven. I was finishing up the last little bit of the dishes, when he asked me if we could sleep in the bed again together tonight. I said, "Sure, tomorrow is Saturday and he'll be sleeping in. He won't wake up until about noon anyways. Unless one of his little girlfriends call him and he goes out tonight. Other than that, we're good."

He said, "Cool," and then said he was going to go hop in the shower. I told him that would be great. I was going to let Bella out one last time then I'd be up. I let her out before I finished the kitchen so by the time I was done she would be ready to come in. And wouldn't you know it, as I was turning on the dishwasher, she was letting me know she was ready to come back in.

As I was turning off lights, about to head upstairs, my dear old brother was on his way out the door. Didn't I call it? One of his little "chick flicks" called him and he was going to stay over her house for the night. Being the quick one that I am, I told him to make sure he called me in the morning when he was on his way back so I could make sure the alarm was off and the doors were unlocked (meaning the garage door) just in case our house guest was still asleep. You know I'd already be woke.

"Oh yeah. YOUNG! I keep forgetting that mutha'fucka is here! You don't mind, do you?"

"No, you're fine, he's fine. He's keeping me company. I get tired of being here by myself sometimes. He's good, though. Go ahead and enjoy. Just hit me in the morning. But not too early!"

"A'ight bet. Goodnight. Love you!"

"Goodnight. Love you too."

I closed up the house as he was pulling off, then I went on up-stairs to get in the shower. B was in the guest room, so I didn't think anything of it. I got in the shower and made sure I was "extra" clean and smelling extra good for Big Daddy. (Laughing to myself.) I knew we wasn't going to sleep any time soon, so I didn't mind.

When I got out, I heard the music on, and he was laying across my bed.

Bell's was laying in the hallway, playing with her chew toy and all was well. I had my own little family. The thought of it was cute. I came out and sat on the bed to oil down my feet and legs (like I always do). He sat up, told me to stop and to lay back. I said no, I don't like going to bed ashy.

He laughed. "Chill. Just lay back. I got chu."

"UGH! Okay."

So, I did. I laid back and he took my oil gel and oiled my feet and legs for me. His strong hands felt so good. As he switched to the left leg, he put my toes in his mouth. I laughed and told him I was ticklish, and he needed to stop. He giggled and nibbled on my toes. Yeah, that felt good, too. Before I knew it, he was lying between my thighs and kissing me down.

The funny part, he stopped and asked if my brother was asleep. I burst out laughing and told him he's gone over some girl house; he'd be back in the morning. We're good, sugga. This fool jumped up, turned the music up, took his shorts off and jumped in the bed. I was already slight naked because I had on my robe. Yeah, he snatched that off me. He climbed back on top of me and we started kissing again. Body to body and chest to chest. That's when he noticed how fast my heart was beating.

"DAMN! Why is your heart beating so fast?"

"Because you have me nervous, on top of hot and bothered."

"What the hell you nervous for?"

"Um, because I'm not ready for the *it* yet."

"Oh, nah baby, we ain't gotta do nothing you don't wanna do. We got time for that. I mean we *are* gonna do other stuff, though, right? I mean, you can't be looking good and smelling good, teasing a brother and think I'm not gone wanna do something. I'm saying, though. Break me off something."

"You get on my nerves. I mean, I *might*, could do something."

We didn't do anything. We just kept on kissing and enjoying each other's company. It was nice. Not only was it nice, but it felt like I had somebody that was all mine. Be it I was only in the ninth grade, but you and I both know I've always been "GROWN" (as my elders would say).

I loved that he was older than me and not into the bullshit or games either. We talked the rest of the night and laid all our shit bare right in front of each other. The things that we have in common are unparalleled.

Once we started talking more, we realized that we even had some the same people in common.

Remember I was telling you how Uncle B had his "issues" and "run-ins" in the past? Um yeah, so we have BIAS in common. And DAMN IT! That was enough. Not only did Grams love him but Uncle B loved him as well. That alone made me give him the side eye again. Once he mentioned how my uncle and his mother were cool. I sat straight up in the bed.

Wait a minute MF! What do you mean they are cool?"

"YUP! Your uncle has been over to my house quite a few times. Him and Ma always hang out or talk. He cooks, brings her dinner or lunch everything."

"*You know what?* I'm *not* surprised. That's how he is. But keep going. I know you're leading to something. I can tell."

"Well, don't judge us, but my mother used to sell dope."

"HA! I knew it. Where do you all live?"

"Southeast. Anacostia. Why?"

"OOOOOOOOOHHHHHHHH! If you tell me your mother's nick name is "Silvia" your ass is going home!"

He burst out laughing. "Get the fuck out of her! How do you know my mother?"

"NO WAY! B! Your mother is one of my favorite people! It's because of HER I know how to do certain things. Like a keep a blade with me at all times! LOL! I LOVE YOUR MOTHER! Oh my God!"

"A'ight, damn! CALM down!" He laughed.

"I'm so serious! I LOVE YOUR MOTHER! Oh, we going to see her tomorrow! I'm not playing with you!"

"You said you had church stuff to do tomorrow."

"FUCK THAT! That shit can wait! I'm going to see Aunt Silvia tomorrow! OH YES, WE ARE!"

"CHRISTIAN! This some bullshit." He shook his head.

"And I can't wait until I tell Grams and my mother. They are going to flip!"

"WAIT A MINUTE! All of them know Ma?"

"YUP! They asses used to slang dope together. BOOM!"

"WAIT."

"NO, BOY! I mean my uncle and your mother. Stop playing."

Once we were done laughing about his mother and my uncle, we went downstairs for ice cream. We were sitting outside on the deck while Bell's played in the backyard for a few. I couldn't help but to think, everything happens for a reason. Everyone we encounter in this life; we are supposed to. Be it good or bad, happy or sad.

I went in to get us some water and was stopped dead in my tracks by the, thought of all of this. A rush of heart fluttering emotions ran through my body. I ran right back on the deck, straddled him and kissed him so passionately. I didn't care who would have seen us or caught us. Usually when my heart flutters like that, it's because of my nieces and nephews. So, for it to flutter like that, at just the thought of him, sent me over. Yeah, he's definitely the ONE for me. He didn't even stop me; he just went with it. Although afterwards, he did ask me what he did to deserve that. I told him it was from my heart to his.

Form that day forward, we were ONE. All through high school, college and after. The funny part, though, NOBODY knew we were dating except for the select few that we agreed we would tell together. It was a very small list, too. His mother, my uncle, my brother Keith, his sister, my father and godfather, his father and my best friends. That was it. I know it may seem like a lot, but nope. Only the ones that could keep a secret. I mean obviously grams was in the mix. But she was funny. She knew right off the break.

It was more so me protecting him than me. I know how people can be asses. Not that he can't protect himself, but in our community, you know a mutha'fucka will try you quick. Especially if they think they can punk you or get away with it.

#Pause Remind me to tell you about the fight we had leaving the movie theater with these goons later. Chyle, it was a mess but funny. *#Continue*

What are you asking me, Love? Just say it! The sex? Oh no, that didn't happen until later on. My senior year to be exact. We definitely did other things, though. I couldn't do my man like that. LOL. Trust me, he was fine. Just fine with what we were doing.

That's the story of us. My Human Teddy Bear of a husband.

Thank you for asking.

TT4N.

Love You much,

Eskimo kisses.

THUG PASSION 101:

Love,

I've been thinking about Kevin a lot lately. I miss him so much. That boy KNOW he could kiss. Whew! Wait, I thought I told you about him. My bad boo. Yes, hunni. Kevin was my last love after B. The only thing was, I knew it wasn't going to last long. Sure, I'll tell you all about him. Go get you a cocktail doll, you may need it.

Kevin was my little "Thug Warrior" I met on Facebook. I know, I used to tease him all the time about that. "Boy ain't no real thugs on Facebook. UGH!" But there really are, though. Oop. LOL! He was one of my favorite "Homo Thugs." I met him in one of my Facebook groups. I remember him commenting on a few threads and he was ripping folks in half. I was loving it. He was a shit starter in the way of making you think about things twice before you say them out loud. Let alone before you post them online. Naturally, people thought he was a bully, a jerk or just another Facebook jackass. I don't know what it was about him that turned me on so much. I think mainly because he was so fearless. Not only was he book smart, but he was street smart as well.

I remember commenting under his comments or laughing hysterically at his comments while "@-ing" him. Then, about a week later he popped up in my DM (direct message). I slightly geeked. I did, though. I was like oh my God. He's in my inbox! Now let me figure out a way to get him IN, MY BOX. Ow! He was just so... Ah! He was that breath of fresh air that I needed from all the other lames I had come in contact with. We were talking about a good two months before I even decided to give him my real number (you know I'll give out my Google voice number in a heartbeat). He cussed my ass out for giving him my Google voice number, too! About the third month in, we decided to meet up. It took a while for us to meet because he lived in another state (of course, he did). Why else would I be so damn attracted to him (eye-roll)? Nobody I want is ever in my backyard. That would be too much like right. TUH!

Anyway, I remember when we were talking about finally meeting up. We had been talking for quite some time now and it was time. I made sure I had enough leave at work to take off from Thursday through Sunday. He told me that he'd meet me in Detroit. I remember it was in November because I went to meet up with him a week before Thanksgiving.

Right, of all places to choose, he chose cold brick ass Detroit. I had to buy myself a real winter coat, hunni. I remember not telling anyone where I was going on purpose.

I told my BFF and my sister. Those were the only two who knew my exact location. Flight numbers, hotel name, and address. Chyle, everything. Once I landed at the airport and made it to my driver, I texted him to tell him I was on my way to the hotel. He texted me back to tell me he was riding the bus up to Detroit (I almost passed out). I told him what hotel I was staying in and to give me a buzz when he was on his way to see me. He informed me that he had some business to take care of fist, then he'd be over to see me about 4:00 p.m.

I'm thinking, *Great,* as I got out of my car and walked into check-in. I couldn't help but be in awe at how beautiful this hotel was. The entrance and lobby were surrounded by glass. The way the sunlight bounced off the windows gave it a beautiful glow. Absolutely gorge. It smelled amazing, too. Anyway, as I was checking in, I couldn't help but notice all the eye candy walking around. It was "Old Money", too. They were some old sexy "Kat Zaddys" walking through that lobby hunni. As I was being escorted to my suite by the hotel personnel, I could barely hold in my excitement.

I was finally about to meet my "Kevy." I was super giddy. I wasn't nervous at all. Just extremely excited.

Since I had some time to kill, I decided to get a massage then take a nice hot bath. The massage was great. That little man had some strong arms and hands I tell you that. He had my body feeling, right? After my bath, my body was so relaxed I took a nap. I slept for about three hours before I was awakened by my cell phone going off. It was Kevin telling me he was on his way. I told him my suite number and to call me if needs me to come down and get him. I jumped up, ran in the bathroom to get myself together and made sure I was cute! Oh yeah, I had already made up in my mind that if he was the real deal, we were gone flat out FUCK. I'm so serious, though. NO FUCKS GIVEN! AT. ALL.

I put on my sheer underwear with the matching tank top, my ripped-up Levi's (my fav's), and a cute T-shirt. That way if he decided to undress me, he'd see I had on the underwear he likes #ClockedT. Um yeah, well we've talked on the phone a lot and he would ask me about some of my guilty pleasures. You know how I LOVE under-wear. Especially sexy underwear. We were talking about how many pairs I have, how often I buy them etc. We've face-timed so that he could see the drawer's full of underwear for himself. Yes, I've mod-eled a few pairs for him as well. Oh, he's very familiar (wink). He's been quite vocal about which ones are his favorite as well.

Anyway, I gave myself the once over and let my hair down. I sprayed my cologne and put on some gloss.

As soon as I was done applying my lip, I heard that knock on my door. I squealed, shook my hair and gave it a whip, inhaled, exhaled and then walked to the door.

"I'm coming."

"Well hurry up then shit!

"Boy, shaddap! *Opens the door*

He looked up and smiled. "Wassup, baby?"

Oh my God! He smelled so good. As I was sizing him up, he was everything and then some. He was leaning up against the wall on his forearm, he had his baseball cap turned backward, his jean jacket was fresh with his polo shirt on underneath it, and his blue jeans that laid right on top of his new J's just right. Then he looked up at me, smiled at me while flashing those pretty white teeth, then responded with a "Wassup, baby? You gone let me in or nah?." I was smiling so hard at him. I said of course you can come in. He pushed the door open, grabbed me and hugged me so tight while kissing me on my neck.

Boy, you better stop!

"Why you faking you know you don't want me to. Smelling all good and edible and shit!

You so simple. HI KEVY! *grabs his face*

"Wassup, baby! You happy to see me?

YES! *Kisses his lips*

Love, his lips were so soft, his breath smelled and tasted like bubble gum. We kissed for a good minute too (and oh my God his beard was so soft). He was extra sexy to me at that moment. I think it was because he had a fresh shape up, head was freshly shaved, I mean just, everything. Whew Lord! I had to pull back from him a little bit. The energy I was getting from him was that he was ready. I wasn't ready just yet (I know what I said). The emotion that flooded me right away was like nothing I had felt before. So I made myself calm down and break away from his grasp. But I did it in a way that he wouldn't catch on to it. I wanted to talk to him and just experience all of him while I had the chance. Yeah, while I had the chance. I don't know what it was about him, but I felt like I needed to be in his life for the time being.

I said okay Gut instincts, I'm going to go with the flow. And you know what, I did just that. He took off his jacket, hat and sneakers, then sat on the sofa beside me and we just talked and laughed until about 9:00 p.m.

We both were hungry, so we decided to go downstairs and eat in the restaurant. As we were leaving my suite, he was in front me and I couldn't help but to admire his thick ass from behind.

He was six foot, with pretty brown cocoa buttered skin and walked with a certain swag. That thick bear cub was gone get ALL THIS BUSINESS hunni. I already knew it. I think he knew it, too. He looked back to see why I was walking so slow. He slowed down, so he could walk beside me, but slightly behind me. Enough for us to walk together, but with his hand on the small of my back (OOP! Exactly). We all know what that means (wink).

We were on the elevator and he backed me into the corner threw my hands up and we kissed all the way down to the first floor. LOVE LISSEN! The way THAT LEG went up and around his waist, Baby! It slightly went down in the elevator boo. *giggle* I don't know if there were camera's in the elevator or not, but if there were, the got an eyeful. We stopped kissing right before we reach the main floor. I was reapplying my lip, he was um, adjusting himself because he was on BRICK (I felt it NOT BAD either). Nice piece of man meat (HA).

We were walking off the elevator, when his phone went off. He read the message and told me to go get us a table and he'll be right in. I didn't think anything of it. I just said okay, then went to go get us a table. When he came back in, he seemed a little different. Like he was kind of antsy but didn't want to let me see it. Naturally I picked up on it. Not in a bad way, more like he was in that headspace where something had just happened, but he was trying to shake it off because he handled it. That's the energy he was giving off.

You alright?"

"Oh yeah, I'm cool. Just hungry. Let's order.

Okay.

I glanced at him as she shrugged it off. I could tell there was something wrong with him, though. I left it alone for the time being. The waitress came to take our order. For starters, He ordered a beer and I ordered a glass Prosecco. He moved closer to me and began to rub my leg under the table. I smiled:

Um, can you stop rubbing my thigh please sir?"

"No, this my thigh. Fuck you mean?"

"Whatever. So wassup with you?"

"Fuck shit. I'm glad you agreed to finally meet me, though. You had me nervous for a minute. I just knew your uppity ass was gone stand me up.

I would never. You've been talking to me long enough to know how I am. If I'm NOT interested, I'll just flat out say it. But I like you, so I wouldn't do that to you (wink & smile).

"That's wassup. Well I appreciate it and you.

You better. Everybody doesn't get this kind of treatment."

"They betta NOT. You mine now."

ANYWAY! Are you staying here tonight or are you going... wait, where are you staying?

"Nah, not tonight, but I got you tomorrow night, though. ALL NIGHT, too. I'MA BEAT THE BREAKS OFF YOU."

Boy answer me!

"I did. And I'm staying over my boy's house with him and his wife tonight."

Oh ok, cool."

"Why wassup? You got something for me?"

I don't think so. We'll talk about it later."

"We sure are. You might have your mouth full, but we'll talk about that, too."

That was cute."

He's such a clown. Which was one of the reasons why I loved him so much. He kept me laughing, I kept him laughing. We ate dinner and just laughed and talked until about midnight. By this time, we were sitting close and he had his hand back on my thigh (of course). It was very intimate. I noticed the lighting in the restaurant had dimmed and it had that soft glow feel and look to it. Again, very intimate. It was nice. The waitress came to tab us out, naturally I was ready to put my credit card down; I went to reach for it, and he grabbed my hand;

"Christian stop fucking playing with me. I wish you would pull your money out."

What?"

"Here you go sweetie. Keep the change. We good."

Waitress: *SMIRKS* Thank you. You all have a wonderful evening fellas."

Thank you, but I wasn't going to assume that you were going to pay for dinner. Calm your ass down."

"Whatever. Stop that shit. You know damn well I got'chu. Now let's go."

"Ooh! Forceful. Alright now, Big Zaddy! Ow! I like's that shit. You better be careful. Fuck around make me give your ass some lil' thug babies!"

"Thug babies? You always fucking playing. Let's go."

As we made our way back to the elevator, we noticed we had more people this time. So, there would be no chance of another elevator kiss fest. At least not according to me. As we piled into the elevator, he stood behind me on purpose.

The elevator was quite full, he and I were standing in the far-left corner, when I felt him push my hair to the right side of my neck, slide his hand around the front of my stomach to hold me in place, then he begins to softly kiss my neck. I laughed and shook my head. He kept right on kiss my neck. YES! He had jokes. He knows exactly what that does to me.

Then he pulls me closer to him, so that I can feel his um "girth and growth" in his jeans. But no, this is the gag, there was a lady looking right smack dab at us. That heffa was lovin' every-single-bit of the show he was putting on. When it was time for us to exit the elevator, he deiced he wanted to be cute and lick my neck while looking at her. I told you he's a simple ass. LOL. We were walking down the hallway to my suite when I heard him deeply inhale then exhale. I kept walking until I reach my suite door. As I was taking my key out, I turned to him and asked him what was wrong?

"Nothing, I'm good...."

No, you're not. Don't make me read you completely. I'ma ask you again. What's wrong?"

"It's just, I'm really enjoying you. I don't want it to end so fast...

As we walked into my suite...

It's fine. I'm not leaving until Monday morning. We have time sugga. No worries.

"Yeah, I know. It's just...

Stop it, don't say it. I already know. We will link up tomorrow after you're done and spend the rest of our time here together. Go home, get you some rest, then meet me tomorrow."

"See, Christian, that's what the fuck I'm talking about! You be on it. That's why I love your stuck-up ass. Straight up off the no Bullshit. I'm being one hundred right now."

Thank you. I think...

"What?"

"I'm kidding. I love you, too, sugga. It's okay."

"Now give me a hug and go get some rest."

We hugged, I kissed his face, then he left. As I shut the door behind him, I stood there for a few seconds to let it process. You see, I knew something was wrong with him by his deep heavy sigh. It was like, it felt like a dagger to the heart. Matter fact, when he did it, I got that weird feeling in the pit of stomach. I knew what was wrong with him instantly. I could tell he was tired of the hustle and the game he had to play, in order to survive.

Of course, I knew he was a "Hustler" or "Dope Boy" as we call them now. It wasn't my place to judge him or make him feel some kind of way about his life (I would never). That's like spitting in my uncle B's face.

You know about my uncle and his "hustle hard" days. We've talked about those before. Honestly, I think that also played a big part in my attraction to Kevin as well. You know I have a soft spot for Dope Boys. Kevin is just like my uncle and godfather. His swagger, attitude about the whole lifestyle, along with how he treats others. They are a very down to earth type of people. They tend to wear their hearts on their sleeves with their sleeves rolled up. That was Kevin to a T. His heart was heavy. I could tell when I hugged him goodnight.

While I was undressing, I was still thinking about him. I turned on my music to help me not think about him so hard or so much. I found myself worrying about him the way I used to worry about my uncle and godfather. That's when I knew I needed to have a heart to heart with him. As I was laying in that super comfortable ass bed, I couldn't help but to breathe in and out deeply. I had to say a little prayer for him. I prayed for his safety, his heavy heart and that he'll gain mental clarity to pull, though. I know, heavy, right? But it is (or it can be shall I say).

It was about two in the morning when he texted me and told me he was at his homeboy's house. I dozed off shortly after he told me he was good. That's what made me exhale hard enough for me to fall asleep. I woke up about 8 a.m. (I know, you know I don't require much sleep) to my stomach growling. It was like I had ate nothing at all. UGH! I ordered me some room service. I ordered a nice little spread, too. Everything from waffles, eggs, bacon, fruit, apple juice and mimosas. I knew he was going to be over for breakfast, so I just took the liberty of ordering enough. No sooner than I was done ordering breakfast, I get a text to my phone: *Wake that ass up! I'm omw to you and I'm hungry.* Naturally I laughed then responded with, *"You just get your ass here! How about that?"* Literally as I was getting out of the shower putting on my robe, he knocked on the door. I opened the door to him smiling at me. He grabbed me, then kissed me so passionately but with a little more ease and JOY.

"Well! That's different. And very nice. What has you so excited this morning sir?"

"I don't know! I woke up with so much joy in my heart this morning, Christian."

Well GOOD! I'm glad to hear it sugar."

"(goes into the bathroom) I slept good and everything. I think it's because of you

Your welcome!

"(Peeing with the door open)!!! FUCK YOU! But you probably right. SHIT."

UM! I DO NOT WANNA HEAR YOU PEE!

"I'm done now! *comes out drying his hands*

At least you washed your hands. Hmph."

"Always. So, what you got on under that robe. Can I see?"

NO, and open the door."

"Who is that?"

Didn't he just say room service dum-dum?"

"Oh, shit! You ordered breakfast boo? THAT'S WASSUUUPPP!"

Yes, I woke up hungry as hell. UGH!

"ME TOO! Like I ain't fuck that steak up last night."

You definitely DID THAT!

"Don't clown me just yet."

We were beginning to eat breakfast when I jumped up and opened the curtains the rest of the way. I had to let that beautiful sunshine in. The view was gorgeous. I didn't even realize that my view was on the lake side of the hotel. It was very nice. When I turned around, Kevin was leaning back in the chair, looking at me smiling. I didn't realize I was gazing out the window for so long. I couldn't help it. You know how I am with sunlight and views.

Why are you smiling at me?"

"I'm just taking in the view."

Mmhhmm. I bet you are."

"I am. Matter of fact. *walks over to me*

"Gimmie a kiss."

Oh, NOW you gone ask for one."

"I was try'na be polite and shit!"

I kissed him then I pulled away so that I could eat. I know what he wanted to do, and I wasn't ready yet. I wanted it to flow. Not that it wasn't, but I... I don't know. I just felt like that moment wasn't it. He laughed.

"Oh, I can't get none"

Not yet. You will, though. TRUST ME. YOU WILL."

"That's wassup. So, what we gone do today beside eat this old lavish ass breakfast you done ordered?"

Um, I'm going shopping. I DO know that much."

"Nah, WE going shopping."

That's fine. But I WILL be at somebody's mall today. I need new loafers. Besides, I've never been here so I wanna see what their dept. stores have that we don't."

"That's wassup. I want some new J's anyway."

Well we can go when we finish breakfast."

Once I was finished eating, I began getting dressed. It was pure coincidence that I had on another underwear set that he liked. Well, kind of. I packed it on purpose, but I forgot when I went to go put it on, it was the one of the sets he likes. Me, not thinking, came out the bathroom with it on and BAM! He was on me. I burst out laughing.

"Oh, fuck no!" he yelled, jumping up off the sofa. "Christian, why the ruck you playing with me?"

"What the hell are you talking about now?"

"Where the fuck you going with that on?"

I bust out laughing. "Boy! These are my underclothes. You acting like I'm about to walk around the streets in these. Get outta here."

"I bet I'ma fuck! Keep it up!"

I was still laughing. "I bet you are, too! Now leave me alone so I can finish getting dressed."

"Yeah, okay. Play with it. Balls deep on that ass!"

You are so damn stupid!

Once I was finished laughing at him, I managed to get dressed. You know he had jokes for days. And Kevin is simple as hell; I kept laughing at him even, though I KNEW he was dead damn serious (SMH). I was calling the front desk to make sure my driver was downstairs before we came down. You know me hunni, I hate waiting when I'm ready to go. The attendant told me he was in front and waiting on me.

"Christian! You got a hired driver?"

Uh yeah. I don't know where I'm going and I'm not in the mood for no damn cab."

"OH MY GOD! We could've caught the bus. It goes right to the mall."

Cut to me just looking at him and blinking, when that bus comment came outta his mouth.

"Oh shit! Never mind. Come on then wit'cha stuck up ass. You betta be glad I like that shit."

And I'm sure you know I wouldn't give a damn if you didn't. *wink*

"I'ma still fuck!

Come on fool!

We made our way down to the car and baby! It was BRICK outside!

Whew! I knew about Detroit's cold winters but Wow! You know he had "Rich White Woman" jokes because of my coat, hat and scarf. I had on my blue fox stole and he was just tickled pink. He was laughing but that ass was cold, and I wasn't. TO be honest, he was glad I had a driver. The freezing air would have had us shaking like a leaf at that damn bus stop. SHIT NO! NOT ME! That was a different kind of COLD I was NOT ready for.

While we were one our way to the mall, we laughed, talked, kissed a little bit and just enjoyed the ride. It was very nice and very intimate. We were getting closer to the mall when he grabbed my hand just to hold it. I could tell that he was enjoying the private time, along with the intimacy. I could feel his energy through his hands; if that makes sense. It was like the minute he grabbed my hand, there was a calming that came over him again. I guess you could say, I became his comfort zone. Which I'm not unfamiliar with so it didn't bother me. It was just, yet again; I don't know. His whole energy left me feeling unsure at times. I couldn't quite pinpoint what it was at first.

We pull up to the mall, and the driver gets out to let me out first. Kevin jumped out in front of him to tell him don't worry about it he got it. I'm looking like what is he doing? He wanted to open my door. He made the driver get back in the car. Actually, he told him "Nah slim. I got it. Get'cho ass back in the car. We good." I had to laugh. I said aw shit now. I'm about to have a "Dope Boy Hubbz". Yes,

I definitely laughed to myself. As we're walking into the mall from the dept. store entrance, he grabbed my hand again.

Now Love, you know me. I don't force anything. Especially with his "kind." Those super masculine, thug, dope boy kind'a fellas. It shocked me for a second until I remembered he DID slob my neck down in the elevator in front of ol' girl. So, I said okay fine. I just went with it. We were in the store near the shoe area so I let his hand go so I could take off my coat. I swear I think he caught a slight attitude. RIGHT! I'm like damn! Can I take my coat off first? I took my coat off and he put his hand on the small of back again while we continued to walk. I went over to look at the loafers he went over to look at the sneakers.

Naturally the sales clerk came over to greet me to see if I needed help with anything. He was fine too. He was about six-foot-two, salt and pepper hair with a sexy beard. Tall, chocolate and handsome. AND HE SMELLED GOOD! Yeah, I had to get myself together. He told me if I need anything to let him know (as usual).

I found me a nice pair of loafers, then I informed Howard (the salesman's name) of the size I needed. I'm sitting down waiting for him to come back, and I can see Kevin on the other side asking questions about a pair of sneakers that caught his eye. I chuckled, as Howard was coming back with my shoe and he asked me "what was so funny" I said I was laughing at a customer.

He kneeled to help me with my shoe. I told him he didn't have to do that, and it was okay. He insisted on it. That's when I knew for sure he was "family." Not only did he take my sock off to put on the dress sock, but he caressed my foot as well. I'm thinking to myself; okay, this joker has a foot fetish. Yup! I was right.

"You have very nice and soft feet."

Why thank you Mr. Howard. I use coconut oil.

"Very nice. Now, tell me how that feels."

Its heavenly. I love it! But...

"Uh-Oh. But what?"

It's nothing bad, I just want to know if you have it in brown as well. That's all. LOL."

"Oh OK! Let me go check. I just may."

As Howard went to check for the brown ones, Kevin came back over with his bag and sat down beside me.

What did you find?"

"Just a black pair of Nike's I wanted. Something simple."

Oh Okay. Cool."

"How many did pairs did you find?"

One for now, but he's checking for the other color."

"I knew it, I know you."

I guess."

Howard comes back smiling with my box in his hand. Of course, I got excited."

"It's your lucky day. Just try these on to be sure, though. You know colors run different in sizes."

OH YAY! I sure will. Thank you."

"(kneels again) Let me help you with that one."

Thank you."

"I just love your feet are so soft. Wow."

I see."

"Yeah you been down there for a minute now. You can get up. He can do it!"

"Stop it. And thank you Howard. This shoe feels great as well."

Howard got up and gave Kevin a look. Chyle, Kevin gave that look right back. Like I wish you would say something MF. Girl! He was about to knock his block off. Howard smiled and walked over to the register.

I need for you NOT to act up like that."

"Nah Fuck that. He ain't gone be doing that shit. Not while I'm sitting here."

He doesn't know that we're together. Calm your nerves."

"Oh Shit. We together now boo? AWWWW SHIT!

You know what I mean jerk."

"Christian, will that be cash or charge?"

Its charge. Thank you."

I was giving Howard my card, when Kevin snatched it outta my hand."

"Nah, its cash. Here!"

Aww Boo! Thank you. You try'na get you some tonight ain't you?"

"Shit! That's a given! I'm fuckin' tonight!

You get on my nerves. Howard thank you and don't laugh at him!"

We were leaving the store when Kevin grabbed my hand again. Yet again, I was shocked. I'm all for PDA but I just didn't see it coming. Let alone from him because of how he is. Not to mention, that's NOT "Dope boy behavior." Hey, if he loves it, I like it. Again, I just went along with it. We made our rounds to a few more stores then went and had lunch. We ate seafood for lunch, and he paid again. I made sure he understood that he didn't have to do that.

He said that it didn't bother him, and he wanted to. He said he felt like it was the least he could do since I had helped him out so much by just giving him advice, or just listening to him talk. I told him I understood, but no more. He said he understood but I was still his main bitch. He tried me (LOL). I was sitting at the table when he excused himself to go to the restroom. I didn't think anything of it. I was talking to the waitress about hair and all those kinds of boring gay things.

He came back smiling and asked me was I ready to go. I told him I was, the waitress was wrapping up my food to go.

"Cool, I'm ready when you are."

Why are you smiling so hard? What did you do?"

"I ain't do nothing."

"Whatever, boy. You did something. You are smiling too damn hard."

He just kept on smiling at me. I knew he had done something; I just didn't know what yet. The waitress came back with my bag, he tipped her, then said let's go. We get up to leave, mind you; he's still smiling. Now, I'm laughing at him because he's smiling so hard. I mean straight up cheesing. We walked to the front of the restaurant;

I'm looking for my driver when Kevin says "SURPRISE" in a super cheesy way. He hired a new driver. It was one of those black SUV's (which I didn't mind) but I liked my driver. He was with me since I first got to the D. He was so excited, so I didn't want to burst his bubble. I kept it cute and got in.

It was a nice gesture, but it made me side-eye him again. I know, but it made me feel some kind of way. It was like he was doing it to show me that he can hang with me, or he can give me what I needed. Which again, I'm familiar with this behavior because of my uncles and B. The driver was putting our bags in the back, when Kevin leaned over and kissed me. He caught me off guard, but it was nice the way he did it. I had to laugh, though. Not at him but at myself. I felt like one of those "Kept" women. I did. It was funny to me. I just told him his beard was tickling my face.

We were on the drive back to the hotel when Kevin decided he wanted to get super fucking freaking in the back seat. Um sir, we DO have a driver. Chyle, the SUV had a partition in it. I said wait a minute FANCY. YES, it did. I never knew you could get a SUV with a partition in them. Not like that, but okay! He rolled up the partition while we were kissing really passionately and naturally, he went up my shirt, which was fine, but I wasn't in the mood for car sex. I stopped him and asked him what had gotten into him. "I'm just enjoying you so much (talking while kissing me)

Yes, I can tell."

We kissed for another two minutes, then I made him get up off me (I know, but I did). Like I said, I wasn't in the mood for car sex. We pulled up to the hotel and while the driver was getting our bags out, he told me he wanted me to relax and trust him. I told I was fine, and I do. He kissed me again, but this time it was different. I felt the difference in his kisses. It was more relaxed yet filled with love but very passionately. I think I needed that, too. When I got out, I felt different as well. It was like he took away what I was feeling, and made it all better, with just that kiss.

I jumped out the truck and thanked the driver. He was cute

too! This time, I grabbed Kevin's hand (of course he had jokes). "Oh shit! You learning." We made our way back to my suite, as I was putting my bags away, I heard him on the phone telling somebody (probably one of his clients) that he wasn't coming out because he was spending the day with his "shorty." I chuckled because I thought that was cute. Exactly, flash backs. Anyway, I told him I was going to go shower because I was feeling gross. You know how I get excited whenever I go shopping, so I always end up sweating. I just end up feeling gross when I'm done. Ugh. Although, that was key for him to get ready because I was about to give him the BUSINESS! At least so I had thought.

I heard him when he came in the bathroom. I said oh shit! Here we go.

Then, I heard him peeing, so I didn't think anything of it. My music was on and I was singing along with it. I was washing my face when I felt his beard on my back. I laughed.

And who told you I wanted some company sir?!"

"My dick."

HA! Now see. Here you go."

"You feel it."

I DO. But can you hold on while I wash my body please and thank you."

"Gone and wash that thang off. You already know what time it is."

I sure do. And I'm game. So, once I'm done, don't you be too long behind me."

"SHIIIIIIIIT!"

I washed off my body and jumped out the shower. Love, I ran in that room and put on my smell good so fast. I know, but I wanted him to remember my scent. Every time he smells it, he'll think of me. Oh I know. I did it on purpose (wink).

I plugged in my iPod and let it do what it does. He came out that bathroom Guns Blazing! He was READY. He jumped on me like a fat kid on free cake baby! Naturally we started kissing right away. He LOVES to kiss! He can kiss very well too! So, I didn't mind at all. He went from vanilla to WILD quickly. Again, I didn't mind at all. I know "Dope Boy Sex" very well. I told him to FUCK ME LIKE HE DIDN'T LOVE ME. Baaayabey! That is EXACTLY what he did, too. Before I knew it, we were in there sounding like "Biggie & Lil Kim"! Straight FUCKING. We were loud, too. Not one fuck was given on our parts.

There was hair pulling, ass smacking, deep throating, spitting, face smacking, splits, spread eagles, gagging, tears, growling, cursing, name calling, frogging, riding, bouncing, throbbing, then the ultimate screams of "I'M CUMMING!." We definitely had a good time. It was needed. All that teasing I was doing to him, he definitely made me pay for it. While we were laying on the floor (don't ask) we burst out laughing because it was quiet, and we were breathing heavy AS FUCK! I was thinking about B. Usually when I had sex like that, it was with him. Kevin was laughing because he said he didn't know I had that in me. Oh hunni, don't let the demureness fool you boo *wink*.

We managed to climb back up onto the bed (after fixing it back on the box spring the proper way) he flopped on the bed, snuggle under me, then dozed off as I checked my messages on my phone.

Once I was done, I went over to the mini bar and grabbed me a water. Um yeah, you can imagine how thirsty I was after that work out. I climbed back in the bed, set my alarm for 8:00 p.m., then dozed off myself. When my alarm went off, I was already awake. I was laying there, looking at him; thinking about his story. He's had to fight so hard for most of his life. His grandmother played a major role in raising him (like mine did), then he got into trouble when he got older, then locked up, got out, put on probation, got off probation, got into the drug game via his probation officer (exactly, hot mess) then ended up talking to me and now lying beside me asleep; temporarily without a care in the world.

I knew all of this because he told me all on his own. Not once did I judge him or mke him feel any less than what he was (which you already know). I just loved him anyhow. More than anything, that's what he needed. We've spent so many nights on the phone talking, with tears in his eyes because he was tired of the game and games. I had to give him props, though. He managed to enroll himself into school and stay the course. He was doing pretty good with it. I told him a number of times I was very proud of him. He wasn't hearing that from anyone else and I could tell. I'm just thinking about all of this while his ass is still snoring.

I had to shake it off. Hell, he was with me for the moment, so I decided to just enjoy him like he was doing me. I got up, hopped in the shower, then woke him up when I got out. He was snoring down hunni. I hated to wake him because he was sleeping so good. I didn't wanna go to dinner without him. I would NOT have heard the end of it. I climbed back in the bed beside him and started kissing his face, then I pinched his nose.

"Come on Shit! Why you playing?!"

"Because it's 8:30 and I'm hungry. I can go without you if you like."

He stretched and yawned. "Don't get fucked up."

"Exactly. So, get up and get it together. Sir."

"You showered already?"

Of course, I did."

"You could have waited on me. You petty."

Mmhhmm, all that. Now go."

While he was showering, I was cleaning up the mess we made. I was picking up his clothes when a bank roll fell out of his jean pocket. I laughed, shook my head, then put it back. I figured he had cash on him, but wow. Yeah, I knew what it was.

I put it back because I didn't want him to think I was trying to steal from him, or I was stealing for that matter. The boy already had trust issues, he ain't need no damn help from my end. I was on the phone talking to my mother when he came out the bathroom, took the phone from me and they started talking about FOOD (as usual); and what they were going to MAKE me cook for the Next Holiday dinner (LOL Right). My mother? Yes, they spoke on the phone multiple times. She didn't know where I was. All she knew is that I was out, and Kevin and I were together. I didn't tell her until later. Anyway, we go down to dinner, but I didn't eat that much. I wanted to check out the club next door in the hotel after dinner.

You know I was ready to dance. As soon we were done dinner, I went to the bathroom to do a self-check, then we bounced right next door to the little club. Baby, listen! When we were walking, I felt that bass, I knew it was a song I knew, I just wasn't catching it. The bouncer opened those big double doors and "Lil Kim" was on (The Jump Off). You know damn well I ran straight to the dance floor! I sure did. I left Kevin's ass right there. I didn't even look back. The DJ was killing it with the "Brooklyn" mix. Lil Kim, Biggie, Junior Mafia, The Lox I was getting all my life. I forgot I was even with Kevin! By the fourth song I remembered. When I glanced up, he was in the corner booth with his beer, smiling, watching me dance.

Once I was done, I ran over to him and jumped on his lap and planted one old mean kiss on his lips. The other fellas fell out. They didn't see that one coming. I'm assuming because the girls were trying to flirt with him, but he was paying them dust.

"You always starting shit! I ain't know you could dance like that."

You love it. Shut up. And you never asked me if I could dance or not."

"You ready to go? I wanna fuck."

DAMN! But okay. Let's go."

Ass smack

"Aiight fellas, y'all be easy.

"You, too, thanks."

We made our way back up to the suite and got right to it. This time it wasn't as wild as it was before. This time, it was more passion. I think because he knew I was leaving soon, and he wanted to enjoy our *us* time as much as possible (as did I). Once we were done, we just laid in the bed talking for the rest of night until we dozed off. Sunday morning, I woke up, showered, order me some coffee and breakfast. He was still asleep, and I let him sleep for as long as he wanted. I kind of figured he would, though. I was sitting in the chair looking out the window, listening to my gospel, drinking my coffee and nibbling on some toast; when I heard him grunt.

I looked over my shoulder:

Well good morning sir."

"Wassup."

How did you sleep?"

"Good as shit! Damn. I need to get me one of these beds!"

I know, right? I said the same thing."

He got up to go into the bathroom, to clean up (shower and all that stuff), and when he came out, he came over and sat with me at the table. He smiled at me poured him some orange juice, grabbed a piece of toast, then said out his mouth

"Why you don't stop bull shit'n and marry me?"

I choked on my coffee. "WHAT?!"

"But I'm serious, though. You know we click. We both need to stop with the bullshit and make it happen. I know you know where we can make it happen."

I do. Ok, if you're really serious, in your heart of hearts, we'll revisit this again in a month or two. How about that?

"So, you're NOT saying No, you're just saying not right now?

Pretty much."

"Okay. I can respect that. Just know, that I DO Love you and I have fallen in love with you. Straight up."

"Aww boo, I love you too."

I kissed his face then I excused myself. I went into the bathroom. Love, I had to sit on the toilet for that one. I turned the water on, and I was just sitting there in shock. I think I was thrown off because he was DEAD ASS SERIOUS, and I knew it. Oh, he had me straight shook. I had to inhale and exhale a few times. Hell, I did so many breathing exercises I got slight light-headed. WHEW! I got myself together then went back out to the room. I told him I had food in my teeth. He was laying in the bed, so I crawled beside him. I asked him what was wrong.

"Nothing, just thinking."

"Pair of loafers for your thoughts."

"Only YOU would say some shit like that."

"Cute right?"

"Yeah okay. Anyway, I'm just thinking about life. I met you over the internet, we talked, and bullshitted around, met up and hit it off right away. I mean like I fucks with you for real.

You know how many of my so-called friends and buddies would have sold me out or did sell me out over some fuck nigga bullshit?! Yet you know all my shit and you still here".

"Yes, I'm aware. We all know that loyalty is hard to come by now a days. Doesn't matter if its family or not. I know right off the break who I should and shouldn't talk to. I follow my own mind and gut instincts. My heart told me that there was something familiar about you and clearly it was right. You just remind me of my uncle and god father so much. They lived that life like you, for a little while. So, I get it. If people choose to judge you, then you tell them to kiss your ass and you be on your way. I've told you this before".

Tears welled up in his eyes. "Yeah you did. That's why I fucks with you. You have no idea what you've done for me. I truly appreciate you for real."

Of course! Now suck it up and figure out what we are going to do today. You've got me for another twenty-four hours, so you better make it count."

"You right."

He rolled over, opened my robe and pushed my legs up. Yes, I was turned on. We went at it again. We had that "Belly" kind of sex. Baby! OH HE DID THAT! After we were done, we showered and went down for lunch. He said he wanted to hang out in the city for a few. Which was fine with me. I was tired of being indoors anyway. This time I had my driver back. I think he was slightly excited to see me, too. He took us to some of the popular spots downtown. You know I'm not a "touristy" type person. Kevin was funny. He asked him for his aux chord so he could turn on his music. He gave it to him, too. So now we are riding around Detroit listening to Biggie and other Rap music in a town car. I'm like dude really?! SMH.

We got back to the hotel about 7:00 p.m. I went straight up to my suite so that I could gather my things and be ready to walk out the door in the morning for my flight. Kevin told me he'd catch up with me in a few, he had to handle some business. I noticed room service had cleaned up a great deal so all I had to was figure out what I was going to wear and pack up the little stuff, along with the things I had just brought. Which was fine by me. You know I HATE packing anyways.

Kevin came in the room smiling until he realized what I was doing, and his face dropped. I think the reality of it all had set in. I told him to fix his face and what did he want for dinner. Naturally his response was steak (as if I really didn't know). I saw he was feeling some kind of way, so I turned up my music and danced with him to make him laugh. It worked.

He was back in his happy place. His laughter was very LOUD and contagious. You could tell he laughed from his belly. I loved it. Then his favorite song came on "I Love your smile" by Shanice. Oh, he opened ALL THE WAY UP for that one. Like, he really shocked me. I didn't know my little "Dope Boy" had it in him. He was grooving and everything.

Just looking at him get his life off that song made me feel one hundred times better and I wasn't even feeling bad! I said okay! I see this is your song for real. He grabbed me to dance with him. I couldn't stop laughing at him. Oh hunni, Shanice had him in a zone for real. Alright now. After the song went off, I went in the bathroom to freshen up for dinner. He was standing in the door looking at me smiling. I turned around and told him to stop being a creep. He laughed then said, "I'm your motherfucking creep, though!"

Anyway, let's go. We made our way back to the elevator with his hand on the small of back again, then it he put his arm around me. That was nice. Look, it is what it is now. Hell, the boy done already asked me to marry him so clearly, he's love'n me and feeling some kind of way. I low-key was love'n him, too. It was nice to be with somebody who gets you, lets you be you and everything. The same thing with him. Just love, fun and enjoying life. Let it flow. That's what we did. Even, though something about him would NOT let me get but so excited, I knew I had to suppress it for the time being. I've had this feeling before and I was right (yeah, regarding my Hollywood sis). A part of me feels like this won't last long, then I'll be pissed because I didn't listen to my gut.

So again, I decided to just enjoy him. Be present in the moment. He made us reservation at the steak place, which was a great idea because it seemed like everybody wanted steak that night, or at least wanted to eat in there. The waiting time for a table was thirty minutes at the least. I thanked him for his smarts. I was NOT in the mood for that wait. As we were escorted to our table, I noticed there were drinks waiting for us. He took the liberty again and ordered some wine for me and him a beer. I don't even drink beer, but his beer was looking good as fuck! He was on point. I like it when a man takes things into consideration. See, it's the little things that I like.

We ate so good. He made an excellent choice. My seafood platter and salad were just to die for. It was so fresh. His steak looked good, too. If I ate steak I would have asked for a piece. But I'm sure he would not have given me any by the way he fucked it up! Once we were finished eating, he grabbed my hand, then told me he wanted to show me something. I smiled at him then said okay.

We got back on the elevator and went to the top floor. Those doors opened and the view was so spectacular. A view of the city line under the stars.

"Have you been here before?"

"I have."

"Clearly. You know this area and hotel too well. I love this! Oh my God!"

"I figured you would. I decided to wait until your last night. One last gift from me to you."

"And you know what? This is, by far, the BEST one!"

"I agree. The way your face lite up was priceless.

"Great job."

We kissed then jumped back on the elevator down to my room. He stayed the night, which I figured he would anyway. He said he wanted to ride with me to the airport. I didn't think anything of it. I woke up Monday morning to him kissing my neck. He said he wanted one last round. This time, he wanted to take his time and enjoy it. I was cool with that. We had some great intimate sex, showered together then, went downstairs for a quick bite to eat then I was off to the airport. We sat out in the terminal talking, laughing, people watching and just chilling until my flight. My flight is only an hour, he was acting like I was flying across the country or out of the country.

Just before it was time for me to board my flight, I went to the store to buy me some gum and water (per my usual). Kevin was on my heels. I laughed at first and told him to relax. As my flight was called for us to begin lining up to board; and as we made our way over to the gate, I noticed he was quiet and slightly stand offish. I turned to him, told him that we will see each other again very soon. I hugged him, grabbed him by the face and then kissed him again. I was walking to the line to board when my instincts told me to look back at him.

He was standing there watching me looking like a little kid. He had his hands in his pockets, his snap back turned backwards, and tears in his eyes. I instantly jumped out of line to go hug him again.

"Why are you upset? Kevin, I need for you to chill."

"Nah, I'm good. Just go 'head. I'm good."

"No, you're not, but you will be. I had a wonderful time and I really enjoyed you. I know you enjoyed me as well, and I'll see you soon.

"I'll let you know as soon as I land. I promise. Now straighten up and gimmie a kiss. This ain't dope boy behavior."

"You right. These thug tears. I'ma miss you, homie."

"Ha! There it is."

"*smiles* I love you."

And I love you right back sugga."

I hugged him, kissed him then went to board my flight. I sent him a text message when I was sitting in my seat. It was pic of me sitting down in my seat winking at him.

He responded back with "I love you & have a safe flight." It made me smile and I responded back with I love you, too. When I landed then turned my phone back on, I had five messages from him. I guess it was all the things he wanted to say to me that he felt he couldn't say in person.

Everything from he loves me, to thanking me, to me taking him serious about his proposal, being his friend, etc. The only thing I said was, was that I landed, and I'll hit him back once I'm home and settled. I talked to him off and on throughout the rest of the week. He was loving life. He was just so excited that we had finally met in person and spent the entire weekend together.

I was glad that he didn't say anything to anyone. Oh no, I'd never be ashamed of him. You know that, but he knows how private I am. Hell, he's just as private as I am so he wasn't going to say much anyways. He would crack jokes and say random things on Facebook, but only he and I knew what they meant. As time went on, we kept in touch and linked a up a few more times. After that, we hadn't seen each other in person for a quite a few months. We did revisit the whole proposal thing, I told him that I do love him, however, I'm not ready for the whole marriage thing again. Not right now.

He told me that he totally understood and that he could respect my choices. He also told me that he loved me even more for telling him the truth. We remained very intimate friends and talked on a regular basis. Even, though he deiced to try and date other people, it never really worked for him. He couldn't be honest with them or let them into too much of his life the way he had let me in. Something we talked about on the regular basis. Time passed us by, we still kept in touch.

I finally figured out why my heart wouldn't let me get but so excited for him. You see, Kevin and I often talked about how he didn't want to grow old. He said that he wanted to die young.

I would often tell him not to say those things or to even think like that. He was very adamant about it too. As time went on, he was slipping away from me more and more. I would keep in touch with him on purpose and make sure he was alright. He would talk to me, but I could always tell when something was wrong with him. We would talk it out and he'd be alright briefly, then he'd slip right back into his funk a few days later.

Life kept going for both of us, so we would talk on the phone in passing or I'd call, text or Instant message him to check on him. As another month passed by, I decided to check on him, not knowing it would be our last conversation ever. Yup, the unthinkable happened. The last conversation we had was our usual checking on each other, catching up, cracking jokes and telling each other how much we loved one another. My greatest fear happened.

I was on Facebook checking my highlights and checking on a few folks, when I got a notification that Kevin had passed away. My heart dropped immediately, and I fell to my knees. As I went to check for myself, it turned out to be true. Kevin was killed in his own house by someone who he thought loved him or had his best interest at heart. I cried so hard to the point I was sick. I knew this was going to happen. Not him being killed that way, but him dying young. That's why my soul wouldn't allow me to connect to him but so much. It was like my sixth sense knew. Again, I've been down this road before.

I called his cell phone just to make sure because I just, I just wasn't ready to come to terms with it. His sister answered the phone because she saw my face pop up. When she said my name, and I could hear the grief in her voice, I whaled all over again. Once I finally got myself together, all I could muster up to ask her was, what happened? She told me that he and his roommate got into an altercation, the boy caught Kevin with his back turned, choked him and drug him down the hallway with something around his neck. I felt the air leave my body; and all I remember was waking up on my living room floor. So yeah, I passed out.

I called his sister back, and all I could do was tell his sister, thank you for telling me. I told her to forgive me for going silent on her. I didn't tell her I blacked out. I told her to text me her number from his phone and I'd call her back. I just needed to get myself together. I hung up, ran to the bathroom and laid on the floor. I was there for twenty-four hours. The more I laid there, longer I cried and asked God what had I done?! I felt like it was my fault.

Like if I would have just married him like he asked me to, he would still be here with me. Had I said yes and moved him in with me, out of harm's way, or SOMETHING, he would be fine and still with me.

Even now as I'm telling you this, I'm fighting back tears. I know, but that's just how I felt. I know that wasn't right, but at that moment, that's how I felt. It was too much for me to handle. But I KNEW he wasn't going to be here with me long. Not to mention, what was marrying me going to fix? I went through an array of emotions. I just knew I had to get myself together to say my final goodbye to him.

I managed to get myself together enough to go to his services. I left the night before so the morning of, I could just go to his services and then get back on my flight to come back home. I wasn't in the mood to linger around. On the flight out, I smiled and laughed a little thinking about him. The next morning, as my driver pulled up to the funeral home, I just sat in the car for about ten minutes watching his family proceed into the building. I just needed a few minutes to get myself together. I finally got out once the foot traffic died down. I decided to hide behind my shades, dark clothes and hair. I just knew I was going to be able to sit in the back and not bring any attention to myself.

When I walked in the funeral home; and saw his body lying in that damn box, my knees got weak and I had to sit down right away. I began to cry all over again. The tears would just NOT stop flowing. My baby was lying in that damn box because his life was taken away from him over foolishness. I was crying on top of being angry, all while trying to keep it cute for his family. The last thing I need is "Who are you and how did you know Kevin" etc.

I went to the restroom to get myself together. I was met by his sister when I came out. She hugged me and thanked me for coming. She and I sat down in the foyer and talked for a few minutes. She informed me that she knew who I was because Kevin often talked about me.

He told her that he finally had a real friend. Which made me tear up all over again. She was so sweet. We talked, laughed and cried. Then she walked with me in the service. I told her I didn't wanna see him up close. I could see enough from where we were standing. I sat down in the back and told her to go be with her family, I was fine. I sat there for most of the service and slide out right before the very end.

I sat in my car and waited for them to proceed to the cemetery. I sat in my car until the very end of the cemetery service, then I walked over to him once his casket was closed and said my good-byes. It was very hard for me to do that because I knew that was it. No calls, text messages, dirty jokes, the kisses, his smile or his loud infectious laugh. That was the END. I talked to him for a good forty-five minutes. His sister sat right there and let me. She didn't allow them to lower him into the ground until I was done. I thanked her for that.

I gave her one last hug before I left. I went back to my car and had the driver take me to a hotel. I got a room for a about 4 hours, got myself together, changed my clothes, then checked out. I went straight to the airport. My driver offered his condolences then hugged me before I went into the airport. He said he could tell I needed one. "The strongest people need hugs as well." And you know what? He's right.

I remember me sitting on the plane back home, and once I was in the air, I exhaled one good time, then I fell asleep. I slept better than I had, since I had heard of him passing. I got back home, took a shower, then began to unpack. Something came over me to the point where I felt like I was covered in love (if that makes sense to you). It was like a rush of good emotions all at once. Not that I was complaining! It just felt really good. Once I sat down and thought about it, it was because I knew that he was finally at peace. He had been battling too long with too many demons. Past and present. Now, he was at peace. It's a bitch the way he left, but the end result was his peace.

Now, when I think of Kevin, I smile, laugh or I get that rush of being covered in LOVE. I no longer cry or weep for him. It took me a minute to really get over the fact of not being able to hear his voice, but I'm okay now. When I hear his song, I light up and just laugh. I may tear up a little bit, but that's all joy now. I do still very much so love him and miss him a great deal. I still hear him laughing at me every once in a while, when I do something stupid or act like a "Becky".

That's the life you live when you date a "Dope Boy," "Hustler" etc., or fall in love with one. Those are the emotions, choices and chances you have to live with, make or take. It is what it is. You are either blessed enough to see his change, or your stuck with the emotions of burying him and living life without him. I hate the way it ended the way that it did, but I don't question God or life. Yeah, I know. He'll always have a place in my heart though. My favorite "Dope Boy" whose smile I'll always Love.

Love, I'm glad you asked. I needed that.

Thank you.

I'll ttyl,

Eskimo Kisses.

COOKING WITH HEART FROM THE MATRIARCH

Love,

You know what's nice? I'm sitting here just thinking about everything I've been through in the past nine years since I started my "Soul-full" makeover. It has truly been an experience for me. I was learning myself from the inside out. Now that I'm done (for the most part) it was enjoyable. A lot was learned and lost. I've lost a few people, yet I've gained some great ones in return. I could not be happier honestly. I literally find myself laughing out loud at any given moment. Be it a thought or something that triggers a memory. I know, get the designer straight jacket now. HA! I'm sure there's more to come (it usually is) and I'm ready for it. So much was taken for granted, on top of me being allowed to be taken for granted.

I remember when it started because it was right after Grams passed away. I was reeling so bad from her passing; I didn't even realize it. At least not until B and my older cousin Cindy brought it to my attention. I remember that Thanksgiving after she passed away; I cooked until I couldn't cook anymore. I literally had food all over my kitchen. It was so much food that I literally had different people coming to get food every day for two weeks. That was the beginning of the transformation. YES. Just that much. Hmph.

Shortly after Grams passed, my mother and I went AT IT! She was just all kinds of fucked up. Just being mean for no reason at all. Then she lost her job; I laughed at her trying to be mean, but that didn't do anything to me but make me even more upset because I stooped to her level of ignorance. Then on top of that, I still had to take care of home. I still had to look out for my husband, siblings, cousin Cindy along with my nieces and nephews. I really didn't get a chance to have a moment to myself. No bereavement period or anything. At least not until I started cooking and SNAPPED.

I remember me not being in the mood to cook a big holiday dinner "Rose" style, but I knew I had to cook because I had too many people depending on me to do so, just like she would have done. I made myself go to the store, and no sooner than I was in the store, I started remembering all the things she would cook just for Thanksgiving. Before I knew it, I had gone to three grocery stores and had spent about $500 on groceries (if not more). Just for one damn day! Lord, I'm laughing out loud just thinking about it. When I pulled up, B was looking at me like I had lost my dayum mind. I told him, "Well, y'all wanted me to cook and Grams isn't here to help me, so hey."

He shook his head and helped me unload the car. I went upstairs to change into sweatpants and a T-shirt, then I began my prepping phase the way she taught me. This was on a Monday afternoon. I prepped everything all the way up until Tuesday evening. I think I slept a total of four hours between the two days. By Wednesday, I was cooking full speed ahead and in my groove. I think I had very little interaction with the people in my house. Even my own damn husband hadn't seen me. I wasn't sleeping in our bed or anything. I wasn't mad at him or upset even, I just wasn't in the mood for anything extra. In order for me NOT to come off in a hateful way, I just let him be. I still fed him and made sure he was alright.

I was just cooking and getting things done. That's when suddenly, I began to cry. I started crying and fussing. I didn't even realize I was doing it out loud until B told me later. I was looking at her cookbook—cooking, fussing, cussing and having an all-out war go with God and Grams. I was so pissed at her for leaving me here by myself, I didn't even realize I was just that upset. I was remembering how every month on the twenty-sixth; she would teach me how to cook one of her dishes. This went on for about sixteen months before she passed away. Sometimes, we would start cooking on the twenty-sixth, and we would cook the entire week straight. I don't know what it was about the twenty-sixth, but that was our day. If we weren't cooking, we were talking about recipes or what her special ingredients were that she was using. It was just us, and she made sure it was that way on purpose. Very intimate and filled with love. Heart-to-heart and one-on-one. The more I thought about it, the madder I got.

As I was cooking, I began fussing at God and asking him why....

"Why did you do this to me? Why did you have to take her away from me the way that you did? Why was it so soon? How dare you! Then you didn't even give us a chance to say goodbye. The NERVE OF YOU!"

Then I flipped on Grams...

"Why did you leave me? How dare you leave me and not think about what I would do without you. Then you have the nerve to tell me everything is going to be okay. IT'S NOT OKAY! You Left ME! You left me here with these jackasses all on my own; I have nobody to talk to, no body to protect me anymore. Why? WHY DID YOU DO THIS TO ME!?"

I was saying these things out-loud while continuing to cook. I'm thinking that I'm saying these things in my head. Yeah, no. Before I knew it, I turned around and my God! - I had a mean spread throughout my entire kitchen. My countertops, table, and even my island was full of food. It was everything she taught me how to cook before she passed away. Even the things we talked about cooking one day but never got to. I had things my grandfather used to make as well. Like, just a ridiculous amount of food. I was steady pulling food out the oven and putting food in the oven. I mean, just all over the place. By Wednesday night, I was in full on chef mode. I did not sit down until all my food was finished, laid out, covered, or done.

Mind you, I was still in my mood. Once I was finally finished, I stepped back, looked at everything I cooked, and I fell to my knees and sobbed like a baby. That's when B came in and tried to help me up. I just couldn't move. I couldn't do it. I told him to just leave me alone. "Please, just leave me alone." He got upset because he didn't know what was wrong with me and I wasn't talking to him. That's when my cousin, Cindy, came in the kitchen and told him to leave me be. He didn't want to, but I told him, "I'm okay, and to please just go." Cindy told B "Come on sweetie. He'll be fine. Christian, work through it!" See, the thing with Cindy, she had already made peace with grams passing because her mother passed well before grams did. So she knew how to handle it. She also knew how to handle me and how to get me going so that I would move on. I sat on the floor for ten minutes after he left. Matter fact, I sat on the floor so dayum long my ass and legs fell asleep; I was no good. Just thinking about it still makes me laugh out loud. The way I had to roll around and move because my dayum legs were asleep. LOL. Anyway, I went upstairs, took my clothes off, showered, then sat in the bathroom for another forty-five minutes. B knocked on the door to ask me if I was okay. Then he peeked his big head in the bathroom at me to see if I was good.

I told him I was fine (not looking at him) even though I wasn't. I kissed him goodnight and he went to bed. I was still in the bathroom and I began to cry again. This time, it was different. I could feel my broken heart begin to heal. There was a rush of love that flooded my soul in a way I had never felt before. It was refreshing, but it made me nervous at the same time. It actually took a lot out of me. The last thing I remember about that feeling was me laying on the bathroom floor with tears flowing down my face before dozing off to sleep. I DO remember my dream very vividly, though.

In my dream, I was lying in bed when I heard a noise in the kitchen. It sounded like someone was cooking. I jumped up to run downstairs to see who the hell was in my kitchen and what they were doing. I turned the corner and it was Grams. I ran to hug her, and I began to sob again. She hugged me back, but Baaaybeey! She let me have it! Not only did she tell me to cut my shit, but she told me to sit down because we needed to talk.

I sat down at the table and she sat right across from me in her normal seat.

"First off, I'm sorry. I am. You know that I love you and I would *never* leave you. I am *always* with you. Don't ever forget that," Grams said.

"I know but—"

"No buts. You know this. Now listen to me. This is *not* about you. It's beyond you. How dare you question God? I taught you better than that. You know better."

"I do."

"I know you do. Not now or ever have you heard me say it's okay to go against God's will or *HIS* plans. I am *fine*. It was time for me to go. I have fought long enough. You are grown, my children are grown. I've seen my grandbabies, and all is well with my soul. You never once considered how I might feel or others around you. That was very selfish of you. Stop shutting people out. You deal with it and you move on. You will *not* waddle in this. You are *not* allowed to." She took my hands in hers. "*I am fine.*"

"Well, you seem fine." I laughed.

Grams laughed, too. "*I am.* And I need for you to be, as well. Listen to me. I'm good, you're good. I need for you to get over this. I don't need you falling apart at the seams. I taught you better than that. We grieve and we move on. And don't let me hear you question God again. He's not the issue *now* or *ever*. And I mean it!"

"Well, doesn't that seem easier said than done? And yes, you're right. I apologize. But I miss you so much. I was not prepared for this." I began to cry.

"But my baby, you were. Why do you think I've been teaching you how to cook and spending so much extra time with you? I already knew what was coming down the line. I made peace with it well before you even had an idea. *I made peace with it*, she emphasized. "But you were prepared, you just didn't catch it."

"You know, you're right." I laughed. "I see where you're going with this."

"Now, apologize to my baby. He doesn't understand. He's not like you and I. He needs a little help with understanding all of this. You know I love you."

"I will. I Love you too Grams."

Grams stood up. "Deal and move on. I mean it. Whenever you need me, you know what to say and where to go. I love you, my baby."

As she made me hold on to her hands, I began to feel that rush of Love, Comfort and Peace flow through me again. We hugged, then she kissed my face, then told me "It's alright. Let it go". She walked around the corner to the patio, then disappeared. I was smiling at her because my flowers on the porch bloomed and there was a sweet soft fragrance of her in the air. I woke up immediately after that and ran downstairs. Love, my right hand to God, I ran to the patio and I could smell her. I said, "Yeah okay. Dreamscape my ass! That heffa was really here." I had to laugh at myself. I went to the kitchen, made me some hot tea, grabbed my blanket and sat on the porch while watching the sun rise.

I was a little more at ease. No, that's a lie. I was at ease! PERIOD. I felt absolutely nothing after she left me. Which was funny because she did that to me a lot. She would either walk up behind me or place her hands on my back in a way, that would rejuvenate me, or take away whatever anxiety I was feeling at that moment. Even though Grams gathered my ass right on together, I felt better than I had in a while. It was nice. I still had tears flowing a little bit, but this time, they were tears of joy, comfort and relief. I was finally over it and I could feel it. It was like she was that calming peace that I needed to wash over me. I sat there for about a good two hours. Once I was done apologizing to God and coming to terms with everything, I got up and went back in the house.

I went upstairs then climbed back in the bed with B (who was still asleep) and I snuggled up under him. He threw his arm over me, kissed my check and went back to sleep. I woke up about 10:00 am and went back downstairs to finish cooking. I was chilling with the fam for a bit, while I made sure all my loose ends were tied up and everything was ready to rock. I left the fam for a few minutes while I went upstairs for a few minutes to talk to God again, while my family was downstairs talking amongst themselves. As I was sitting on the side of my bed, Bella came in the room and sat at my feet while resting her head on my lap. She knew I was having a moment. I told her I was fine. Grams made it all better. She licked my leg and laid down. I had my moment with God then got in the shower. After my shower, I laid down and took a nap for a few. It was one of those naps where I just drifted off in peace. If I did dream, I have no memory of what it was. AT ALL. That's how I knew it was one of my peaceful sleep moments. B woke me up about 3 p.m. so I could get dressed and do any last-minute things I needed to do. He knows how I am about my table and entertaining, so he leaves it be. He's no fool. "Bree" will have his ass! LOL. I got up, I threw on my cute little Thanksgiving dinner "outfit", then bounced back downstairs.

When I came around the corner to the kitchen, they all stopped talking to look at me. I laughed. "Y'all just staring. What?"

"Well! Don't you look better," Cindy said. "You good now, Rose?"

"Yes. I'm fine now. Thank you (as I hugged her). You all can go get dressed. We can eat as soon as you want to. No need to wait for others. I don't know who's coming by anyway. Not that I care. So, when you all are dressed and ready, we can eat. Cindy I'll fill you in later"

They all ran upstairs and to the basement (Keith) to get dressed for dinner. I always make them put on real clothes for the holiday or major dinners. It's the way Grams did it and that's the way it will continue to be. Especially if it's going to be at my house. They were more than happy to oblige. That and they didn't want me to pop off. HA!

We had a great dinner and they truly enjoyed everything. I just...GEEZE that was A LOT of food. They ate until they were dizzy. I didn't eat much. I enjoyed watching them eat what I had prepared and hearing them say "You can tell Rose taught you. It tastes just like she cooked it herself." That part made me tear up a little bit. Little did they know, it *was* her that cooked it. Once dinner was over, I went back up to my room for a few to change my clothes and just chill. I turned on my music and just mellowed out.

I was felling one percent better. That dream, on top of me smelling her and feeling her essence, I knew I was fine. I knew she was. Everything was okay.

B came upstairs to check on me. I told him I was fine and kissed his face, which led to other things. Yeah, a quickie. Then after that he was fine. LOL. He asked me afterwards

"Are you ever going to tell me what happened?"

"One day, just not right now."

"Cool," he said and then went back downstairs with the fam to watch football.

I went downstairs to clean up the kitchen a little bit, when in walked my cousin, Cindy, again. She hugged me. "I knew you had to come to terms on your own time. She loves you and she's so proud of you. Especially after what the fuck you did today. You cooked your ass off. I don't know who the fuck you thought was finna eat all this food, but you did it! It was good. Just like she prepared it herself."

"Thank you so much. I'm fine now. I just needed to deal. Thank you."

"She came to you didn't she?"

I burst out laughing "YES! OMG! How did you know?!"

"I figured she would. I thought I smelled her this morning when I went to let the dog out"

"Yup! That was her".

"Mmhhmm. I figured that".

"Thank you Cindy".

"Anytime. I love you. Now please cut these cakes so we can fuck'em up already, child!"

"Yes, ma'am!"

I did just what she asked. I cut all the cakes and pies and let them have it. I went outside with Bella for a few and let her play in the backyard. Even that gave me comfort and joy. Just watching her play and playing with her gave me great peace. Everything had come full circle. As I was walking back up the deck steps, I stopped and looked at my family sitting in the family room, just enjoying each other. The laughter, talking and love that filled the room made me smile. That's what Grams was all about. That's what Pop-Pop was about. That's what my family is about. We get through and we get over.

If Grams didn't teach me nothing else, she taught me how to stick to my guns and have faith in God. Everything else would fall into place. That's exactly what happened. Dealing with her and my issues gave me a whole new outlook on life. It taught me how to deal with things and people. Whenever I need a reminder, I just pull from her and what she taught me. Breathe, Pray, Focus, then Kick Ass! I'm glad I did catch it early on though. It's been a nonstop battle since. I haven't given up or given in. You know my stubborn ass will fight until the end. Like I said, I've lost a few, which didn't bother me, but what I've gained in return...whew Lord!

I have no complaints. I thank God first, then my Ancestors. No mess, no fuss and no regrets. Not to mention, I learned how to say *NO* and I love it! Others hate it, but I LOVE IT! And that's ALL that matters.

I know, all in a day, right?

I love you Love.

Ttyl,

Eskimo Kisses.

MEXICO LEFT ME BREATHLESS

So okay, Love,

I know you've been itching for a scratch about this year's Mexico trip with the fam. The funny part is, I wasn't even in that mind frame this time around. Like…I wasn't looking for another "Louise" or anything. I was just going with the flow. You know, as I always do. Go get a cocktail, doll. You'll need it *innocent giggle*.

Well, as you know, we go on a trip every year for the Queen's (Lady E) birthday. This year, she decided on Mexico, again, just a different resort, which was cool. She always picks the best places. Since the Diva (Lady J) and I were leaving on the same day, we decided to fly out together. We caught an early morning flight out, with an hour layover in Charlotte. Of course, we were geeked the whole time. Laughing and talking as we always do. Enjoying each other's company.

When we arrived in Mexico, our driver was waiting and ready to rock. With that heat, you know I was not complaining. The driver took us to our resort (which was beautiful). As we were walking in, we were greeted by a super friendly staff and decor that was immaculate. The entrance to the resort was very fresh. It was open and brought all the four elements inside. Multi-shaded brownstone walls with shapes carved into them, accompanied by glass waterfalls with fire pits in front of them. They really put some, thought into it

We were a little early for our check-in, so J and I decided to get something to eat at the buffet restaurant. The concierge told us it was okay for us to leave our bags with them while we dined for lunch. We walked to the door of the buffet, and as we were greeted by the hostess, I couldn't help but notice all the beautiful glass doors and windows. Not to mention the two full-service bars we passed to get there. We were seated right away and greeted by the restaurant staff. The waiters, servers, and chefs were too cute and adorably funny. They were all very friendly. The restaurant was nice. Food went as far as the eye could see. Everything from seafood to barbecue, desserts to salads. You name it, hunni they had it. Not to mention the tequila-based drinks. Oh hunni we had a ball! She got me to get a drink. Something green, fruity and sneaky! It was hell'a GOOD though. LOL.

No sooner than we were done with lunch, our birthday girl showed up. She walked in, we were lit up and geeked all over again. We did our usual hugging and making noise.

Since E said her and hubby had something they needed to do, we were going to link up later. J and I checked into our rooms.

The front desk clerk gave us adjoining rooms, which made me nervous at first, but I shook it off. What? Why was I nervous? Because I know me. If I was to get...um...lucky, I don't want her hearing all the business or vice versa. As we walked into our rooms, we noticed that they were beautiful and freezing cold. I turned down the air and opened the sliding glass door and was taken aback by the private swim out pools. It was very nice. The headboard changed colors to set the ambiance in the room. Yeah, all of that. I'm sure somebody went home pregnant, but it wasn't us. HA!

We settled into our rooms and changed our clothes. It was hot so you know I needed me a shower. Yet, I took a shower to go back outside to sweat all over again. I know, don't ask. But it made me feel better. Any who, we met back up at the center bar in the middle of the resort. We took some cute pictures together and just chilled with lots of laughter. Drinks on deck, the fellas were eye candy, the ladies had their titties out, it was *real!* But hey, that's why I prefer "Adult Only" resorts. As the time went on, we got hungry again, so we slide over to the tapas bar.

After tapas, we slid right on over to the beach. Again, the sights. Oh-me-oh-my. You know me, shades on, head low enjoying the views. YES! LOL! Catching all of the T!

We did the beach for about three hours before we headed to dinner. We went to the Buffet restaurant for dinner. We laughed, drank, talked and laughed some more. It was just really nice. Love, you know me, I made sure I played nice with the workers as well. The waiters, hostesses, chefs, all of them. They were so nice and down to earth. Just loveable. Some of them even joined us at one point for a little convo. I think we sat in the restaurant until one in the morning, which was cool because it was open twenty-four hours. Afterward, we made our way back to our rooms. I wasn't sleepy, so I changed back into my shorts and sat outside on my balcony. Once I remembered it was still warm out, I put on my sarong and bikini briefs with my tank top.

I sat on the edge of the pool, with my feet in the water, enjoying the night. I had my music down low since J was asleep. I went back in to grab me something to drink and came back out when old boy who was in the room next to me on the right side, came swimming by. He asked me what I was doing out so late, and I told him just enjoying the night. He introduced himself. His name was Jerry. He was about five-ten, two hundred twenty pounds, white boy with dirty blond hair and gray eyes. He was handsome. Not my type, but cute, nonetheless.

We sat outside and chatted for two hours. I stayed on the edge and he stayed in the water. His other buddies swam down to us for about fifteen minutes and went in their room. Jerry was cool. He told me he was visiting from Florida with his buddies and they just came down to enjoy and cut up a little bit. I did notice him trying to look up my sarong every once in a while. Slick ass (or so he thought).

I went to my room at about three-forty-five and slept until about eight in the morning. I jumped up, got dressed and went outside for a little walk on the beach. That's when I met Truck (Danny). He was from Chicago. Now HE was my type. Baaybeey! He was a cute chocolate bear; six-two, two hundred forty pounds, low Cesar haircut and one hell of a beard! He was sexy! We passed each other on the beach. We spoke and he smiled at me.

I said, "Oop! You got some pretty teeth!"

He laughed. "Thank you."

He complimented me on my legs and sarong. As I was smiling back at him, all I could think was "Hook, line, and sinker! *Gotcha!*" I thanked him while smiling away. We talked for a few minutes. I told him which side I was staying on. He said he may have to come and visit me later.

"By all means, please do," I said.

Baby! I would slide away from the crew to give him some ME time! I returned to my room and slipped into my shorts. I got a text from the Queen telling me she'd meet me for breakfast in thirty minutes. I texted that I would meet them over there since I was already dressed.

I got us a table and waited for them to arrive. I had the waiter to bring me some coffee and water. As I'm waiting, my stomach started growling, so I went to get some food. I was trying to be polite, but it wasn't working. I got some French toast and all the fixings to go along with it. I'm talking chocolate sauce, sweetened condensed milk, caramel sauce, raisins, almond shavings, whipped cream, and fruit. Hunni, it was laid out! Since it's been a while, I decided to make me a sauce to drizzle on top of my French toast. As I was making my sauce in a bowl, there was an older lady standing near me. She wanted to taste it. She was so cute. I told her I'd bring her some so she could taste it before she put it on her food. Once I was done, I went over to her table and allowed her to taste it. As I was giving her some on a small saucer, her son was walking around to her table. I looked up and yup! It was old boy. Mr. Truck himself.

They were on a family trip. As she introduced us, in my usual unlockable fashion, I just made it seem like we were meeting for the first time. I saw his facial expression and I automatically put two and two together. I shook his hand, introduced myself (again) then winked from my right eye. I knew she couldn't see it, so it was cool. His reaction was hilarious. I could tell he was nervous at the thought of me saying something, but you and I both know that is NOT my cup of tea. After the wink and smile, he smiled back and gave me that good ol "nice to meet you" etc. She told him what I did for her and how good it was. He said, "Thanks for taking care of ma Christian". "Anytime. She's a doll. Enjoy your breakfast hunni".

I told her to enjoy the sauce and if she needed any more to let me know. Then, I showed her where I was sitting. Truck said, "Thanks again Christian". I told them to enjoy the rest of their breakfast. She hugged me then kissed my face, then I returned to my table. No sooner than I sat down, the rest of my crew walked in. I had to laugh at their timing. We had a wonderful breakfast. We decided to make the second day a great one. We were just going to cut up! That's exactly what we did too. Cut. THE FUCK UP! We walked around the entire resort so we could see what was really good. They had a party pool area that was always jumping. From 10 am to 6 pm they were in the pool, drinking, and eating, with the music going. It was a cute setup. That pool was grossly packed the whole time it was open. Yeah no, I didn't get in it. Matter of fact, none of us did. Um like uh no. Some folks ain't NEVER get out. Ew.

Anyway, after our exploration, we returned to the beach and found us a spot to sit. As E and her hubby found us a spot, J and I decided to go to the bar and get us some drinks—the first round anyway. I went to drop off the drinks to E, and she and I began to talk. Just about life, work, thoughts, and everyday BS. How much we were enjoying everything so far. Before I knew it, we had talked for about a good forty-five minutes, when I noticed my little Ms. J wasn't back yet. I decided to go look for her. Low and behold she met a friend. He was a cutie pie from Chicago. A light-skinned thug with cornrows in his hair. He was really cool and down to earth.

When I walked up to the bar and sat beside her, he peeked over at me, spoke and dapped me up.

He figured that we were together. He was quite comical, too. As we sat and talked to him a little longer, he opened up. I guess he figured she and I weren't together, or I wasn't a threat per se. Although me sashaying around in a sarong and sole'less sandals should have given that away. But okay! He went on to tell us about his home life, a little about his family and how he loved his gay sister as well. Like yeah, he went there. I didn't think anything of it. That was just his way of saying how he wasn't intimidated by me or anything negative (I caught it). You know how hetero boys can be (bless his heart). E and her hubby had a spa appointment, so J and I stayed on the beach. We walked over to the other side and found lounge chairs out of the sun. We were sitting there, talking and chilling until she dozed off to sleep. As she was napping, I walked back over to the bar to get me a ginger ale.

Mr. Chicago and some of his buddies were at the bar laughing and talking. When I walked over, he gave me that loud *"Aye!"* thing that drunk boys do. He introduced me to his friends as "my buddy Christian." It was cute, for what it was worth. One of his buddies was fine as fuck! He was about six-five, two hundred seventy pounds, caramel complexion, juicy lips, solid, with a deep-ass voice. I remembered his name because he turned me the fuck on! Baby liiiissssssten. That motherfucker was so fine if I was driving, *bitch I would've crashed!* His name was "King". I wanted to show him my royal hind parts. Love! Yes! All me!

He shook my hand with a mean grip and gave me that sexy ass "Wassup?" *Baby!* I think my culo winked at him. I swear! You know when I get really turned on my eyes and mouth start watering. I had to make myself break my attention away from him.

Mr. "Chicago" wanted to know if we were going to be free later. I told him I wasn't sure. I'd find out and let him know. He told me he was staying on the club level. He gave me the room number and to give him a ring if J and I wanted to come by later on. I said, "Cool," and got my drink and walked back over to J. She was still napping so

I didn't wanna leave her there by herself. I sat back in my chair and took a couple of selfies and posted them to social media. She woke up about thirty minutes later. After she woke up, we decided to walk the beach one last time before we returned to the room. We walked over to the neighboring resort which was a clothing optional resort. Again, shades on and sights were seen. *Yes, God!* It was some "Kat Zaddy's" over there that were ready for the taking (my hot box ass)!

We returned to the room and chilled for a bit. We texted E to see where they were. She replied that they were coming over to our rooms to party. That's exactly what we did. We had our wireless speaker, a bottle of *"Veuve Clicquot Rich"*, some snacks and it was on! We were partying in our own little private pool areas just having a ball. That's where all those selfies came from. Yeah, those were taken in my room. I even turned on some Gloria Estefan. I slightly queened out on that part. Leave it to J to notice that right. Just so happen I looked up, and "Big Daddy King" was standing on the other side looking at us cut up.

You see, the gag was that our rooms were directly behind the party pool area. We were tucked behind a cabana, some bushes, two feet of concrete and another row of flowers and shrubbery. Our pool divided the rest. So, it wasn't like you could just walk over to our room or pool from the party pool area with easy access. When I looked up, I saw him standing on his buddy's balcony up on the 5th floor adjacent to our rooms, looking down, nodding to the music; I was over. I saw him, but I wasn't sure if he was looking at me or J or E for that matter. I kept it cute and cool. I took my sarong off and put on my orange shorts. And they were truly short too. All the yams were viewable hunni. When the music changed to hip-hop, we kept on dancing. I looked up again and he was still looking at us. This time I wanted to be sure, so I smiled and winked at him. He gave me a nod and winked back. Yeah, that wasn't enough for me. I needed that real confirmation.

After we were done parting, we decided to take showers and get dressed for dinner. That's when we noticed Ms. J had caught a cold. Going from the heat to the air, from the water to the air, made her sick. The kind of head cold that's filled with congestion. Yeah, that. We made dinner reservations at the Italian restaurant, so we had to be cute for that one. Like really get dressed. Everything was good, we just had to make sure she was alright. That kind of cold can drain you fast. Once we were done with dinner, we went back to our rooms to chill for a few. We wanted to make sure J was good and could still party with us. She's so resilient, she went to her room, drunk some hot tea, took a pill and she was good!

I changed into my jeans and sneakers, and we bounced right on up to the club. The club was near the buffet restaurant. We had to walk up the stairs near the restaurant. As we were walking up the stairs, I looked up and saw old boy looking at us. He must have seen us coming across the walkway. He winked at me again and walked back to the room. I knew then, that's what I needed to get it popping. We walked up the stairs, looking for the club. We kept seeing the signs on the wall, but we couldn't find it. We walked back around the corner and those huge double wooden doors opened, and BAM! The music, along with the base, came booming from behind those wooden doors. We were not ready.

I said, "Those damn doors are no joke," making us all laugh. There are rooms on that level right across from the club. So, it would make sense to have noise reduction walls and doors.

After we walked through the club doors, we had to walk through a set of glass doors before we were actually in the club. The club was nice. It wasn't, too big or, too small. The deejay sat up on a platform, so he wasn't in the way or anything. The dance floor was in the middle with booths, tables and sitting areas around it. It was cool. We sat down in our booth and looked around for a few before we got up to get drinks or dance. You already know who I was waiting on. We people watched for about an hour before I decided to jump up and start dancing. I figured I would walk over to the bar to get us some drinks and to scope out the room a little better. You already know it was dark, smoky from the fog machine, lights flashing and whatnot.

I needed a better view. As I was walking to the bar, I saw Mr. Chicago walk in with his crew. I was standing at the far end by the bar, looking at the front entrance. As they were walking up the right side of the club, I got our drinks and walked down the left side of the club. By this time the deejay was playing some real music and something that actually made us want to dance. I gave them their drinks and headed toward the dance floor. Of course, I knew what I was doing. Are you kidding me? I wanted some of him. And those white jeans were fitting me like a glove on a fat man's hand. BOOM! Oh I was ready for Big Daddy. As the night went on, my shot kicked in. I decided to show off. There was a pole beside our booth. Well, you know me. I jumped up and did a little pole tease. I was dancing and throwing these hips, dipping and straight up working it. Tossing my hair and everything. I made it fun, sensual, and cute. While I was pole dancing, I managed to glance over, and they were looking at me. King was sipping his drink and watching me dance. Naturally, my girls were cracking up and loving it. They didn't catch it. At least I don't think. They did manage to catch me on video (that damn J) working the pole.

To be honest, that made it worse for me because I was really ready to dance then. Once the deejay kicked it up a notch, I jumped my ass right off the pole and on to the dance floor. You know if the music is right, I'm gone straight cut up. We had a whole ball. After we were done dancing, we chilled for a few minutes, then danced and partied for about another hour then we made our way back downstairs to the buffet restaurant. We were a little hungry. Some of us were slightly drunk, but I'm not gone say no names, though—J! She was *five alive* when we were outside dancing earlier in our rooms, in the pool. That's when she got sick. She was cutting up! We loved it! She let her inhibitions free and went for it. Between her still being slightly drunk from earlier and me being tipsy, yeah, we needed some food in our stomachs. We didn't eat much, just nibbled. Chicken wings along with other finger foods. Once we were done, we went back to our rooms. Since she and I were next door to each other, I told Lady E I would keep an ear and eye on her. J told me she needed some Earl Gray tea. Since I knew the coffee shop was still open, I changed my clothes and went for her tea.

As I'm walking over to the coffee shop across the walkway, I heard a man's voice that sounded familiar:

"Aye, Christian, you were working the fuck out of that pole. Can I get next?"

I turned around. "It wasn't me; it was the alcohol moving through me."

"Oh, is that what it was?" He smiled.

"Oh, that's definitely what it was."

"I think you're lying. I think that was all you. Especially when you grabbed that pole and rolled your hips on the way down."

"Wait a minute! I didn't even see you. And walk with me. My girl needs some tea."

"Cool. I know you didn't see me. I was standing over in the far corner by the bar with my brother and cousin. I was watching you the whole time."

"Yeah, that's not creepy at all!"

"Oh shit! Nah! Not like that at all. I'm just saying." He shook his head. "Man, never mind."

Exactly! Creep! (as he laughed)

I went to the café at the right time. They were about to close for the night. I ordered her two teas and we left. Truck and I chatted more while walking back.

"So, what you gone do now?"

"I'm going to take my girl her tea, make sure she's good, then I'm gonna chill. Why wassup?"

"Shit. You know why. I'm tryn'a come chill with you. So, what's good?"

"That's possible." I smiled.

"A'ight then. What's your room number?"

"1126."

"A'ight bet. I'ma go change and I'll meet you."

"Call me when you're on your way."

"Cool. I'm going to check on ma and change. You be ready."

"Ow! Alright now."

"Aye, go 'head."

"See you in a few." As we were smiling at one another.

I went to drop off the tea to J and to make sure she was good. She was kind of surprised that I found some. She forgot about the café across the way. I made sure she didn't need anything else before I made my way back to my room. As I was settling in and putting on my swim trunks, Truck called me to tell me he was on his way. Love, I had to clean up my room.

I had clothes all over the place. I just threw everything in my suitcase and closed it. I moved it over to the floor in front of the sofa. That way it was kind of out the way. I turned off most of the lights and dimmed the rest. I turned off the flashing headboard as well. That bitch was bright. I opened the doors to the balcony and sat outside until he showed up. I saw him as he was walking into our building, so I got up to open the door. Baby catch this tea: how about as I was walking to the door, I straight up bust my ass on the floor. I just laid there laughing. I had my feet and legs in the water, so I jumped up to unlock the door. As soon as my feet hit that floor, yeah. Feet in the air and ass to the floor. Naturally, Danny knocked on the door as I was laying there, laughing. I got up to let him in as I was in slight pain.

I was rubbing my arm when he asked what happened. I told him and he started laughing.

"Yeah, thanks for the support."

He kissed my elbow and said, "Shake it off."

I told him I was going to go back to the balcony, and he was welcome to join me. He grabbed a beer out the mini fridge and came out and sat beside me. We both had our legs in the water. Love, he smelled so damn good. Oh my God! As we were talking, he slid that famous line in there.

"So what's good?

"I knew that was coming."

"I want to. You down?"

"Sure. Let's do this."

I jumped up and started taking off my clothes. When I told him to hold on, I peeked around the divider to see if J was awake or not.

"What you doing?" He was standing behind me ass naked.

Well, damn.

"I'm checking to make sure my sis is asleep."

"Shit. Your fam next door?"

"Yeah. So."

"Well if you don't care, neither do I."

"That-a-boy."

As I came back over (and yes, she was asleep) I started taking off my clothes too. I was taking off my shirt when he snatched off my shorts. Like yeah, *snatched off* my shorts. Then he kneeled down and started kissing my stomach. Now we both know how ticklish I am, so I started giggling:

"What's so funny?"

"You're kissing my stomach and your beard is tickling me."

"My bad. You want me to stop?"

"No!"

"Good. Cause I wasn't."

Baby! We made our way to that lounge chair in the corner of my balcony and let loose!

His tongue game was *serious!* He rose up to kiss me and made his way back down. My neck, my chest, each nipple, my belly button. Love! This Chocolate Adonis took my legs and tossed them on his shoulders and went to *work!*

That mouth went from front to back, back to front. Whew! Then he came back up to kiss me again. He could kiss too. He had a wide, yet juicy, tongue. I told him we needed to go in so I could stretch out and really make it worth his while. He agreed. We got up off the chair and went inside. As I was closing the screen door, I noticed we had an audience.

It was Jerry from next door. He was watching the whole time! Well, I wasn't interested in a third party this time, so I locked the screen door. I ain't give a shit about him watching and beating his dick. Do you, boo, but no third parties. I noticed Truck was fumbling and looking for something. So I asked him what he was looking for. He said he was looking for a rubber and asked if I had any?

"Of course, I do. But that can wait for now. It's my turn." I pushed him back on the bed so hard I think I scared him.

So okay! I was not ready for this. Love! This motherfucker had a baby arm! Yo, no bullshit! I was not ready! Girl, I had to gather myself. Shit!

"Hold on."

"What's wrong?"

"Nothing. I need a drink for this one. Just hold tight."

"What the fuck?! You need a drink now?"

"*Yes!* Hold tight!"

I went to the mini fridge, drunk a beer straight, then chased it with a shot of tequila that Jerry had given me earlier that day. It kicked in, in no time flat. I was doing my stretches while it was working its way down. He was laughing because he, thought it was so comical. I'm like shit. You ain't got a penis, that's *dick!* I gotta get ready. Shit I might need a blunt too. *Fuck!*

"A'ight. I'm ready."

"Good! Hurry up. I'm excited."

So I started giving this joker some head. I'm working him and going to town on his shit. Then I noticed the harder he got, the more his dick changed. *Bitch!* He had a *curve!* I was like, *okay!* Now we are talking! I can work with that (by the way, his dick was pretty too). You know I love a pretty dick. Balls all fresh and everything. Yes! He rinsed them balls the fuck off before he came to see me. That's what I Liikkeeee…

So I stopped with the oral and said, "I don't think I have a rubber that will fit you." We both laughed, and then it hit me. "Wait! Yes, I do. Hold on." I went right to the bathroom and got a shower cap. BOOM!

"What the fuck is that?"

"It's a shower cap!"

"Oh shit." He laughed. "If you think it will work."

"Oh it will. Let's get it, big daddy! Ow!"

I slathered his dick down in coconut oil, slapped that shower cap on it, put some coconut oil on the outside of the shower cap, and then mounted him. Hold up, I'm lying! Now that I think about it, it took me a minute to position myself right. I remember leaning over, turning on my iPod to my "freak bitch" playlist to help me with my groove (and it did). Once I mounted him and made sure I was good, I had to position myself on his hook just right. Once I did that, oh baby, it was take off time. I was rocking and riding that dick so damn good his motherfucking toes were popping, eyes rolling back in his head, mouth open and his ass started cussing! Oh baby, it was getting good. Then he flipped the script on me.

"Oh shit Christian! Grab my beard!"

I grabbed it.

"Grab it, baby! Yank that shit!"

I'm like what the fuck? So I'm grabbing and yanking his beard while riding his dick. It was turning him on! I was like, *wow!* This joker right here though! He was really getting turned on. So after riding him, when I started pulling his beard, he nutted within five minutes. He came hard, too. I was just like, *oh, okay. You good? You finished? Alright!*

I got up off of him and put my shorts back on. He was laying on the bed, shaking and going on. I'm just looking at him like, *the fuck?* Yo! The shit was funny! I made him sit up so I could take the shower cap off. He filled that bitch up! If I could get pregnant, it would have been multiples. Yikes. So anyway, I cleaned him up and made sure he was good. He put his clothes on, kissed me goodnight and left.

I brushed my teeth, showered, and I went to bed so fast...I was laying in the bed, laughing. I'm thinking, I just know these heffas were gone yuck this up whenever I finally tell them what happened. I shook my head. Only me. Besides, that wasn't who I really wanted anyway. I wanted King. I went to sleep at about three in the morning and woke up at about nine. I remember rolling over looking at my door. It was still open, which made me burst out laughing.

I texted them to see what time we were meeting up for breakfast and learned it would be in a few minutes. Apparently, everyone was dressed already or close to it and was ready to go. We went to breakfast and sat there and talked for about two hours.

Not only were we enjoying each other, but we had the perfect table. The sun was shining in through those beautiful windows, the background noise of the hustle and bustle from the breakfast crowd was going, but we tuned it out and it was just us. Since it was my girl E's birthday trip, I surprised her with a birthday song after breakfast. I had the crew to sing the Happy Birthday song to her after we ate. She wasn't expecting that. I think that was my favorite part of the trip. The look on her face was priceless and so was her reaction.

After everything was calm, I wanted Lady E to tell me the whole story about what happened between her and the "Basics." You know who the "BASICS" are.

Those dry face hoes, we were so called friends with that tried us. Yeah, them. The "Slithering" crew. I wanted to make sure I wasn't overreacting to the situation between us. I wanted to make sure I knew the whole story. I had her to break it down to me. Once she did that, I was good. I told her I didn't wanna discuss it anymore in life. It was confirmation that we both made the right decisions. Learning the story wasn't only the nail in the coffin, but it was the lowering of the casket into the ground hunni. Ashes to ashes, the BASICS's are now dust. PERIOD. Once we cleared that up, I was good. Not only did I exhale again, but I had a better understanding of the situation from all angles. It made me look at E, her hubby, and J through a different lens. I had a whole new appreciation for them. A new level of love and respect.

After breakfast (since it was her birthday dinner day) we decided to change into our swim clothes and go back to the beach. We made reservations for the Hibachi restaurant first so we wouldn't forget.

There we were again, on the beach chilling, laughing, drinking and enjoying. J and I took a walk down the beach shore, from one end to the other. We saw the little fish swimming along or nibbling on seaweed. They were too cute. It's funny how that time we spent outside flew by. It was time for dinner before we knew it. Since J and I were ready first, we left out to go stand in line, also to make sure everything was in order. On our way to the restaurant, I saw King walking down the steps from the main entrance. We locked eyes. As we passed each other, he slick grabbed my hand and kept on walking.

Baby! I started to leave J's ass right there and go follow him! Whew! I kept it cute though. But Love, when I tell you! HMPH. He was smelling so good. As we stood in line, I texted E to see where she was. She responded that they were walking over to us now. Let me tell you about this heffa! She gone sashay her old fine, thick ass over to us in this ol nasty-ass piece of jungle green dress boo. That bitch was bad! But it's the Queen, so I really wouldn't expect anything less.

But she didn't have to upstage us like that though. Bitch makes me sick! If I wasn't dressed in all white, I would've "death dropped" for her ass. My baby was showing the fuck out!

I said "Gon' girl and put that bitch around ya neck! Ow!"

I didn't even want to take a picture with her. I'm so serious. Okay but catch this, King and his buddies, he told me later on that she passed them when she was walking to the restaurant for dinner. She had all the heads turning!

His simple ass said he and his friends wanted a picture with her so they could go back home and lie to their buddies that didn't go and tell them those were the kinds of "baddies" they missed out on. I told him he was a dork for that. See how boys lie?

So anyway, we had a ball at dinner. You know whenever you dine at a Hibachi restaurant, the chefs cook in front of you. He did all kinds of tricks for us. He made hearts and shapes with our food and everything. They even fried the damn ice cream. Everything was delicious. We took more pictures, had more drinks, more laughter, more love, and my baby enjoyed herself. That's what truly mattered the most. I ain't tell her, but I ate just enough. I needed to be ready for later on. I was gone take that King out for a test drive. I needed my stomach light and body ready! We left dinner and returned to our rooms to change our clothes. We managed to make our way back up to the club for a few minutes, but it was dry, so we left. We came back downstairs and sat at the bar for a few hours. We listened to the band play a few songs before we watched the water and light show. It was really nice.

Once we were done with that, we retired to our rooms. J was a little worn out from her cold, so we let her chill. I told her to text me if she needed anything. I was laying in my room across my bed, becoming more and more restless. I said, "Bump this. I'm going outside and look for this motherfucker." I knew where to go. I went upstairs to Mr. Chicago's room and knocked on the door. Chicago opened the door all loud, but I assumed by the aroma coming from the room, he was high and drunk, or just high.

"Christian," he exclaimed, slurring my name. "Wassup, man! Come in! Chill! Enjoy!"

"Thanks."

"You want something to drink or you good?"

"Nah, I'm good for now. Thanks."

I walked in and spoke to everyone (like I always do) and sat down on the sofa next to King.

"What are y'all up to for the rest of the night?" I asked him.

"This is it. We're just chilling, smoking, drinking and bullshitting."

"Cool."

"Aye, Christian, where hunni dip at that had the green dress on?"

"My... the hunni *dip* is in her room with her *man*! WHY?"

"Oh, shit. My bad. Aye, tell her if she ever comes to the Chi and wanna have a good time, tell her to holla at ya boy! "

"I will not!"

The room erupted in laughter.

"Come on, Christian. Don't block me, man."

"I'm not, but I'm sure her big protective husband will. You know, the one you, thought was our body guard earlier? Yeah, Him."

"Oh, shit. Ne'mind," he slurred.

"Exactly!"

"So, Christian, what's good? You fucking around tonight or what?" asked Chicago.

"I would like to. Why? Wassup? What y'all got going?"

"You do?"

"Yeah, why?"

"What do you normally get into?"

"Well now that depends on my mood. Why?"

"Because my man's over there feeling you."

"Oh, so you know already?"

"Hell yeah. What I tell you earlier? I don't fucking discriminate. I told him how cool you was and he wants to see for himself."

I looked at King. "So is that true?"

"Hell yeah," King said.

"So we good now?"

"Hell yeah. I'm tryna get a taste. So wassup?"

"Well shit then! Let's go!"

"Oh, shit," said Chicago. "That's wassup. Aye, y'all do y'all. I'ma go find me a little thottie or something, shit."

I shook my head.

King asked me, "What's your room number?"

"1126."

"A'ight. Give me a few minutes to hit this blunt and I'm come holla. Be ready."

"Whateva. You just make sure you ready!"

"Oh shit. It's like that?"

"Oh sir, you have no idea. I'll catch you in a few." I winked.

I ran my ass over to my room to get ready! I was itching for that scratch, got damn it. He called as soon as I walked in to tell me he would be over in forty-five minutes. Which was perfect. I needed to clean up my room anyway. I showered first and then cleaned up. That way, it would give me time to "clean up" the right way. I went outside to peek around the divider again to check on J. She was asleep. She was actually snoring. I've never heard her snore before, so I was too tickled. She was getting that good sleep. I wasn't mad. I was relieved actually. That way no jokes later on. HA!

I didn't have any clothes on while I was cleaning up, so when I received a knock on the door, I grabbed my robe to cover myself just in case it wasn't him. I opened the door and it was King. He was standing there in his tank top, basketball shorts and Nike sliders. Everybody knows that when you see a dude late at night in that particular "outfit," there's a booty call about to go down. That's his "Hoe Gear". And Love, you know that look always turns me on. Makes me swoon! I gave his ass that once over and dropped my robe.

He laughed and said, "That's wassup!" He walked in taking off his tank top and kicking off his shoes.

I jumped right on him and we started kissing and going at it. I kid you not. It was funny because we fell on the bed and I just knew we broke it. Whew. We were rolling around all over that damn bed like nobody's business.

His heart was beating so fast, I pushed back from him and asked him if he was okay.

"Yeah. Why?"

"Because your heart is beating so damn fast! I'm just making sure."

"Shit! I'm Excited! And I smoked a blunt. Let's do this. I'm good."

"Okay. I'll go slow and be gentle then."

"Fuck that! I can take it. I'm a grown ass man! I wanna fuck!"

"Well shit! Okay!"

That joker smacked me on my ass, and it was on. I really enjoyed kissing his juicy ass lips though. I made sure I kissed and licked him from head to toe. And he had some pretty feet! I sucked his toes and made him giggle like a little bitch! Okay, but this was the gag though, he got me. He nutted three separate times and kept right on going. His stamina was sick! The first time, I was giving him head, but I think he nutted so fast because he really was excited. His nipples were sensitive. I was sucking, licking and pinching his nipples while giving him head and he was going crazy. Then POP! He was done. So I laughed.

"My bad. You done?"

"Hell no! You see I'm still hard, don't you?"

"Why yes, yes, I do. DAMN!"

"Exactly. Keep going."

So that's exactly what I did. I kept right on going. He flipped me over where he was on top, then we started kissing again. This time, he reached over, grabbed my iPod, turned on some rap music and baby! We went the fuck in! I think the music was giving him everything he needed to rock. The funny part was, nut number two came while he was orally pleasing me. He was so turned on by me being turned on by him, he nutted again. I laughed when he started shaking and growling again.

"Did you just cum again?"

"Yes! Fuck! My bad."

"Oh no boo, don't be ashamed. It's all good. You wanna stop?"

"Fuck no."

"Okay Good. Because now I'm ready."

I made him lay back and relax. I just mounted him but didn't slide down on him yet. Our conversation went something like…

As I'm grinding slowly on top of him, "Okay, sugga, I need for you to relax (as I kiss him)…Your heart is still racing and it's okay (I kiss him again). I'm not going anywhere just yet. You have me for as long as you like (I kiss him again). We can do anything you like. We don't need to rush. Just take your time. I got you" (I kissed him again).

We started kissing again and locked hands. I needed him to relax. I had to take another route with him. As the music slowed down, I decided to go with the flow of the music. He was enjoying that particular pace a little more. That's when I took control. I made him get up and let me be the "Pillow Princess" I'm known to be from time to time. I made him continue orally pleasing me. He was more than happy to do so. I told him to do as I say so. If he wants this to be enjoyable for both of us, he has to listen to me. He agreed.

As he lifted my legs, I told him to take his time. "Kiss it first." He did. "Now French kiss it." He did. I made him French kiss my inner thighs and V for a bit. Then, I made him use his tongue. "Now lick from top to bottom. When I tell you to, go into overdrive." As he was eating me, I felt his grip get tighter, so I made him stop.

"STOP! And you better not."

"Shit, okay," he panted, breathing hard.

We had to wait for a bit for him to get himself together. He didn't catch what I was doing to him. So once he was good, I made him continue. He kept servicing me. Once I felt his grip get tight on my hips again, I made him stop.

When I grabbed him by the head and ears, it turned him on. I told him to get up here and lay down on the bed. I wanted to ride his beard.

He laughed and said, "Oh shit."

I made him lay down. I stood up over him, made him throw his arms back.

"I'm 'bout to ride you until I get seasick."

"Fuck!"

I was riding his face in a very sensual way. I could tell he was enjoying it. I wasn't going to be rough with him at all. I could have, but that wasn't the time for that. I leaned forward and begin to kiss the head of his dick, where I licked the shaft of his pretty dick. Oh my God, it was so pretty! Forgive me, but again, you know how I am about a pretty dick.

Anyway, as I was kissing and licking his shaft and made my way to his fat mushroom head, his toes curled and popped. Oh hunni, I was teasing the fuck outta his ass.

Again, I felt his breathing change, so I stopped and stood up. He was breathing so hard.

"Fuck! Why are you teasing me?" (As he balled up his fist while inhaling and exhaling).

"Because I'm not ready for you to be done. Open your eyes and look at me."

"Shit."

"You ready?"

"Yes. *Please!*"

He came back over to the bed, I grabbed him then made him lie down. I leaned over and grabbed a little coconut oil (we didn't need much, we were both juicy enough). When I slid down on him, he let out a grunt that was followed by a groan. I smirked and told him I was ready. I began to rock on him back and forth when I realized I wanted to make him remember this. So I squatted over him enough for me not to come up off of him completely. I started twisting my waist. He grabbed the pillow to cover his face because he started getting extremely loud. I'm glad he did, though. I did not need J hearing this!

I started slam-fucking him while his face was buried under the pillow. I would ease up off him, then slam back down. I figured he'd like that. I could tell it was something that he was slightly used to. I did that for about a minute before my damn legs began to hurt. I made him cross his legs Indian style, then slam me back. He was feeling that. Oh, he started talking big shit! Oh, so we we're confident now? Okay. I'm not gone fake, though, he was fucking me up! I had to take control again. That didn't last long though.

Once I let him do whatever he wanted, that joker flipped my ass over and took it doggie style. He jumped behind me and DAMN! He had me cumming like a damn faucet. Once he made me cum, I turned over on my back and made him get it missionary. Since he had a nice ass, while he was beating me down I was spanking him. Then I gripped and ripped him. Once he was close to cumming, I slid my finger right up his ass and made him cum hard and loud!

Again, if I could get pregnant, yikes! Once he was done shaking, growling and grunting I asked him if he could get off me. I'm like dude, you're crushing my lungs! LOL.

He didn't get up off me, but he shifted his body weight. He just laid on top of me for a few minutes while I caressed his head and kissed his ears and his face.

I was under him thinking, I might need to make more trips to Chicago! Shit! If they look like this and do it like this, bitch! I'm game! But of course, I didn't tell him that. Once he finally let me up it was four o'clock in the damn morning. I didn't even realize I had been with him that long. He went to shower; I went to the minibar to get me something to drink. Then I joined him in the shower. Once we were done, we went to sleep. I woke up about nine to put his ass out before my buddy next door made her way over. I looked over at him; he was snoring down! Geeze. I ain't heard a mf snore like that since ex-hubbz. I figured I'd wake him up the same way I used to wake up B. I rolled the comforter back just enough. Then I buried my face right between his legs. Once he caught on or woke up for that matter, he said, "Oh, shit."

Once he was awake, I tossed his long ass legs up on my shoulders and let him have all the throat! I was sucking his dick, eating his ass and everything. He wasn't ready. I straight went slight freak on that ass. Literally! He came in no time flat. Then this joker gone say, "Why you ain't finger pop me again? That nut was intense. I liked that shit!" I cackled. We cleaned up and he left. I sent out my good morning text to the fam to see what we were going to do for the day and what was good with breakfast. I'm sure as you could imagine I was hungry. We went to breakfast and enjoyed. Since it was the Queen's last day, we did whatever she wanted to do, which was just chill at the pools and on the beach. Fine by us.

We spent the day on the beach while eating food from the party pool area. Just dancing, eating, drinking and enjoying life. They didn't realize I snuck off to go meet King for an afternoon quickie. I just told them I had to use the bathroom. Since E., was leaving before us, because she got there before us, we had an extra day. Well somewhat. We just left the next morning after she did. King and I were going at it. We had sex about four more times before I left. Look! The boy was *it* for me.

I was enjoying all of him and him me. Then his old bucket head ass friend, Mr. Chicago, asked me what I did to his friend. I asked him what he was talking about. He said, "That big nigga been walking around smiling and fucking bugging. He ain't been this fucking live since we been here. The fuck did you do to my homeboy, Christian?" I laughed and told him I'd have to charge him if I told him. He just shook his head and walked away.

King was in the room with me as I was packing and making sure I had everything ready to go. As I was packing my bag, he was looking in my suitcase. I asked him what was he looking for.

"These," he said, holding up my black sheer bikini briefs. "Can I have these?"

"And what exactly are you going to do with them?"

"I want them to remember you by."

"Ummm sure."

"A'ight bet, but can you do me a favor first?"

"And that is?"

"Wear them for me."

"Now?"

"Yes. I want them to have your scent on them. So when I wanna beat my meat thinking about you, I can sniff them and get my nut."

"Oh! Okay. I got'cha Poppa."

I had to laugh. It was my fault. I freaked his ass the fuck out and now he stuck. I put them on for him while I was packing up and cleaning up my room. He spent the night with me even, though we didn't sleep much. Look, he was willing to give it to me and I was surely going let him. The next morning as I was getting dressed (after we had sex and I showered) he asked me to unlock my phone so he could put his contact info in it. He said he wanted to keep in touch. He's always in DC and since I haven't been to Chicago in a while, he would love to show me around and chill with me whenever I do manage to surface. That blue coffee cup I brought back, he brought that for me from the gift shop. He said since I brought my own creamer across international waters, I should be drinking it out of a real coffee cup. The cup was cute. That last sex round made me loose as a noodle for my flight back home. I don't think anybody noticed it, but then again, those little heffa's of mine notice almost everything. They just don't realize it sometimes.

He and I still text on a regular basis. He got a new job and a new place. I told him I was going to be in New York in October, he said he would meet me. I'm definitely going to make that happen. BOOM!

Okay, Love, I gotta go now.

My dinner guests are arriving.

Love you much.

I'll fill you in on N.F.Life later.

Ttyl,

Eskimo Kisses.

SHAKE MYSELF LOOSE!

Love,

I'm sitting here, shaking my head, as I ask this question: *What the hell is wrong with me when it comes to Dom?*

So okay, remember Dom? The football player I kicked it with for a little while? Yeah, him. I don't know what it is about him or us, but we could not keep our hands off each other.

Let me backtrack. Remember I met Dom when I lived in Rockville and he lived in Silver Spring. We met at the Pancake House in Bethesda. When I walked in with my friends, he was sitting in the corner, chilling. You know how tight the waiting area is there, but as the door was constantly opening and closing, his cologne caught my attention. So, when I said out loud, "Whew! Somebody smells good," the girl he was with burst out laughing and said, "That's my boyfriend. We were just talking about that. He got it lit, don't he?" I laughed and replied, "Yes, the hell he does!"

We were all called to our tables at the same time. Apparently, because we had small parties, it wasn't a long wait. Yup, you guessed it, he was sitting at the table across from us. His girlfriend's back was facing me, so I could make as much eye contact with him as I wanted. I was with "Butta", his husband, and another friend of ours, KC. As the waiter came over to take our orders, I kept glancing over at Dom. Every time I glanced over or looked up, he was already looking at me.

Now, let me give you his stats. Dom is about six-foot-four, a little under three hundred pounds, and Dominican with gorgeous hair and a kick-ass beard. Now you know damn well Butta noticed his beard well before I even said anything. Butta and I had a quick side convo about how cute Dom was and his sexy beard. He's definitely a "Beard'y". While we were waiting for our food, I told the fellas I would be back. I needed to go wash my hands. I knew Dom would hear me, so if he was game, he'd follow me. And just like a moth to a flame, he followed me. He came in the bathroom with that "So wassup?" line. Yes, I laughed. I told him we ain't got a lot of time, so make it quick. We introduced ourselves, swapped contact information and went back to our tables. His girlfriend had no clue and neither did Butta. Yes, Butta had jokes, but little did he know that everything he was saying, ended up being the truth. Of course, I didn't tell him. Please! Are you kidding me?! At least not right away anyways.

So later that night, Dom hit me up, asking if he could come by to see me for a few. I told him it was cool, and I'd meet him in the garage because I still had company at my house. I didn't want to invite him up just yet until I got the backstory about him and ol' girl he was with earlier. So about 10:00 p.m., I got a text asking for my address. I responded, then proceeded to primp a little bit for that simple cute look. You know, fresh breath, juicy lips and smelling good, legs out and simple t-shirt. You know how I do. And of course know Butta's nosey ass was on me!

"Who you getting' cute for? Hold up! Where are you going? You didn't ask me. You old harlot!" Exactly. That's why I said nothing to him! I just shook my head and laughed.

Dom texted that he was downstairs, so I could buzz him into the garage. I told Butta I was going down to the store and I'd be right back. Just to make sure he wouldn't follow me; I took the steps down three floors and jumped on the elevator.

As I came out the side door looking for Dom's car, I saw lights flash at me. It was a very nice murdered-out Chevy Tahoe. I got in, he leaned over and kissed me right away. I laughed.

"Well okay! That's what we're doing?"

"Shit, I wanted to do that since I saw you earlier. Old juicy lip ass."

I laughed. "Well, we gone hold off on that until we talk a little bit first."

"I already know. She's not my girl. She's just a friend with benefits. She always introduces me as her boyfriend because we been fucking with each other for about a year now."

"You do realize how that makes you sound, right?"

"Yes, I do. Now I really do. Oh, shit." He laughed. "Nah, listen. I told her I love her, but I'm not in love with her. I even go out with other bitches. She knows this shit."

"Again, sir." I laughed.

"Aye go 'head. Look she knows what it is. I'm about to cut her ass loose anyway. She's, too fucking attached for a benefit."

"Sounds like her heart is her vagina to me. But okay. As long as we have an understanding. But I knew it was something when I looked at you. That's the only reason why I gave you my number in the first place. I sensed the bullshit. So wassup Dom, what'chu good for?"

He smiled. "Shit. I mean, Wait." He covered his face and shook his head.

Exactly! I cracked up laughing. "It's all good. Mean what you say and say what you mean, boo."

"See! You fucking me up."

"Nah, you're telling the *truth*. That's all that is."

"So, wassup with you? When can I get a taste?"

"Well, it can't be tonight because my folks are still with me."

"The dudes you were with earlier?"

"Yes, that's my fam from New York."

"Oh okay. Cool. I mean, I do drive a truck I got space back there. I chuckled. "Really?"

"Hell, yeah! Shit. Don't sleep on the fat boys. I can make it work."

I smiled and licked my lips at the, thought of having truck sex with him. He was smelling so good. It was intoxicating to my senses.

I don't know what cologne he had on, but it mixed with his body chemistry perfectly. The more he moved around, the closer he got to me, the more I got turned on. Before I knew it, I was leaning into him on the center console, and within a blink of an eye, he was kissing me again. Not only was he doing it right, but he just, like... I don't know! All I know is, I was on top of him in that driver's seat and we were kissing down! Then on top of that, he had a deep voice. So, while he was kissing on my neck, he was talking all kinds of shit! *My, God, he had me rock ready!*

Like, you know how you're in a moment of passion right before the sex happens with all the kissing, touching, titty groping, lip biting, slight hair pulling, neck kissing and sucking? I mean just *hot ass foreplay. Yes, That!*

I was so glad he pulled in that corner parking space. Baby, listen! The way he slung that got dayum door open while holding me up and still kissing... we climbed in. He was not lying when he said didn't sleep on the fat boys (not that I was unfamiliar anyway). He pulled my shorts down, undid his sweatpants—with one hand—and we got right to it. He threw my right leg up around him and slid right on into home base! That fat

Dominican had dick, hunni. Grown man dick too. I said bitch OOP! I see why old girl was claiming his big cute ass.

But what's funny, he had the music on, and when "Notorious B.I.G" came on he got super turned up. I was like wait a minute! But why did that shit turn me on even more? All I could think was *"What the fuck is even happening right now?"* It was the "Notorious Thugs" song. He was in it. Literally and figuratively. And the shit had me gone.

My mouth started watering, tears were flowing, and I mean everything was happening. Then he flipped me over and started grinding, *bitch! I was o'vah!* We both nutted at the same time. The fucker made me scream. I've only screamed with two people. B. and Beast. It was amazingly intense. Once we were done, we both burst out laughing.

He said, "You fucked me up."

"Right back at cha, playa." Whew! Powerful. "I think I'm good now." I chuckled; as my mind was still blown and I was still reeling from the moment. My body was saying what I was not physically capable of verbalizing just yet.

"Shit. I'm not. I wanna see you again. You had my dick hard as shit. Fuck! I'm still hard. I could fuck you again, for real."

"Um yeah, I gotta go. You got my leg shaking. That's why I'm still sitting here. I slightly got water legs."

"I did that?" He smiled.

"Oh definitely you did. More than you know."

"I gotta piss. Don't move."

"Oh trust me, I'm not."

I jumped down out the back to fix my clothes and stretched. He finished doing what he needed to do. He walked up to me, grabbed me and kissed me. And yeah, he wasn't lying, he was still brick hard.

"Yea, you feel that shit, don't you?"

"I do, but I'm good for now."

"I will definitely be back. So you better be ready to go until I tap out."

"Yeah right! You are not living in my cookie jar."

"The cookie jar shouldn't be so damn sweet. Besides, I wanna experience those lips. We doing everything. *Everything.*"

I chuckled and shook my head. "Goodnight slim."

"I'm gonna hit you when I'm home."

"Okay, cool. I'll be right here."

"A'ight."

We kissed again, then I walked away, and he pulled off. He honked twice and chucked me the deuces while going down the garage hill. I laughed and returned the deuces. I got on the elevator and rode it up to the clubroom. I needed to gather myself before I went back to the house with "Nosey Rosie." He would have sniffed it out. I was slightly flustered and had to use the bathroom. Go figure, Butta texted me to say I was spending a lot of time at the store. I texted him and told him I was upstairs in the clubroom. I be damned if three minutes later, that fool came flying through the door asking me who was I with. Once I finished laughing at him telling me "you smell like fucking", I told him.

"I knew it. I knew it. I can always tell. And you got that sex glow, you hook'a."

"Butta, it was so damn good. He did everything just right."

"Clearly. You haven't stopped smiling yet. I can see it all in your face."

"I'm in love with his *fat boy* sex. OMG!"

"You harlot! The harlot is a tramp."

"I am! I really am!" We both laughed ourselves to damn near tears. "Okay, we can go now. My nerves are calm now."

"Damn! It was *that good?*"

"It was a quickie, but baaayybeeey, when I tell you he literally made me scream. And you know how I am about that. All I could do was shake my head."

"Damn. I wish my sex with that fool downstairs left me like that. It's been so long."

"Stop it!"

As we got up to go, Dom was texting me to tell me he was home and how much he couldn't wait to see me again. Again, nosey leaned over my shoulder and was reading it. He burst out laughing and had even more jokes. It was a long holiday weekend and they were not leaving until Monday morning to go back to New York. Dom and I had sex in the garage two more times before they left. We quickly became friends with benefits. After a period of time, we ended up seeing each other so much, he broke it off with ol' girl for sure. He said she was upset because she knew he was "fucking other bitches, but now he wasn't even making time for her." I let out an OOP, then smirked. I ain't gone lie; I laughed and flipped my got dayum hair.

He told me how it all went down. She was blowing his phone up while he was on travel with work and everything. He said he would have been cool, but she was getting beside herself. He liked being single and having options, but she wasn't with it.

I told him I definitely understood. Even though he and I were just sex, it quickly developed into a friendship that started off as a physical attraction. Not only were we having sex on a regular basis, but he was spending the night, we were hanging out for lunch and or dinner. And Love you know me; my ass will cook in a heartbeat. He'd come over for dinner quite a few times a week. He was a big fella and clearly, food was one of his things. So I knew what it was okay.

Anyway, we would have sex a couple of times a week. It was nice. We were truly friends with the benefit of sex.

Even if we didn't have sex it was no biggie. However, I do remember one day, we happened to see each other out and about in the streets in DC. Matter of fact, we were in DC on U Street at the same time. He was with some chick (she was hella cute) and I was on a date with a dude from around the way. We both had the nerve to catch feelings. We both texted each other like a minute apart: *I know y'all ain't fucking.* The shit was hilarious. Yeah, we were serious about not fucking with other people unless we both cleared it. It was like our unspoken rule.

It was weird. It was like we were in an open relationship. Love, we both know that is not my cup of tea at all. But again, it was, what it was. Like clockwork, we met up at my place and had sex that same night. The only difference this time, he flat out told me, "Christian, we gone have to chill for a few, but I can't quit you. You are so chill, and you just get it."

"Well, we both know what this is. I'm honestly content like this."

"Yeah, me, too, for now. But I feel myself getting attached to you. And for real, ain't nobody I ever been with be having my dick this hard or making me this satisfied before or after fucking."

"Why thank you. I feel so honored." In my hypocritical voice and facial expression. As I gave his round head ass a side-eye.

"Nah, I'm serious though. Like, I really felt some kind of way when I saw you with slim. I was ready to square the fuck up."

"Um, that would have been a bad idea. He's a dope boy that's a professional trainer."

"I would 'a sat on that nigga."

"You stupid! But wait a minute, weren't you on a date yourself?"

"Come on ma, I was just fucking that bitch. I was gone get right back." As he let out a loud hardy laugh.

"Get punched!"

"Sike nah. She was cool on me, but it wasn't going any further though. I can't fuck with a silly bitch. She was silly as fuck."

"And you didn't know that before you took her out?"

"Yeah, I did. I just wanted to fuck. Her ass was phat."

"And that's what you get!" I laughed.

"You're right. She was annoying as fuck. Then all she wanted was money. You got all your own shit; I can come over here chill, smoke whatever. You don't ask for shit."

"Because I don't need anything from you sugga. Besides, what I want, you give it to me."

"You're right. And just know that anything you need I got you. All you gotta do is ask. Straight up."

"Thank you. Right back at you."

"So, can I get that neck?"

"Only if you return the favor."

"You know I'm down. Shit. Now throw them legs up again. Let me see how far back your ankle's can go."

So I did just that. I put my ankles behind my head, and he lost it. He had to stop because he said I was gonna make him bust too fast that way. Anyway, we did that whole "FWB" thing off and on for about six months straight. Then his job sent him on travel for a few months to Colorado. We still kept in touch while he was gone. Then, shortly after he was settled, my job sent me to Texas again for a few weeks. He told me he would come for a visit on his first free weekend. Just so happened, when he and I linked up again, it was Memorial Day weekend.

He flew in from Colorado on that Friday after work and stayed the whole weekend. He left Monday evening, heading back to Colorado.

We cut up in Austin. We were fucking 6th Street up. Just living and having a ball.

Of course, he found a group of dudes that were into the whole sports car/racing car thing like he was. What was even funnier, when they asked who I was, I cut him off and said that I was his god brother.

If you could have seen the look on his face. I think it turned him on even more, to be honest. I think mainly because he wasn't sure of what to say or how I would react. Shit, it doesn't bother me none. I said it and kept moving. I knew he was going to bring it back up that night when we got home. He told me later on that he was taken aback by me. He was going to say that we were good friends, but he was stuck for a second. It's all good. He was laughing at me, then he was kind of freaked out because I wasn't tripping. Clearly, he's had some bad experiences in the past. I mean, the way we first met was proof enough, so hey.

We had a great time in Texas. As I said, he left that Monday and I went on about my business. He came down a few times while I was still there before he left to go back home for good. The last time he came to visit me in Texas, he stayed a week. All of that was fine and dandy. No problems, issues or anything. We were just friends who were hanging out, enjoying each other's company, with sex always being an option. It was something about our chemistry that had us both sprung and open for one another. We just...clicked. He was very easy, laid-back, easy to get along with; on top of that, no kids, good credit and good sex. Marriage material, right?

The first week of December, I went back home, and I texted him to let him know I was back. He responded that he was happy and couldn't wait. He had some pinned-up things he needed to express to me. In other words, he was ready for a fuck session. Again, I was home, we were having sex again and hanging out. Then, one day in February, it all came to an end. He just disappeared on me. I sent text after text, email after email. Now I was worried and wanted to make sure he was all right. When people get quiet like that all of a sudden, it makes me nervous. After a while with no replies, I just asked God to take care of him, if he's still breathing, wherever he may be. Then I moved on. From February to July, I hadn't had sex or showed interest in anyone. I wasn't interested in that "getting to know you" stage all over again. I was just blah. I said July because that's when the "Snobby Fam" and I went to Mexico.

So um yeah, we both know how that turned out. LOL! Drought over hunni. Bloop! Another Dominican. Go figure. Anyway, he was just as attentive and passionate as Dom. He didn't make me scream, but he damn sure hit all my spots and sent me over a few times. We already talked about him, so anyway.

Now cut to the present day. Dom was still M.I.A. As usual, I was in DC doing some light shopping before going home, minding my little cute thick-ass business, when in Bloomy's, my nose picked up a scent. I was standing there looking at a pair of shoes when I smelled something very familiar. I literally had to step back and get myself together. I started smiling, giggling, and then I got turned on. I immediately thought of Dom.

When I said out loud to myself, "Dom, where are you big baby?" I just knew I was having a moment. I went to the register, paid for my goodies and left.

As walked across the street to another major department store, I heard a horn blowing. I didn't think anything of it. I was in the store jamming to my music because my headphones are always in my ears; I smelled him again.

Now I was irked. "Okay, now look damn it! Where the hell is he?" But I said it while I was still looking through the rack. That's when I felt a nudge on my shoulder. I turned around to see *him!* I gasped, then I burst out laughing and we embraced each other.

"Where the hell have you been?!"

"I was out of the country. It was for work. I got your emails, but I kept forgetting to reply. I was always getting them while in meetings or on my way to do something work-related."

"Yeah. Mmhhmm."

"Christian, I swear. You know I would not treat you like an old bum bitch. I fuck with you too hard for that."

"I appreciate it. You look good. Done lost some weight, shaped your face up. You just showing off," I said, licking my lips.

"You don't look too bad ya'self pa. And don't start licking ya lips. You know that shit fucks me up."

"It has been a while." I bit my bottom lip, as I smirked at him.

"Christian, please stop. You have no idea how much I have missed you."

"I think I have an idea." I chuckled. "So wassup with you?"

"Follow me out, I wanna show you something."

"Ha! Do I look dumb to you?"

"Aye go head. Just follow me."

So I went to the register and told the clerk to hold my things because I would be right back. I followed Dom out to his truck in the garage, and damn if we ain't fuck in the truck again! He knew what he was doing. And low-key, so did I. It was too funny. I followed him to the driver's side to see what he wanted. Baby, he opened that back door and BAM! It was on again.

I don't know what it is about him, but I don't mind whatever that IT is! I'm never left with an empty feeling after he and I have sex (no pun intended). This time it was even more climatic because we were in a parking garage that was not residential. Let alone my residence. There were people walking about and everything. No fucks were given on our part about that. *None.* This time, I rode that nut up outta him. I wanted him to be the one making all the noise. I know, I'm petty, but that was payback for him making me wait for so long with no response. I climbed on top of that belly, situated myself and slid down on that oh-so-pretty shaft and went to work!

#Pause So you know how I have a thing for pretty dicks, penises and man parts, right? Well, Dom's is *gorgeous!* It's a pretty caramel color (like his skin) with the perfect matching mushroom head, a fat vain on the top (that I use to my benefit) *and it is never ashy! Baby,*

yes! You know how much I hate ashy dick. I know, sounds weird, but it's true. Hell, when you lotion or oil down your body, don't leave out your dick. Get that too. It's a part of your body as well. *No*, don't neglect the dick. You don't want me neglecting them balls when giving you head so don't be rude and ashy. I'm just saying... Even, though he's uncut (uncircumcised), when he gets hard, you can't tell. The way that turtleneck rolls back like the top on a convertible when you hit that button... Yessuh! That skin rolls back on its own and that pink head pops out. POP! Hey, less work for me. Did I mention he has a slight curve? Baby, listen! All my spots! I crowned him Dominican King of my Labia! WHEW! *#Continue*

So, I digress. Back to the story. I was riding that pretty fat caramel colored 7.5 dick for my life, baby. I missed it. I was rocking him right along with that damn truck. I was bouncing, then started twisting so I could use him and that vain to hit my spots to make me cum. I was hitting him so damn good his mouth was open, and he was gripping the seats. Then he covered his face and started cussing. Got him! I made him cum so hard, he turned redder than normal.

"Christian, you a bitch for that one! Whew, shit!" he exclaimed.

"And you loved every minute of my bitch-ass just now. That's why you won't open your eyes."

"Fuck you! You're right, though." He laughed. "Whew! Shit! Don't move yet. *Please," he begged in deep, heavy breaths.*

So you know what my hard-headed ass did? I slammed on him again. His ass cussed at me.

"Stop, you fucker! Shit. You better chill. I'm trying not to get hard again, and if I do, I'ma sit right here and fuck the dog shit outta you." His eyes were still closed.

Oh baby I fell out laughing. "Okay, I'm done! Ima chill"

"Please do."

While he was still recouping and I was still sitting on top of him, I just began to kiss him. He responded right away. One thing about Dom though, that boy knows he can kiss. He will kiss at the drop of a hat hunni. I love that his kisses are full of passion.

I think that's what makes me love them and him so much. ...Unh-unh! Stop it! Now, wait, I love him, but I'm not *in love* with him. Let's be clear right now. I turned that part of me off quick. You can't be friends with benefits and have your emotions all up in the shit. Or as I like to say, "Have your heart in your vagina." He did say how much he missed *us* and *this,* while we were kissing. I'm not going to lie, I high-key missed it as well. But get this, while we were kissing, I'm supposed to be on the other side of DC meeting my Diva and my boy Jussie for a quick dinner and drinks before we go to the movies.

I jumped up.

"I have to go now. I have plans. I almost forgot."

This jerk gone say, "Oh shit. A'ight, Cinderella Puss. Make sure you hit me later on tonight."

I burst out laughing at Cinderella Puss. I kissed him and ran back into the department store to cash out so I could go.

I'm so glad I keep my "just in case" bag in my bag. I needed to freshen up. I cannot be walking around these streets smelling like "The Sex" or another man (ew). Besides, I like to smell like me. I never know who I'm going to bump into. I made it to dinner on time. Jussie was there before Diva, so I was able to talk to him for a few minutes. Oddly enough, when he was leaving, Diva was coming in. I know they had to have walked past each other. They were, too close in time not to have passed each other. I had had two drinks by the time she had gotten there so I was good and loose. Little did she know, in more ways than one. Later on, I was telling her about Dom and what happened.

She laughed and said it was because he and I have history and a special connection. So naturally, when we see each other, it's an instant attraction that may or may not result in sex or physical connectivity. I didn't really think of it like that, but she was right. That connection that he and I share is what made us not ask any questions and just fuck on sight.

It's only happened to me a couple of times. It's like something that just pulls me and that person right toward each other.

Even before we got to know each other, we had sex right away. We just knew what it was. What's funny is, I swear he would be my one that, if I was to ever cheat on my husband, it would be with him. I already know it. Whenever he and I see each other, it's automatic.

Ever since he and I reconnected, we've been making up for lost time. He has not missed a beat either. We picked up right where we left off. If he decides he wants to make it official, I totally would for him. But first I would have to close out my black book files. You know I don't like leaving loose ends just lying around. RIGHT! I had to laugh at myself. WHEW!

Speaking of which, I ain't tell you the Bishop is trying hard to get me to come to NY one last time before he gets remarried. Yeah. I'll tell you about Ol' boy later. See, it's shit like that I would have to close out before Dom, and I make it official. If we were to ever go down that road. What? I told you about the Bishop. Chocolate, bald, dimples, sexy, a freak, meat and body for days. My bad, doll. I thought I told you about him. Okay, give me a few minutes and I'll come back and tell you about him. Love, he makes me scream "Oh, God!" every time we're together. Hmph. Bless him. I know. I just got hell'a hell points. HA!

Anyway, Dom and I are good. We have recently taken a break from one another. I felt like I was getting in too deep. Yes, my feelings were reactivated. It was all his fault though. He started introducing me to his fam and best buds. It went from "FWB" to constant intimacy rolled up in love and affection. I saw the difference, but he didn't. Or he didn't want to admit to it. For whatever reason. Blah. It turned me off and made me step back. No love lost or anything, I just need to figure out a few things. I had to shake myself loose from falling into one of those places, where you're aware that your floating, but don't want to come down because of temporary bliss, but it that temporary feeling seems to last longer than you intended for it to. If that makes sense. Yeah. THAT! No thank you. I'm good. However, I will admit, that for a little while, I allowed it because he was keeping me company and I was afraid that I would lose him as a friend and lover. TUH! Fuck that. It passed. I'm good. We still talk, just no sex until we figure this all out. UGH! And you know I do NOT take kindly to feeling like I'm spinning out of control. So yeah, we're good. I just moved on to other things. Fuck that "open ended, don't know just doing this" shit. That's not me, nor has ever been me. And I'm NOT about to start now because a MF got good dick and we cool. A NO SIR! I think once we figure it all out, we'll be fine. If not, then I'll continue to do what I need to do for me. Move on and be well. Period. Still haven't had sex with each other in over 3 months now, and you know what, perfectly okay with it. That emotional roller coaster was not for me. I got off quick.

Blah. All in a day.

Okay Love, I have dinner plans. I'll talk to you later.

Love you much.

Double kisses.

CONFESSIONS FROM A GENERATIONAL CURSED GENTLEMAN

Love,

GIRL! Let me tell you about this joker! Baby, I couldn't make this up if I wanted to. Why do I have to always end up with the fellas that are damaged goods? I can *never* just have fun. It's always a mf that gets attached. I can *never* just have sex and be done with it. I think part of it is my fault for being so damn lovable and likable. HA! Go get you a glass of wine, chyle. This is another doozy.

So, as you know, I love going down to the National Harbor here in Maryland. I always enjoy myself there. Whether I'm with someone or alone, it's my favorite place to get away and chill. There are so many new stores there, so I've really been enjoying myself lately. I decided to go down there for the day to get away for a few hours. I did a little shopping, had a little lunch and sat by the Ferris wheel to shoot the breeze. As I was sitting there, I, thought, *I should get me a room at the resort hotel and spend the weekend here.* Hell, I was already there and had new clothes anyway. So, I did just that. Walked my cute ass right on up to the hotel.

I went to the hotel to see if they had any last-minute vacancies. That spot is *always* booked up, hunni. Go figure I'd bump into an old friend from high school who was working the front desk. Her name was Anastasia (I called her Asia for short). We were so ecstatic to see each other; we hadn't seen one another since graduation. When I heard her say, *"Oh my God! Is that Mr. Jackson?"* I looked up and started smiling. I ran over to the desk and we hugged each other and laughed like two schoolgirls. She's still a total sweetheart.

"Christian! What are you doing here?"

"Well, I would like a room if you all have any available."

"We sure do. For how many nights?"

"Oh good. Until Monday please."

"Sure. I'll put you in right now and make sure you have all the perks. Since you took care of me in high school, I'm returning the favor, boo."

"You're so sweet, but you don't have to do that sweetie. I'll take a regular room."

She gave me a great deal— a king suite for the price of a regular room. Alright now. As I made my way up to my room, I peeked over the railing down below on the lower level to see what was going on. Someone was taking wedding photos and the crowd was cheering. It was beautiful. It made me smile. As I picked up the rest of my bags; I turned around and bumped into a bellhop standing behind me. I apologized and we both laughed.

"Ms. Anastasia sent me over to help you with your bags," he said.

Yes, chyle, I had that many bags. SMH. You would have, thought I went on a damn shopping spree. You know I hate crowded and heavy shopping bags.

Anyway, as we made our way to the elevator, then boarded; I looked up and locked eyes with a very handsome gentleman walking past. He smiled and winked at me right before the doors closed. Hunni, he had me *hot*. He knew he was handsome! I just knew he smelled good. He looked like he did too! I got off on the 7th floor and made my way to my room. When I walked in, that big gorgeous window met me with a beautiful view. I wasn't surprised; the room was beautiful (as always). Asia hooked me up with a waterside view and I could see the Ferris wheel as well. Even if I didn't have a view, I would not complain hunni. The cute bellhop put my bags down as I walked around the room to get a better look. Yeah, my girl did me right.

Once settled in, I ventured to the wine and cheese store. I wanted to indulge little more, so I decided to treat myself to some "Fancy Wine & Cheeses". I'm sure the hotel would have supplied me with goodies, but I wanted to do it myself. Besides, the weather was beautiful. The sun was still shining and there was a cool breeze. I was itching to get back outside. I got my goodies, but what's cheese and wine without chocolate? I went right next door to the candy shop and got some dark chocolate to go with my wine. Since I was flirting with the store owner, he hooked me up on the chocolate. Clearly, he wanted some of this chocolate, but I wasn't there for him. I just used what I got (my legs) to get what I wanted. Boom.

LOL. So, I was making my way back up the sidewalk to the hotel, enjoying the weather and taking my time. You know me, being cute and playing off the sunlight while the wind blows giving me all sorts of hair drama. On top of, me having my legs out (that's what they're for). Why hide them? *wink*

Anyway, as I'm walking with my headphones in when I heard a car horn. Now you know me, normally I don't pay that kind of noise any attention when it's beyond me. The car pulled up right in front of me before I could cross over to the other side of the street. It was black-on-black "Big Body" Audi (a8 Series). I said, "Well shit!" Girl, it was hella sexy too. Nah, it wasn't murdered out or anything, just the classic black-on-black. The window rolled down and it was the "Kat Zaddy" that winked at me earlier. I smiled at him as the sounds of smooth jazz played through his car speakers. *Alright Zaddy. I see you.*

His smile was mesmerizing. "Wassup? What room are you in?" he asked.

"Well damn. You just straight to the point hunh Mr. Transporter?"

He laughed. "Oh you've got jokes?"

"Oop! You caught that?" I laughed. "Quick I see."

"Yes, I caught it. I'm trying to catch you, if you let me."

I chuckled. "Cute."

"Thank you."

"How about I catch your name first?"

"I'm Matthew." He extended his hand through the window.

I stepped closer to shake his hand. "Nice to meet you Matthew. I'm Christian."

"Likewise." He smiled, looking me up and down. "So where are you on your way to?"

"Well, I was on my way back to my room until I was blocked."

He chuckled. "Okay, okay. Can I join you? You look like you're in for a great Friday night. You got wine and chocolate."

"Oh baby you have no idea. Humph."

"I kind'a do. Can I join or what?

I smiled and tilted my head. "I'm in room 726. Call and clear it before you decide to knock on my door."

"I will definitely do that."

"Now, if you'll excuse me, I'll be on my way sir."

"You are excused. Wit'cha cute ass."

"Right back at you. Talk to you later." When he pulled off, I yelled, "Call first!"

Girl, it was like I could smell his sex pheromones. I really believe I did though. That's why I moved away from him as abruptly as I did. The air from his car was blowing right into my face and it was *all him.* As soon as it hit my nose, my mouth watered, my eyes watered up a little bit and my nipples got hard. I knew then what it was. The last time that happened to me, I jumped right on the dick (I'll tell you about that one later).

So, I made my way back through that beautiful hotel lobby when Asia yelled, "Christian! I left a surprise in your room. I know you'll Love them." I was super giddy and thanked her.

Now you know I was feeling extra excited now. I talked to Kat Zaddy *and* I had a gift in my room. I was geeked. I got off the elevator and shot down that hallway to my room. I opened the door and Asia had me two bouquets of flowers in my room. One set of roses in an array of colors on the desk when you first walk in and the other bouquets were tulips in an array of colors sitting on the table in front of the window. The note on both said, "Thank you," but I couldn't, for the life of me, remember why she would be thanking me, but okay. I called her right away and thanked her.

She laughed. "I knew you'd love them. I remember that tulips are your all-time favorite flowers."

I love people like her. Seemed so simple, but so *big* to me.

My excitement was quickly killed by the growling of my stomach. I went to the restaurant on the lower level to find me something to snack on. The elevator is all glass, so you know what I did, right? Yep! I was giving Janet T's. I was dancing, going down like I was putting on a show, being lowered to my stage. I sure did! But look though, I looked up and Asia was looking at me, cracking up! She was already on the lower level, waiting to take the elevator up.

The doors opened, she burst out laughing all over again. *"Boy!* You ain't gone never change! Always dancing."

"You know me, boo. Any chance to Boom Kat and I'm here for it! *Ow!"* We laughed. I told her "I want some buffalo wings and fries."

She directed me to the sports bar. That's where she was coming from and she told me how good they were. "Ask for Greg," she said, "he'll hook you up. Tell him I sent you." She's just such a doll. I ordered my wings to-go. I wanted to get back up to my room and chill.

I turned on my music, took off my clothes and ate my wings. Afterwards, I took a shower, then tried on new clothes to see what I may need for the next day or so. As I was jamming while doing a slight inventory, the room phone rang. Yup! It was Matthew.

"Is it cool if I come down for a few minutes?"

"Give me a minute to make myself decent and I'll ring you back."

No sooner than I slipped into my shorts, he knocked on the door. My music was still playing when I let him in. I mentioned that because one of my favorite sex songs was on and I hurried up and skipped to the next track. As handsome as he was, it was something about him I couldn't quite pinpoint. It was something familiar about his energy though. He came in, smelling so fucking good.

"So, what are you up to besides listening to some rap music?" He laughed.

"Ha. Just snacking and enjoying my own company. That's all."

"I see. I also see you did quite a bit of shopping, too."

"I did! It was a very good day. I plan to do more tomorrow. I need a few accessories and a couple more pairs of sneakers. Then I'll be all done. For now."

"Well damn. Leave some for us." He laughed.

"I can't make any promises."

"So, wassup with you, Christian? What's good?" He sat down at the table and took off his shoes, which was presumptuous of him.

"Um, nothing is up with me. What do you mean?"

"I think you know what I mean."

"Actually, I don't. Elaborate."

"You single, live around here, what are you trying to get into? I'm sure you can tell I'm feeling you. Or at least would like to," he said, with a smirk.

"Hmmm. Yeah, that's what I, thought. Yes, yes and I'm not trying to get into anything in particular."

"Well good, I don't leave until Monday. I'm going to get to know you as much as possible until then."

"Okay, if you say so."

"I do. Now, do you mind if I get comfortable?"

I looked at his feet. "How much more comfortable can you get?"

Girl, why did I ask him that? He took off his clothes and lay his ass in the bed. The only thing he had on was Speedo-type underwear and a gold necklace.

I laughed and said, "Oh, okay."

He told me to come to lay beside him. So, being a smart ass, I *sat* beside him Indian style. He turned up the music a little bit louder and we began to talk. He wanted to know my age and what was going on with me, etc. We talked for the rest of the night. It was two in the morning when he finally left to go back to his room. We talked about everything from the rising of the sun to the going down of the same.

I let my guard down around him a little more. Doing so, I was able to pinpoint what it was about him. I had the feeling that he's married, was married or something along those lines. But that wasn't it though. There was something else about him that was very familiar as well. That part I hadn't figured out yet, but I know I was close. So yeah, we talked for a good little while. We kissed off and on, we cracked jokes and enjoyed my wine and cheese tray. That mixture of wine and dark chocolate made him horny. It is known to be an aphrodisiac, so I wasn't surprised. I could tell he was turned on because no sooner than he was fully there, I smelled his pheromones again. That's how I knew I was right earlier. People always tell on themselves sooner or later. Some don't even realize when they do it. That's what's funny to me.

Saturday morning, I jumped up, got dressed, went down to breakfast and out the door to the shops. I brought me a few more watches, sneakers, a casual shirt and another pair of jeans. I hit up the wine store, again, and then the candy store before I heading back to the hotel. I went to the room to do a drop-off and grabbed lunch at the restaurant where customers could ride the bull. It was so much fun and hilarious. People drinking alcohol and a mechanical bull...not a good combination but Epic entertainment!

I headed back toward the hotel at about four o'clock. As I was walking up to the hotel, I kept seeing flashing lights. I looked up and it was the rooftop lounge of the hotel. Now you know I would be nosy. I called the front desk and Asia was working, so I asked her about it. She made me a reservation and informed me it doesn't open until nine o'clock, so I had time to chill and get cute.

As I was laying across the bed, listening to my music, coloring a picture on an app on my tablet when I heard a knock at the door. It was room service. I opened the door to another bouquet of flowers. This time, it was a mixed bouquet of carnations, roses, and tulips. It was quite beautiful. The card attached read: *I know it's not wine or dark chocolate, but I know you'll love these as much. Mattie.*

He was right, I sure did. Those were flowers of love or romance.

I was smiling so hard the young lady who brought them to me couldn't help but laugh at my amazement. My face totally lit up. Now, you know I love my flowers hunni. No sooner than I closed the door, the phone rang. It was Matthew asking me to join him tonight at the rooftop lounge for drinks.

"Sure, I'd love to," I said, but little did he know I already had a table. I continued to listen to my music and color on my tablet when another knock on the door bothered me yet again!

It was Matthew, wearing in his robe and socks.

I laughed. "How can I be of service?"

He smiled. "Did you like the flowers?"

"I love them."

"You like me?"

"You're cool."

"Do you find me attractive?"

"I do."

"Would you let me fuck?"

"Depends on my mood. And *not* just because you sent me flowers."

"That's all I needed to know."

He pushed my door open, grabbed me by the small of my back and brought me into him, kick the door closed with his foot and started kissing me dooowwwn! He was so intoxicating. I'm not sure what had him going, but he was going. His pheromones where stronger than before and I could not fight it. Especially with him kissing me in such a way. My body melted in his arms. As bad as I wanted to say *no* and pull away from him, I couldn't. It was like he knew that once I inhaled his essence, it was over. You know how much I love passionate sex, this was everything. Matthew was that perfect "Daddy" type of fella.

He was in his early fifties, chocolate smooth skin, short haircut with a salt and pepper beard (that was cut and trimmed very nicely). He had some belly with thick legs and arms; just very height-weight proportionate. He reminded me an older sexier Jerome Bettis. Like he could be Jerome's father or uncle. Just all kinds of sexy. His cologne I recognized. It was Creed and it mixed in with his pheromones, oh hunni the underwear quickly disappeared! He had my legs in the air with his hands in my hair. He. Had. Me. Gone. He took my body and I gave it right to him.

As he was kissing me, he said things that you would say to someone you loved or have loved for quite some time—married to or have shared very intimate moments with over a long period of time.

He whispered things like, "Tell Daddy what you want; you love it don't you? This is what you've been missing." To some, that may seem like a regular thing, but when it's said very passionately, followed by things like, "Say you love me in spite of..." I'm like what? But I said it anyway...rolling my eyes, of course. There were a number of things he wanted me to say in response. I could tell he hadn't heard it in a while. At least *not* from his other half, whatever that issue may be.

The more I moaned, the more he got turned on. His favorite position was missionary and boy could he go! Our session lasted all of thirty minutes, which was fine by me. Once we both orgasmed, he rolled over, laughed, kissed me, then went to sleep. Of course, I'm like, *What the fuck just happened?* I know what happened, my damn nose and senses got me in trouble again. I laid there for about a half hour, continuing to color my picture before I got in the shower.

When I came out, he was sitting on the side of the bed, still naked but smiling.

"Are you alright?"

He nodded. "I'm fine. Thank you for going along with what I needed."

"What you needed?"

"Yes. I just needed to hear those things and to know that somebody still finds me attractive."

"Wait a minute." I sat down beside him. "Explain, although I think I know where you are headed."

"It's just been so long since I've honestly had any kind of

connection with anybody. Let alone to feel like I'm doing something right and I can honestly make someone happy. My wife and I haven't connected on any level in years. Not to mention we haven't had sex since our grandkids surfaced. Not decent sex anyway."

"Well, did you say anything to her, or did you just do what men do? Grunt and cheat?"

"Of course, I brought it up to her. We even went to marriage counseling. I didn't start fooling around on her until about three years ago. She knows, she's not stupid."

"Hmph. Okay. Whatever works for you. So now tell me, how long have you been a pastor?"

He looked at me and chuckled with surprise. "How did you know?"

I grew up in the church. I can always tell. Besides, my senses are very receptive. There was a very familiar aura about you. When I hugged you, it clicked."

"Wow. Well, your senses were right. I've been a pastor for twenty years. I take it you don't tell everything you know."

"You're right. Lucky, you."

"Yes. Very lucky me. Again, thank you."

"No problem. Now, you've gotta go and get dressed or just go. Because with or without you, I'm still going to the lounge upstairs."

He laughed. "Oh yeah, that's right. We do have reservations. Cool. I'll go get dressed and I'll call you when I'm leaving out."

No problem. As soon as he left, I jumped on my phone and texted my sister right away about him. It was just, too funny. We have a code about this very subject. She thinks it's hilarious how I always end up with these married men or "super down low motherfuckers", when that's not even me. I live my life hunni. I whirl and twirl wherever I go when I'm in the mood. Oddly enough, I'm always the one that's approached. Not that I'm complaining. It's just wild to me now that I think about it. That's all.

Anyway, he went back up to his room to shower and get dressed. I ran downstairs to find something quick and cute to wear. You already know, linen! I brought me a pair of black linen pants, put on the black shirt I brought earlier and threw on my loafers and was set. I called Matthew to tell him I was on my way upstairs. I pumped my way to the elevator and did it. Those doors opened and BAM! The deejay was playing my song. I hit that *"Woooooo!"* I couldn't even get off the elevator fast enough before I started snapping and dancing! Look, it's deep and it's real. That good old "Rob Base". Yessuh!

I was so busy dancing I didn't even notice Matthew was behind me watching all of it. When I spun around, he was standing there with a drink in his hand, grinning and bobbing his head to my groove. He looked so cute. I laughed and made my way over to him. He handed me a glass of wine. We walked out to the balcony to have a seat and chat a little. The outside area was very nice. It had an amazing view of the Harbor skyline. It was glass all around us with sliding doors, nice contemporary furniture, tables, stools, the whole nine yards. Very sleek and sexy.

"I like your spirit of life," he said.

"Thank you. I can only be me baby. Life is truly what you make it. You can either live with regrets or enjoy your damn self. I prefer to enjoy myself until God says enough."

He agreed. "I totally understand."

"Good. I'm glad you do. Now, let's go party." I was in the process of walking away when he grabbed my hand. I turned around to look at the somber look on his face; he hung his head. The energy radiating from his hand was strong.

"What's wrong?"

"Just...please help me."

He threw me completely off with that response. Love, if you could have seen his face. I knew then, it was time to go. I hugged him

"It's cool. We can talk about it."

He thanked me and we made our way to the elevator. As we were going down the elevator, he hugged me again. "I really need someone to talk to about this. I am so tired of people and bullshit."

"This sounds very familiar, but it's all good. We will surely talk about it."

As we were walking back to my room, I told him I would order some room service. He said he wanted some of those wings I had the night before, so we went and got some, which was fine by me; they were good.

While going down the escalators to the restaurant, I asked him, "Why did you change so fast on me upstairs? What the hell happened?"

"Christian, you don't have a care in the world. And if you do, it doesn't show."

"Oh sugga, I definitely do! I just don't let them get the best of me if I can help it." We walked off the escalator.

"You said what I've been feeling for quite some time now. I don't want to give a fuck anymore."

"Then don't."

"If it was only that easy."

"Oh I know." TUH!

We were now back in my room, I told him to get comfortable because this would be a long night. We took off our clothes, I turned on my music, opened the curtains so we could enjoy the night view and skyline lights, opened the other bottle of wine, laid the food out, and we got to it. I went back to my original question.

"What made you snap that fast?" I made him think before he responded.

He gave me the same answer, following up with how he would be looked at as "less of a man" if he truly lived the way he wanted to. Again, I told him to elaborate. "I don't consider myself this or that. I like women and men. I'ma straight freak. I like it all ways. I hate having to conform to this modern day and old fashion way of bullshit."

"I understand. Matthew, it's not all your fault. You must realize, you grew up in a time where you had no choice but to conform. If you didn't, you would risk being ostracized by your family and loved

ones. Many of you can't handle that. You would die. Literally and figuratively. I've seen it many times before. The only thing I fault you for is that you got married and then you had kids. Now it's no longer about just you anymore. You have others to think about. You have a family. The only thing I can say is if you and your wife have this understanding, just be careful and continue to protect your mental health. Don't be messy and don't allow the mess to follow you home. No, you're not going to meet another soul like me, which is why I'm being upfront with you."

Love, the way he looked at me. It was as if he could make us switch bodies, he would have. I think because I was saying what needed to be said and not what he wanted to hear. You know I don't believe in that anyway. I could tell he was feeling everything I was saying. I also told him that he needed to take responsibility for his role in all of this as well. He agreed.

I was just so taken aback by his emotion. Not that I'm not used to it, it was just so sudden. The more we talked, the better he felt. I could tell he was coming back to himself. I also brought up the fact that his church members or the "church folk" aren't going to be as receptive. "So, think carefully how you want to handle this," I told him.

"I'm getting ready to retire anyway. I've had enough of the "Black church" and its hypocrisy," he said, which is very common amongst our community. "Besides, I already, thought about that, which is why I'm ready to step down." He told me, it's not just his issues, he has a problem with, but the disrespect and hate period. Again, I'm familiar. Apparently, this retire thing was already set in motion in his mind well before now.

So, my statement about being happy and living life until God says otherwise confirmed what he had been thinking all along.

"I'm glad I could help," I said. "It's still early, so what now?"

"You want to take a ride with me? I just feel like taking a drive."

I responded with a flirty smile and "Sure." I was already eyeballing his car, so why not?

We were getting dressed when he said, "Put your shorts back on."

"Um, okay..."

"I like looking at your legs."

I laughed. "Yeah, I know! They're totally fucking hot!"

He laughed and shook his head.

I threw on my shirt, my new cute sneakers and we bounced. In the garage, he unlocked his car and opened the door for me. I almost buckled and collapsed. He was getting ready to do what I always do and enjoy.

"Are you alright?"

I laughed. "Yes."

We got in, he turned up his jazz music and pulled off. That was the perfect night for it too. We drove from the Harbor, across the bridged to Virginia, around the outer loop of the beltway and then back to the Harbor. As we were cruising, the night air felt so good flowing through the car. He leveled his windows just right and opened the sunroof. I let my hair down and we cruised. Smooth Jazz was taking us through.

Love, it was *so* nice. We really enjoyed ourselves. All in all, it was a perfect night. He grabbed my hand, kissed the back of it and held it against his chest near his heart. He looked at me, smiled and thanked me again.

"Stop thanking me. Live your life and do epic shit!"

He laughed and said "Definitely."

We made our way back to the hotel about one in the morning after a doughnut run.

We sat in my room, ate junk, drank wine, laughed a lot, and had some good sex. It was a fuck session. Old Kat Zaddy can *go!* He flipped the hell outta these legs. He was shocked a little when he saw how far he could bend my legs back. I have often said, be careful who you have sex with because of the energy they leave behind. Well, I could honestly say that I left some of my energy within him. I allowed a piece of my essence to transfer to him. Notice I said allowed. Yeah, let that marinate in ya soul for a few. Anyway, we truly enjoyed each other's company. I was glad I could help him to move forward and be okay with himself. Or at least give him that push he needed.

We had sex Sunday morning before we went down to breakfast. Again, nice. His kisses were so passionate, and that tongue was an added bonus. *What that mouth do? Put in work!* Okay, we had sex again after breakfast too. *giggle* That was it though. I did a late checkout. We exchanged contact information and he walked me to my car. As my driver was putting my bags in the trunk, he kneeled down by my bag, thanked me again and slid a little something in my bag.

I smiled, then told him "You didn't have to do that."

"I want to. After all, I did drink up your wine and eat your chocolate... All of your chocolate."

"True!" I laughed.

"Christian, I'm serious. Thank you for a wonderful three days. I no longer feel mad at the world or my family for that matter. You have a gift. Don't ever lose it."

"Thank you. As long as you can pay it forward to someone else, then my time with you wasn't wasted. You are an excellent person and don't ever let anyone tell you otherwise. Tell'em to kiss ya ass."

He laughed. "Will do! Thank you. I'll be sure to keep in touch."

"Yes, please. By all means."

"After you did what you did this morning with that mouth, I can't let you get away too far from me."

We kissed one last time before he closed the car door. As my driver was pulling off, I got a text message from him that read: *I think I'm falling in love with you.* I smiled.

Not only was his sex game on point, but I was able to honestly help him with his *true confession* of self. I was really glad I could help him to free himself just a little bit or give him that confident push he needed. Even if we didn't have sex, he trusted me enough to talk to me and tell me what was bothering him. I was able to do what I do. It was a very good weekend.

Asia hooked me up and yes, I took all my flowers home with me.

Yes, I still talk to Matthew. He's doing really well. He and his wife are no longer together, he's retired, he moved to Texas and living his best life. I told him I'll be out to visit him once he's settled. He's having a home built. I told him I don't wanna come until he's done. We talk often, exchange photos and everything. He's lost a little weight and he's truly happy. I LOVE IT!

Okay, Love, I gotta go. I'm hungry now shit.

I'll talk to you later.

Eskimos kisses.

EVER SACRED HEART'S

Good morning, Love,

I know I've been gone a minute. I just needed a moment to get myself together. Another one of those moment's where I needed to step back and gather my thoughts, along with making sure my soul is still anchored in love, truth, and light. I've been just so damn irritated with everybody and everything lately. Like the world was just pissing me off. Chyle, I had to step all the way back.

I visited Lola in New York. She lives in a nice condo near Central Park. Since New York is one of my favorite places and she was home, I figured, why not? I swear I love spending time with her. Her condo is decorated so nicely. Very comfortably as well. It was the perfect mixture of masculinity, with the perfect touch of femininity, which was her to a tee. Her place always smells different every time I would visit her. I would always tease her about that. Not in a bad way, just different air fresheners mixed with her perfumes. She had a huge purple leather sectional in her living room that went around the wall, under a big window that overlooked the park. It's my favorite space in her home.

I loved spending time with her because we would always vibe off each other so effortlessly. We would just laugh, love, eat, giggle, talk and just enjoy each other's company. That's what I needed. She and I would talk about her troubles or what she had been thinking about or dealing with lately. All she wanted was just an ear to listen to her and give her some feedback when she needed it.

The only thing I needed was someone to give my pent-up love to. Meaning, I just wanted to be intimate with someone on a personal

265

level. Hugging, talking, hair stroking or scalp massaging, watching movies cuddled up under the blanket, walking down the street, holding hands or arms locked. That kind of intimacy has always been my favorite. Some people just need a hug; some of us just enjoy giving hugs. There are times when I need to give out hugs or just hug somebody. I knew I could do that with her. Obviously, there was no sex of any kind involved. We just got it. We all need that one person who we love and can be intimate with. Just so happens that for some of us, it is our significant other. Mine just happened to be with my best friends.

"Okay, I'm in need of your hugs and a moment. Let me know when we can connect," she message tell me. I knew what that meant. She was on her way home and she needed to dish. We would sit on her sofa, get comfortable, and just go in. I always brought my own blanket and she always laughed at me. It was just a part of my comfort zone, but she would be tickled pink by it. She would always call me or send for me whenever she was home.

And you know what? She always had perfect timing. It didn't matter what day of the week or time; I was on my way to her. I know she traveled a lot so it would be hard for her to just chill at times. She's a busy girl and I get it. Besides, when your friend is in need, you're supposed to be there. Right? Exactly.

I'd call her to tell her when I was in front of her building. We would greet each other with the biggest and best hug. She would see me and just burst into laughter. I would laugh at her laughing at me. You know how I love to make people laugh, but with her, it is nonstop. I would have her crying and bent over in laughter—one of my favorite things to do with my friends. My other home girl is the same way. She sees me coming and automatically starts laughing.

Once I was all settled in (meaning I gave her the dessert that I brought her or what other little things I would bring for her) we would get right to it. Turn the music on low and just get our talk on. I would sit on the sofa, place her pillow on my lap for her head, then I'd let her talk about whatever her heart desired. She would talk and I would stroke her hair or massage her scalp. It was nothing for her to be talking while I play in her hair. Then she'd fall asleep, which became funny after a while. She does it so much, I have become immune to it. I would watch TV or just look out the window and people watch until she woke up.

Once I made sure she was okay, she would ask me if I was okay. Now that I had her together, she would be that ear that I needed (if I happened to need one that is). She's such a doll. I remember telling her that I feel so helpless or useless at times. Before I knew it, the tears were flowing down my face.

She sat straight up and grabbed my hands. "You have got to release the heartaches of this world. That is not your cross to bear. At least not alone. You always tell me to let go of what I can't control. Now I need for you to do the same thing."

There would be moments where I would just cry and cry. That's what I love about Lola, she gets me, and she gets "it." She never once judged me or made me feel like I was crazy because of my heavy heart, or my state of mind.

"I've often felt that way about the world as well," she continued. Like me, she's been all over the world, so she gets it.

"I'm sorry..."

"Don't you *ever* apologize for having a heart and compassion for people."

I nodded in agreement. "My grams tells me the same thing. And I promise you I'm working on it. But when I tell you it's HARD. GOD!"

Now, I don't have that problem anymore. I just deal and move on. Back then, it was still new to me. Lola knows what to say to me and how to respond to me. She's one of the very few who does. She knows how to make me snap out of it. She would go to her closet and show me all the new things she bought or ordered. I love dressing her. She is my version of the life-size Barbie. She always knew how to take my mind off things the right way.

Before I left her to return home, we went for a walk-through Central Park, where we saw what I call "Elf'kins". They are little kids that are no older than three years old but are so small and just super adorable. They look like little Elf's. LOL. Well, Love, you know me. When I saw them, I ran right over to them.

Chyle, I left Lola standing there, cracking up at me. I didn't do it abruptly because I'm aware of the whole "stranger danger" thing, but I don't know what came over me. You know how I am with babies. They were just so adorably cute! They came right over to me. That soothed my heart and soul right away. I even hugged some of the babies. I spoke to the caregivers of the children for a few minutes, then I gave them some cash so they could treat the babies to ice cream. Once I made sure they were good, Lola and I left.

As we were walking away to the other side of the park, she asked me, "So, when are you going to give us some children?"

"Huh? What? Girl, no.

She laughed. "I'm serious. You are a prime example of what we need more of in this world. The way you just lit up when you saw those kids; the way they were receptive to you. That's not something that everyone has. Your maternal instincts are damn near better than my mother's. Better than many mothers I know."

I smiled at her. "You're so sweet. Thank you. As much as I love them, I can't. I don't want my children in this world. People are so cruel and just downright damn evil. I would kill somebody if they hurt one of my babies. I would kill if they hurt one of your babies. I just...I can't. That's the way I feel right now. I may change later, but as of right now, it's a no. *A strong no.*"

"I can totally understand that. I'm not surprised you said that or even feel that way. Hopefully, God will change your heart. I would love to see you with your children someday. I can only imagine what you would be like. Not to mention the love you have for people, Christian. That shit is *beyond most.* I mean, like dude, you're damn near Jesus. I know firsthand because I've been around you. I've seen and heard your forgiveness. I can only imagine the love you will have for your own kids. I just want you to promise me you'll think about it."

"Eh... I guess."

We laughed, hugged, locked arms, and walked to the restaurant for lunch. On the way back to her place, we stopped at a dessert spot she likes. She punished a vanilla ice cream Sunday. I had a piece of hot apple pie with ice cream drizzled with caramel. It was so damn good! We were, too fat to walk home. We took another break and sat on the bench. We laughed and talked as we people watched while drinking water.

Back at her place, as I was packing my bags, she came over to me and grabbed me by the hand. I looked up and she had tears in her eyes. She always does this to me. She always gets super girly on me before I leave. It's because we have such an enjoyable time together.

"All you have to do is say the word and I'm here," I told her, which she knew already.

My driver called to tell me he was downstairs. She hugged me. "Walk me downstairs."

"No. I'll watch you from the window."

I chuckled. I forgot she's not the goodbye type. She's so cute. "That's fine," I said and gave her a little gift before I left. I actually put it in her bedroom on the pillow. I hugged her one last time, kissed her dimple then left.

On the train back to DC, I couldn't help but smile, and thank God for her and our friendship. Our bond is truly unbreakable. No matter where she is, I always make sure she is alright. To this very day, I check on her. She still laughs at me for having such an old soul. I texted her to let her know I was home, and all was well. I thanked her for a lovely weekend. She said the same.

In that moment, I knew I was going to be just fine. In that moment, I was love, I was with love, I was allowed to give love freely and openly. In that moment, the love that we share is pure and unbreakable. My girl, Lola.

Thank you, Love,

I needed that.

I'll talk to you later

Eskimo kisses.

FROM COLLINS AVENUE
TO ABACOS ISLANDS

Good evening, Love:

What? I'm always in a good mood. I mean, can I smile in peace? My trip was very nice. It gave me the rejuvenation I needed. I had time to sit back and think about a few things. Like, I noticed how I dumb myself down for people who don't understand or grasp my mindset, or rather the setup of my whole being. I noticed whenever I'm around certain people for lengthy periods of time, it would exhaust me. I would have to hold back so much; what I'm thinking, what I'm feeling, or whatever I think about them would go into overdrive. The more they opened their mouths, the more they would annoy me, or I would have a dislike for them. It's been happening a lot. Afterward, I would feel drained. So much so, I'd have to go somewhere alone so I could rejuvenate. Hence, my running away to another city or country for a while and not telling anyone.

Yes, that's how I ended up in the Bahamas. I've told you before how being around certain family members wear me out—those guilty by association from Grams or my mother. Yes *her*, with her begging ass. Always got her hand out or asking for a favor. I spent the holidays around a few of them and I'd had enough. I didn't even let the New Year settle in before I was on the plane and off to Florida. I thought about going to see my sister in Texas, but I knew I would not be in the mood to deal with my nieces and nephews, so I left it alone. I called Danny and told him I was on my way to his area, so we could link up and hang out for a few days since I hadn't seen him in a while. He was more than happy to hear from me. What was even funnier, he won't admit this, but he was super excited I was coming to visit him.

He wanted me to stay with him, but I told him I was using my hotel points before they expired. Yes, hunni, I was straight lying. I wanted to be alone when I wanted to be, you know? I know that in the house with him, it would not happen. He understood and suggested I let him know when I was ready to hang out. I preferred it that way. Since I didn't have a specific timeline on how long I would stay, I brought a one-way ticket. Ballsy of me, I know. So, I arrived Friday morning and checked into the hotel in Miami on Collins Avenue. Once inside my room, I fell in love with it. The decor was perfect. It was rustic meets nautical. Yes, I loved it. It had nothing but white linens with hints of tan, yellow, and soft blues. The view from my room was amazing. It was better than I, thought it would be. To be honest, I wasn't expecting the view or a nice room. It went beyond what the pictures on their website showed (and we both know how that can be). When I walked in, the ocean's view greeted me through the glass doors. It looked as if my room was on the ocean. So fresh, so light and breezy. Just beautiful. After spending a few minutes unpacking, I sat on the balcony, enjoying the views and calming sounds of the ocean.

For lunch, I ordered room service. I wasn't in the mood to go out. I kept it simple with a salad and lobster tail. Everything was just perfect. It was what I needed at that moment. After eating, I opened the glass doors wide and invited the ocean into my room. I sat and watched the sheer, white curtains billow from the embrace of the salty oceans breeze. It was so relaxing; before I knew it, I had dozed off. Two hours later, my cell phone rang.

"Are you all right?" It was Danny. I forgot to tell him I was checked in and fine. I told him where I was staying, and we agreed to meet up for dinner.

"I don't want to be in a super busy restaurant," I told him. "I'm just not in the mood."

"I have the perfect place."

After I hung up with him, I returned to the balcony. I sat and watched as people walked the beach. Remembering I had a coloring book in my bag, I went to grab it along with my crayons. I sat outside on that balcony for three hours, coloring and people watching. It was my little piece of heaven on earth.

I started to get dressed at about six o'clock. We had dinner reservations at seven-thirty, so I had plenty of time. I dressed in my... *yes, I had on linen!*

Look, it was warm in Florida, so I was okay. You do not know my life Love!...Okay, maybe a little bit and *yes*, I had on white, again. It was very light and easy, so I figured, *Why not?* Besides, powder or deodorant wouldn't show up on my shirt. I wore white, fitted jeans with a linen shirt and loafers. Very comfortable. I texted Danny to tell him I was on my way to the restaurant. He responded that a car was waiting for me downstairs, which made my day. I wasn't expecting that either.

I made my way to the car and met Antonio, my driver for the evening. He was a cutie pie, too—about five-nine, Caucasian, dark hair, brown eyes and looked to be a dedicated gym rat. A nice little body on him. Wasn't my type, but cute nonetheless. I'm glad he knew where we were going, because Danny didn't say the name of the restaurant. The view on the way to dinner was beautiful. Antonio rolled down the windows and opened the sunroof for me to get the full view. I loved it. Once we arrived, I gave myself a once over, added a little more lip glass, flipped my hair and proceeded inside. I greeted the smiling hostess, gave her Danny's name, then she told me to follow her.

Love, as I was walking behind her; you know I was all into the decor of the restaurant. I looked up and there was Danny's big, bald-headed, fine ass looking like a whole ass snack. I had not seen him in so long. He lost weight, toned up, shaved his head and just... *whew!* I had to smile through my lust. I was happy to see him; he was looking *good!* All six-foot-three inches of him. I hugged him, and he smelled so damn *good!* I was trying to act right, but he was killing me. Danny and I have always had a great relationship. We've never slept together, just flirting and innocent kisses. Yes, innocent kisses are a thing. Kisses on the cheeks or a peck on the lips. But, baby, the way he was looking and smelling...yeah, I knew it would go further. I could tell how he was looking at me.

Remember, we both hadn't seen each other since 2007 for the Valentine's Day yacht party he hosted. I was still fat and so was he. So yeah, all of that!

Anyway, Danny reserved us a table outside near the water. It was very nice and intimate.

"Well, look at you, sir. You look so good."

"Well, thank you. Right back at you. I love the hair. I see you finally gave in." He smiled.

I chuckled. "I know, right? You like it?" I asked, with the flip of my hair.

"I do. It's very nice. Amongst other things I see. Lost a little weight, have we?"

"Yes, *we did!*"

He chuckled. "Look, I had to. I was borderline diabetic and hypertension was around the corner. I had to do something, baby."

"I hear that. Well, we were in the same boat, sugga. I had completely had enough of that fat shit. I *knew* I had to do better. So, I did."

"I'm glad you did. You look damn good."

"Thank you."

"You're welcome. So now, tell me, what are you doing down here?"

"You look good, too, D. Don't think I didn't notice...Um, I just needed a break from everybody and everything. So, I figured, *Why not?* Not to mention, I hadn't seen you in a while, so that was a plus as well."

"Aww, Cheeks, thank you. I'm glad you did. It's been a while and we need to catch up." He tossed me a flirtatious smile.

"Mmhhmm." I rolled my eyes and smiled. "I love the ambiance here. Very nice choice. I take it you've been here before?"

"It's one of my favorite places. I don't bring many people here. Only the special ones." He winked.

"Oh, I just bet you do."

He laughed out loud. "What does that mean?"

"It means I'm thirsty and ready to order."

He signaled the waiter. He ordered a bottle of wine along with my ginger ale. I didn't think he would remember, but he did. We talked while drinking until our dinner arrived. We didn't realize how much we had missed in each other's lives. His father passed away, my uncle and Grams passed away, he had five new nieces and nephews, I had five new nieces and nephews. We just had a lot to catch up on, so that's exactly what we did. As the evening lingered, I enjoyed the pan-seared salmon and he had the filet mignon while enjoying each other's company. He told me how he was feeling toward his son and daughter both leaving the state. I could tell it bothered him a little bit until he told me they were both in DC with me.

"Why didn't you tell me sooner?" I asked him.

"I didn't want to burden you with the task of looking after my grown-ass kids." He chuckled.

"I'm used to it, so it would've been no biggie."

"It's cool." He smiled.

After dinner, he said, "I want to show you something."

"It better not be what I think it is..."

He laughed. "Oh no, it's not that. Not just yet."

We walked over to the other side of the restaurant where he had another table reserved for us with nothing but desserts on it.

"Wait. Are those caramel dipped strawberries with whipped cream and chocolate sauce on the side? *Oh, my God, Danny!* You didn't!"

"Ooohhh, but I did. I even ordered you some sweet potato pie custard with sorbet, if you want something cold."

Oh sugga, you did a great job! I love it! I wanna taste everything! You are so bad for my new figure." I laughed.

"Don't worry about it; we gone work it off later on."

With a raised brow and tilted head, a smile formed in the corner of my mouth. "I am not even about to pay you any attention right now, you nut!" I took a deep sigh. "Thank you so much Danny."

Danny was cracking up. I sat down at that table so damn fast. I didn't know where to begin. I happened to check our surroundings when I noticed it was just me and him in that area.

It was a private area he had reserved for us. He's a very private person like myself, but intimate and sensual, also like me. He kissed my cheek, then excused himself to the restroom. I ate a strawberry and a spoonful of sorbet before he returned. The waitress brought me some water he was walking back into the room. Danny looked so handsome. He was my own little Cuban "Suge Knight". He looked so handsome in his linen suit with a short brim straw fedora hat slightly cocked to the side of his head. Just *so* cute! He didn't sit down until the waitress left. He sat down beside me and put his hand on my thigh and *whew!* Culo be still!

I fed him caramel dipped strawberries, as he sucked the caramel off my finger before he placed kisses up my arm, to my lips. Oh hunni he's a smooth one. I kissed him and turned my head a little. He started kissing my neck. I made him stop.

He leaned in. "I know you don't think turning away from me is going to make me stop kissing you."

"It was worth the shot."

"Yeah, but you fail to remember I know all your hot spots."

I laughed and made him stop kissing me. I was getting turned on. Danny knows damn well the way my freak is set up; I would have jumped his bones right at the restaurant.

"We must stop doing this; we can just save some for later."

He laughed. "Fuck later. It's sooner than later."

"I know, right?"

While Danny cleared the check, I went to the restroom and checked my phone messages. My mother was checking on me to see where I was. As I said, I didn't tell anybody where I was going. I just left. I told her I was fine. I took a trip to Florida to see a friend and I'd be back soon.

Once I was done, I returned to his side. He kneeled down to take off my shoes. He said I won't be needing them anyway. That's when I knew we were getting ready to walk the beach.

"Um yeah, I could have taken off my shoes myself, sir."

"But where's the fun in that?"

"Get off my feet. You ain't slick."

He laughed. "I had to try."

I kissed his bald head and we made our way to the beach. As we were walking the beach talking, I kind of zoned out. The waves crashing against the shore with the breeze from the ocean felt so good! I just had to stop and take it all in. Before I knew it, we had walked to the other end of the beach near the new luxury high-rise condos. We both laughed as we turned to walk back toward the restaurant. Danny began to open up to me about his life and the struggles he's had to endure over the last few years. I had no idea; then I told him I felt guilty for not calling or keeping in touch with him on a regular basis.

"It's cool, babes. Life happens."

"I know, but naturally I feel bad. And you're right, life does happen, and boy did it ever."

"Exactly. It's not anything selfish, we just get caught up in the everyday struggle and drama of this thing we call life."

"You are so right, Daniel."

"You know, you are the only person who calls me that." He chuckled and looked me in the eyes. "I've missed you, Christian."

"Aw, sugga, I've missed you, too."

As I locked my arm in his, I laid my head on his arm. We laughed and walked back to the restaurant.

I pulled my phone out to call the driver, but Danny took it and said, "You better not! I want to take you back to your hotel." He paused and smiled. "Besides, I want to see where you're staying," which we both know what was going to *cum*—pun intended—out of that situation.

As we walked to his car, I couldn't help thinking about what he said as we were walking down the beach. *"Life happens. We can't control everything. Let go of what you think should happen. It didn't happen the way we, thought it should for a reason. Let that shit ride and find another way to rock."* I was thinking about what he said so much and so hard, I didn't even realize I had stopped walking. It made me kind of zone out again. He pulled up and jumped out to open my door.

"That's okay," I said. Just get in and let's go."

He laughed and said, "You need to chill."

As we were riding down the strip, I asked him to open his sunroof.

"I see not much has changed. You and this whole city light, night air thing, huh?"

"You see right, sir, and thank you." I smiled and winked.

We rode the rest of the way with the roof open listening to Afro Cuban jazz music, still enjoying the moment and each other. I noticed it was taking a little longer to get back to my hotel then it did getting to the restaurant.

"What did I miss?" I asked him.

"I want to make a quick stop. I want to show you something."

I laughed. "Unhunh, Danny, I don't do those kinds of things in the streets, sir!"

He laughed. "Stop lying! Remember I know you!"

"Oh shit!" I said, with an uproar of laughter.

"Nah, I think you'll like this." He gave me that side eye glance and smirked.

We pulled up to a beautiful home that had floor to ceiling windows galore. I sat straight up in the seat. Danny started to laugh.

"See, I knew you would."

"I know you didn't! You finished it?" I exclaimed.

"I sure did. I wanted you to see it personally."

"Danny! Oh my God, this is absolutely beautiful."

Love, you know by now I hopped clean out the car and I was standing in front of his home in shock and awe. It was just so beautifully done. The home had a pretty tan colored stone facade that was given so much definition by the black lines and trimmings of the windows and doors. As it sat there glowing with a champagne colored hue, I couldn't help but smile. I was so excited for him!

As I shut the car door, I walked to the front of the steps where he was standing and hugged him. I could not be happier for him. He finally finished his baby. It only took him a whole five years to complete it. Bless his heart. But it was done, and it was all his. His dad started the house, but when he passed away, Danny picked up where he left off.

"You wanna go in, don't you?"

"You know damn well I do!"

Danny chuckled. "A'ight, Let's go."

"Eeek! Thankies!"

Danny fell out with laughter. "Oh, my God! You still Eek!"

"Yes! Nothing has changed!" I chuckled. "Now open! *Open! Open! Open!"*

I noticed over to the left was a three-car garage. He had his dad's old Chevy pickup truck parked in the first one, his sports car in the second, and his sedan was parked in the third. Of course, he reminded me that everything has its place. He's such a neat freak. When I walked in, a grand staircase stood in the middle of the room, flaring at the bottom like a circle train of a wedding gown. Everything in the house was trimmed in black wrought iron or railing. It was just so perfect the way he and his dad executed everything. He already knew what I wanted to see.

"You ready?" he asked.

"Yes, let's go!"

"Follow me."

We walked to the left, down the hall, around the corner, and then *bam!* We walked right into the beautiful chef's kitchen, with a seven-foot island that greeted us with a black, farm-style sink, with a wine rack next to it. I saw the gas stove and my nipples got hard. It was just so sexy. To the left was a double glass door subzero fridge surrounded by cabinets and other little storage spaces. The color of the kitchen was black and silver.

"Daniel, you all did an excellent job. Your dad would be so proud. I can picture him now, walking around with his chest all stuck out."

"Thank you, Christian. And you know what? I said the same thing. I wouldn't stay here at first because of him, but I got over it. I mean, shit, I'm paying for it. I better get my shit together.

"Yeah, I agree. It's beautiful. I'm sure you know this is my favorite room."

"I figured as much when I heard you eeek!"

I laughed. "Shut'cha mouth."

"So what would you like to see now?"

"Your bedroom. I wanna see your closet and master bath."

"Which is why I had the maid to clean up today. I knew that was coming." He smiled, motioning with his hand to move in the direction I should follow. "A'ight let's go."

"Eeeeeekkkkk!"

"You need to cut it out," he said, shaking his head and laughing.

Before we headed upstairs, he showed me the rest of the house. He has a very nice screened-in pool area, with an outside sitting area accompanied by an outside kitchen. Everything was set in a multi-colored stone with nickel finishes. He showed me the media room, dining room, family room, and den. The entire house was decorated with the bachelor pad overtone, with a slight feminine touch. Very nice.

I finally made my way up the staircase, across the catwalk (yes, hunni, I pumped) . As I peeked in, I could see the television was mounted on the wall at an angle like a portrait at the foot of the California king-sized bed. I took off my shoes by the door since his carpet was a light color and very clean.

He laughed at me. "You are the first to that."

"I mean, I do have class boo." I smiled.

As I stood there scanning the room, which was very nice from just the windows alone. He has a very nice view of the water in the back of his home. I went into the walk-in closet and baby! *Yes!* My knees buckled. You know I *love* when a home designer put's windows in the closets.

Daniel had a very nice sized window in his closet. He also had a skylight that shined right down in the middle over his island. Yes child, he had an island in his closet. His closet was so well organized. From watches to suitcases, duffle bags, backpacks, and suits! *The suits!* Love, he had those color coded. He reminded me of my uncle Rio. I wanted to jump his bones right there in the closet. I bullshit you not. I walked over to the display for his colognes. My God, this man had my culo smoking. I couldn't wait to text the bff (Lady J) and tell her all about this shit. I knew she would appreciate it just as much as I did.

Daniel laughed at me and asked, "Are you all right?" He saw my mouth watering.

I walked out of the closet and we made our way over to the sitting room in his bedroom. We sat on the love seat and talked about how he was feeling.

"I'm proud of you, Daniel. Everything looks immaculate. And you seem to be very happy."

He grabbed my leg, pulling my feet toward him. He began to rub my feet and tell me what he was really feeling. What else but lonely? Although, I really wasn't surprised. Daniel is a very handsome man, sexy even. He had it all. The one thing that most people like him miss, is someone to share it with. His house is empty, all the kids and grandkids are gone, his father is gone....he has no love life. So yeah, he's feeling lonely, or alone, shall I say.

"Well, sugga, are you even dating?"

"Not really. I mean, I went on a few dates, but I wasn't feeling them, so I left it alone."

"I don't think you should give up. We have to be receptive to and for new things. Now, if you're not ready, then say so, but don't say one thing and you feel something else. That's how you mess up."

"You're right." He smiled at me. "God, I love how soft your feet are."

I chuckled and smiled at him. "Thank you. And if you keep rubbing my feet like that, you might end up on child support. You betta quit boy!"

He laughed out loud. "You know I love your feet, baby." He kissed the top of my foot and sucked my toes.

I pulled my foot away. "Stop."

"Give me a kiss," he said.

Yes, I kissed him and then I got up. "I'd like something to drink." That was my way of changing the topic and moving from the bedroom to the kitchen. So I thought! Chyle, this joker had a mini bar in his bedroom. I didn't even see it. It was in the right corner of the closet. It was cute as shit, too!

"What do you want?" he yelled out to me.

"Water."

Why his smart ass brought me water just the way I like it? Cold, with ice and lemon wedges, and then had the nerve to have a bottle of wine with him—*with two glasses!* Oh, he pulled it!

"You know you're not going back to the hotel tonight, right?"

"Um, yeah. I kind of figured that much. Just give me a T-shirt and I'll be fine."

"Yeah, I got you."

We chatted for a few more minutes before going down to the media room. He wanted me to see what he had been working on. It was a film he helped to produce for one of his companies. It was pretty good. I can't go into detail, but it was a great action movie. It kept my attention.

It was around two in the morning when the movie ended. And, of course, I was a tad bit sleepy.

"I want to take a shower and then get in the bed," I told him.

He agreed. "I'm a little tired myself."

I went in his master bath and...*oh my glory!* The floors were heated; there were two tinted floor-to-ceiling windows, a shower that was big enough for four people, double vanity with blue granite countertops, with a standalone deep soaking bathtub. It was very spa like and comfortable. Not overly done, just perfect. Everything I needed was in the linen closet, including the type of soap I use. I grabbed the soap, a towel and did what I did. Since I knew he would want some slap and tickle, I made sure I was *extra* EXTRA" clean, if you know what I mean. He made it quite clear it was going down in more ways than one, so I knew I needed to be ready.

After my shower, I sat on the side of the tub oiling my legs and body. You know how I hate that after-shower ashy dry skin feeling. Danny walked in and showered. I knew he was packing, but *damn!*

He was swinging and sitting just right. That sexy thick Cuban was *alright with me,* with his cute ass. I put on the T-shirt he gave me crawled in bed. Oh my God, it was perfect. That even medium that I love. The right amount of firmness and the comforter was made of down feathers, which was good because his room was a little chilly. I was laying on the bed, on my stomach, with my feet in the air, as usual, playing on my phone when he came in to lay beside me, wearing a tank top and silk boxers.

"You mind if I turn on some music?" he asked me.

"No, not at all."

He rolled over to the nightstand, pulled out a remote and chyle, the lights dimmed, a jazz started flowing through the speakers.

"Oh, you showing off!" I chuckled.

"What are you talking about? This is how I chill before I go to sleep."

"Yeah okay. Whatever. Um, is this Boney James?"

"What you know about Boney James?"

"I know enough to know that this is one of my favorite songs."

He turned over to face me and I started singing "I'm gonna love you..."

"Just a little more, baby..."

"Oh, shit!" He laughed. "Okay. You know a little something. Ya daddy taught you well."

"Oh, please. You're right, but I discovered this song all on my own, thank you."

We talked a little more about music before he leaned over to kiss me. I knew that was coming. His body language was talking to me loud and clear. One thing about Danny, when he's comfortable with you, he's a very "touchy-feely" kind of person. I was still laying on my stomach while we talked about music and him showing me the pictures of his kids on his phone.

It was three in the morning. We both laughed and he leaned over to kiss me, once again. Only this time, it was with passion and a little longer. It was passionate enough for his dick to get hard and pop out of his shorts. It was just a kiss to me, but I guess it was more to him.

I jumped up, rolled the comforter back, and laid down. He climbed his thick ass right on top of me.

"So, we gon' do this or nah?" he asked. "I mean, you and I both know how long we've been bull-shittin' with each other. We need to just go 'head and knock it out."

I chuckled and rolled my eyes. "That was just *so* romanti-cal!" LOL.

"I'm saying though. Besides, I'm gonna take you somewhere this week. But first, I'ma teach you how to roll your R's."

Oh shit!

We started kissing again, but this time he took off my shirt. Baby, Danny started kissing my body from head to toe. And I po-litely let him. He has always been sexy to me. Just, you know; hand-somely sexy. Even his late-night essence turned me on. I know, but just smelling his bald head while he was on top of me was turning me on more than anything. As he pushed my hands and arms up, we locked hands over my head and continued to kiss. I felt my body give in to his passionate kisses.

As soon as he grabbed my thigh, I wrapped that leg around him and let him have it. We were going hot and heavy. We were both naked and rolling around on that bed. He kissed my body all night long, too. I had no idea Danny had it like that. Well, I kind of had an idea, but it was *nothing* close to what he put down. He's very passionate and paid close attention to my body. He reminded me of my buddy from Mexico. We had sex two times before six in the morning. He kept asking why I made him wait so long. I laughed at the thought. Shit, I had to ask myself the same damn question.

We dozed off about seven. He slept until two in the afternoon. I woke up at about noon because my phone was going off. Danny hadn't heard a damn thing. He was snoring down. It was my godfather calling to check on me to make sure everything was fine. I slipped on Danny's robe and went down to the lower level to talk to him on the phone. As I was chatting with him, I heard a commotion in the kitchen. Now Love, you and I both know, when I want to, I can walk light as a feather.

I crept around that corner to see what was going on. It was Danny's housekeeper, Maria. I peeked in the kitchen, gave her a soft "Good morning," She turned around and smiled at me. I told my godfather I would call him back. I introduced myself to her, letting her know I was Danny's guest.

Maria smiled at me. "May I get you anything?"

"I just need a mug for some coffee and I'm fine." Not only did she make a kick-ass cup of coffee, but she also had some great flavored creamer. She made me croissants with fruit and turkey bacon; she was spoiling me. She and I had a great conversation while my buddy was in the bed snoring away. She was so sweet. Just the cutest little thing. She reminded me of Jennifer Lopez's mother, Lupe. Just adorbs. We chatted the whole time I was downstairs. We sat at the island and had a grand old time. When I heard Danny go into the bathroom, I told her to go finish her duties and I'd see her later. I didn't want to get her in trouble. She hugged me and went on her way.

I bounced upstairs to join Danny in the shower. Not thinking we'd end up fucking in the shower too. Hey, I just went with it. He knew what he was doing when he started kissing my shoulders, pressed me against the shower wall, wrapped my leg around him, and slid inside me. I polity let him, too. It's just; like everything about Danny, so passionate and sexy. He pays attention to detail and is not afraid to go there. I think that's one of the things about him that turns me on the most. Even before we got to this point, I was attracted to him. Of course, because we were friends and I was married, I never took it that far or acted on it. He told me he felt the same way. Out of respect for me and my relationship, he didn't bother. I'm just glad him and B didn't know each other like that. This would have been super awkward. Tramp much!

After the shower, we got dressed and went downstairs. Maria had lunch waiting for us. She made a mean empanada with rice. She had me so fat and full! She made a variety of them. So, I was able to eat chicken and veggie ones. So good. I told him she needed a raise. Especially if she cooked like that on a regular basis for him. He's always been spoiled. By all them women and men in his family. Big baby! Again, I can relate. LOL.

Danny told me he wanted to take me to one of his favorite little getaway spots. We hopped in his car, went back to the hotel for me to change clothes and grab my bag. I let housekeeping come in while I was there. I put the *do not disturb* notice on the door. They ain't need to go in there if I wasn't there. We went back to Danny's, so he could switch cars. Now I knew Danny had always been a fan of the finer things in life, but, Love; when that round head fucker drove to the front, he was in his Aston Martin—a Vanquish at that! Now you know I had to laugh. I just shook my head and got in. I put my shades on, let my hair down and went with it.

We were cruising down the street. I finally decided to ask him where the hell we were going.

"Since I know you need to know anyway, I figured I'd take you to see where I dock, then go for a little sail. If that's okay with you."

"Okay. I'm with it. I mean, we've already come this far."

"Exactly. You trust me, right?"

I nodded. "I do."

"Cool."

We pulled up to the docks, got out and, we were going to board his boat, but I stopped walking. He burst out laughing and gave up the details.

"I'm taking you to my place in the Bahamas on Abacos Island."

I had to step back and get myself together. I willed my feet to move. He knows about my past relationship and what that island means to me, but not to *that* extent, which was fine because I wasn't in the mood to talk about it. I softly rolled my eyes at the gut-wrenching feeling that I would have to discuss it anyway.

As we began to make our way to Marsh Harbor, I took it all in. I must admit, Danny looked too sexy in his Fedora and linen while steering the boat. The ride was only about two hours (give or take thirty minutes) it was so smooth I really didn't notice how fast we'd arrived.

Once we docked and unpacked, we took the twenty-minute ride to the other side of the island to Abacos. I was playing on my phone when I looked up and noticed that we were pulling up to this beautiful property. We were greeted by the staff as soon as we walked into the lobby, they knew Danny and were excited to see him. I introduced myself and they were super loveable, while keeping that same energy, as they greeted me.

As we followed the butler down the hallway to Danny's wing of the property, I turned to him and gave him the side-eye.

He laughed and placed his hand on the small of my back then said "Just keep walking. I've got you."

The butler opened huge, wooden double doors for us and *oh my God!* The suite was immaculate. Not that I expected anything less, I just didn't expect that much glam. Danny wasn't the type. Again, so I had thought. Love, you know me, I ran right over to the double doors leading to the balcony to get a view of the beach and water. I took a deep breath; took it all in for just a minute and smiled. As I turned around, Danny was standing behind me smiling.

"What are you smiling at, Mr. Daniel?"

"Just admiring the view. That's all."

"Yeah, yeah. I wanna go to the beach. So, I'm going to change my clothes and then I'm going down to the water. It is definitely calling my name."

I did just that, too. Changed my clothes and bounced my ass right on down to the beach. Even, though I had a sarong with me, I hadn't put it on...yet. I was just excited to get to the beach. As I pulled up my shorts, took my earrings out my ears and let my hair down, I looked up in the mirror to see Danny smiling at me. I smiled, too. I don't know! I was smiling because he was smiling. LOL.

"Why are you smiling now?" I asked him.

"I'm just admiring you. You always make me smile. You always have, Christian."

"Well, thank you. I think..."

"If you're done, we can roll now."

"Okay great. Let's go."

I grabbed my coconut oil, shades and shoes and we made our way to the beach. Love, when I tell you it really *was* paradise. Just the view and the way the water looked like it was filled with diamonds. The sunlight bouncing off the water made it look crystalized. Just simply beautiful. I slapped on some oil and Danny and I proceeded to walk down the beach. As we were walking the shore, the water washed over our feet. We talked about life again, but more in-depth about what he had been feeling for the last few months. With his dad passing and his grandmother shortly after, he really didn't get a chance to grieve properly. As much as I wanted to support him and listen to him, I was zoning in and out of the conversation.

I couldn't help it. I was on this beautiful island that was damn near heaven on earth and all I could think about was absolutely nothing. It was like my soul was relaxed and would not let me feel any emotion but pure heavenly bliss.

I was not complaining either. I grabbed Danny by the face. "We need to take your mind off a few things." I kissed him. "Follow me." We went to the private side of the beach where clothing was optional. I began taking off my clothes, and I told him to do the same thing. He was freaking out at the fact that I was stripping in front of him and all the other beachgoers.

"Christian, what are you doing? Oh my God!"

"I'm going to get in this beautiful water, with or without you."

"We can go to the other side where we *don't* have to be naked."

"Nope. I'm fine here."

Naked as a Jay bird, I ran to the water full speed ahead. Danny was dumbfounded. His reaction had me cracking up.

I saw him taking his clothes off, but he didn't take his underwear off. He finally got in the water with me after about 5 minutes of me floating alone. Once we were deep enough in the water, I made him take off his underwear. He was very hesitant, so I took them off for him. He put them around his neck, so they wouldn't float away. I locked my legs around his waist and told him he needed to relax. Not only did I lock my legs around him, but I made sure my entire body hugged his body intimately. I could tell he needed it. I felt his body relax.

"Well now. Isn't that better?"

"You know, you're very good with that?"

"With what?"

"Figuring out what people need via matters of the heart."

"I try to be as in tune as I possibly can be. You know I lead with my heart. It hasn't steered me wrong yet, so hey. Now back to you..."

"Yes?"

As I laid my head on his shoulder, with my legs still wrapped around his waist, I let the water hold the weight of me, while Danny had his arms around me. We floated in a circle when I said to him, "I need for you to stop carrying all that weight. You and I both know what I'm talking about, and we both know how it can be."

"Yeah, I just haven't had the chance to really deal with it."

"I know you well enough to know that it doesn't take you long to deal with matters of the heart. However, this time is different. Only because it's your dad and nana, which means it's very close. Hell, it *is* your heart."

"Yes, you're right."

"So, with that being said, you need to take some time to yourself and talk to them out loud and tell them what you're feeling. That way, you'll feel better along with that weight being lifted off you. You seem to have some unfinished business with them both. Just say it. They will hear you. So will God. Take as much time as you need for as long as you need. Just don't dwell on it."

"Babe, you're going to make me cry."

"If you need to, then do it. It's no problem. But you need to do something. I could tell by the way you hugged me and again by the way you looked at me when I mentioned them before we left your house. It's all good. I get it, sugga."

"Okay. I'll do it then."

"Thank you. *Now!* Can we go, 'cause I'm hungry."

We both laughed.

"We can, but I can get a water quickie first?"

I smirked with a flirtatious smile. "I mean, I already feel you knocking on the back door."

So, I'm sure you can guess what happened next right? Yeah, he got the goods in the water. It was kind of hot, too, if I do say so myself. *Ow!*

Afterward, we sat on the beach and chatted a little while longer. By the time we were finished talking about him taking a moment to himself, we were damn near dry. We went back to the room to change for dinner. After showering together, we decided to lay on the bed for a few and just enjoy the breeze from the ocean. As the breeze danced with the sheer curtains and over our nude bodies, we couldn't help but to just enjoy the moment. It was nice.

After lying there for twenty minutes, we got up and got dressed. We had to chyle. Not only were we hungry, but we were also falling asleep. You know how water tires me out. Let alone sex in the water. So yeah.

As we got dressed and made our way down to dinner, we had one *hell* of a make-out session in the elevator. I don't know what got into him, but he was full of more passion and excitement. I could tell because his kisses were different. We went from regular tongue kissing too long, lingering, passionate kisses. He had me gone for a second. I definitely enjoyed it; I'll tell you that. When we got off the elevator and, while walking past the front desk to go outside, the concierge signaled for him to come over. As he spoke with the concierge, I stepped out the door to look at the sun as it was beginning to set.

It kissed the water so beautifully. As I was standing there in awe of Mother Earth's beauty, Danny walked out, kissed my neck, and said, "Let's go." I flinched and smirked. As we walked over to our designated dining area, I stopped to take off my shoes because they were not needed. The walkway was lit up with tea light candles, leading us to a private bungalow area draped in cream-colored fabric, with tiki torches lighting the front area, where we were also greeted by the wait staff. Love, I walked in that damn bungalow and to my surprise, Danny had it all planned out.

The spread before me was immaculate. Everything from the menu to the drinks, even my maybes. I looked at him in shock and awe. With a choice of fresh crab, lobster, fried conch, grilled Caesar cabbage, hush puppies, roasted Brussel sprouts with avocado, yellow rice, salad, and bread; we had a wonderful dinner. Everything I love to eat with seafood.

When it was time for dessert, we were escorted over to another bungalow that was like a little apartment. It was so cute. The staff set up another mean spread. This time it was fondue. Yes, another one of my fav's that he remembered. There were two fondue pots sitting in the middle of the table with fresh fruit on one side, which consisted of pineapples, apples, mango, kiwi (gross), peaches, strawberries and bananas. On the other side of the other fondue pot were sweets, which consisted of brownie bites, pound cake, chocolate cake, marshmallows, and waffles. Danny saw my face light up and he burst out laughing.

"I did good?"

"Oh baby, you did *great!*" I ran over to the table to sit down, so I could go in! I looked in the pots—chocolate in one and salted caramel in the other. Oh hunni, I was *over!* I could not sit my fat ass down fast enough. You know how I am about my sweets.

Danny dismissed the staff and told them he'd call them when we were done. They were all so sweet. Before they left, I made the young lady have some fondue with me. She was so sweet and cute. Her name was "Layalah". When she told me her name, I slightly buckled and shifted in my seat. I had to catch myself. Hmph.

After she ate a few things with me, I hugged her and she went on her way.

Danny laughed at me. "You're just so damn friendly. One of the many things I love about you babes."

I smiled. "Thank you. It's one of the things I love about me, too."

He chuckled. "Yeah, okay, smart ass. So now tell me, what was that all about?"

"What?"

"I saw the way you reacted when she told you her name."

"Honestly?"

He nodded.

"She just confirmed something for me. Something I need to do. That's all. I believe God gives me the signs and tells me what my next move should be when I ask. I asked, and he told me."

"Well, if you don't mind..."

"*I do.* And *no*, I'm *not* going to tell you." I laughed.

"I had to try." He chuckled.

"I know. I'll say this, though. I'm very in tuned with me and my who. I've been feeling like somebody has been calling my name since I've gotten here. I refuse to ignore it anymore. So, when the time is right, I'll respond to it."

"Yeah, you've always been with that earthy spiritual, creepy shit. I respect it, though."

"You better. Remember, I knew your grandmother."

"Checkmate. You win. Now kiss me before I don't want none."

I laughed, then I got up, mounted him, and laid one old mean kiss on him. The intimate moment in that room was everything. I think it had more to do with the fruit we were eating. The chocolate didn't help either. Not to mention he did have a few oysters at dinner. So, um yeah, aphrodisiacs all around and we went in. As you can imagine, that didn't last long because he immediately wanted to fuck. I felt all the blood flow to that meat. Not to mention, he had on linen pants. So, um yeah. He asked me if I wanted to go back to the room and get my hair pulled. I laughed and told him only if he promises to choke me a little. He let out another hearty laugh and said, "Bet!"

Danny summoned the staff, so they could clean up and close the room. When Layalah came back in the room, she had her friends with her. They were all smiling at me, which naturally made me smile. She told me she told her friends how nice I was to them and how much she loved my "soleless sandals." I forgot I had them on. I'm so used to them; they don't even phase me anymore. Since I was color blocking, I threw on the burgundy and gold ones. So, when they came in, they looked right at my feet. I laughed and said, "Ooohhhh okay!" we laughed, as I showed them the sandals. Danny was tickled because he didn't even pay them any attention. I told him a good friend of mine makes them for me. I only wear them in beach type settings etc. of course he was loving them. Called them sexy and everything. The girls were adoring them as well. They were all little sweethearts.

I told them to feel free to finish up the sweets. They were hesitant at first, but one of them dove right in. I said, "My girl!" Oh, hunni, Ms. Thang sat down and went in! I was not even mad. Even Danny had to laugh at that one.

While we were walking back to the room, he grabbed my hand, turned to me and simply said, "Thank you."

"Of course, sugga. Anytime."

He smiled and we proceeded to walk back to the main area. As we were walking past the beach, under the moonlight, I felt like something was pulling me toward the water. I wasn't sure what it was, but I knew I would see soon enough.

As we got off the elevator on our floor, Danny was already undressing. He's a free bird, so he doesn't stay clothed when he doesn't have to be (in private). By the time we were in the room good, Danny was naked and laying in the bed. I shook my head at him. I wasn't sleepy just yet, so I took off my clothes, threw on my sarong and sat on the balcony. I wanted to know who or what was calling me. I needed to meditate and align myself to handle it the proper way. At least that was the plan. Love, no sooner than I was in my sarong and standing on the balcony enjoying the view, Danny had me bent over the chair, diggin' in my guts. *Hmph!*

I don't know if it was the food or what, but we went at it! I think it was the strawberries and dark chocolate for me, and the oysters and liquor for him. We were all over that damn suite. We started off on the balcony, eventually making our way to the bed. Danny was already touchy-feely, but this time he was extra passionate. That's what sent me over the top. It was a sex session like we had never had before. Not only were his hands in my hair, but his hands were all over my body, accompanied by his kisses. I was returning the passionate kisses, too. Danny was very attentive to my every move. We've had sex before, but this time, it was a passion to the ninth degree. It felt like we were levitating at one point. Our souls seemed to connect like never before. The feeling of bliss that followed, with us being in the state of euphoria, had me gone. I did not want to lose that feeling or let go and I could tell he didn't either. He was waiting for me to orgasm so he could explode with me.

Now, yes, that was all sexy and romantic and whatnot, but the way that fool made all that damn noise knocked me right back to reality. Love, this fool started growling and yelling and making so much noise. If you could have seen my goddamn face! I was so over him. Then he fell fall asleep on me. *Really?* No, sir. I laughed, kissed his face, and pushed him off me. All that damn noise. LOL!

Anyway, I showered, sat out on the balcony and colored for a few minutes while listening to the wave's crash against the shore. A calm came over me that I hadn't felt since I was there. The level of relaxation was different. It was a soothing peace. I put my coloring book and pencils down. I slid on my caftan and sandals and made my way to the beach.

I sat down on a lounge chair and got sleepy all of a sudden. I felt like I was slipping into a trance. "I know damn well I did not come down here to fall asleep on the damn beach," I said out loud. The more I tried to fight it, the heavier my eyes got. Before I knew it, I was asleep.

It was just so weird, so I had, thought. It kind of freaked me out about how fast I started dreaming. Not only was I dreaming, but I was talking to Grams.

Dressed in one of her nightgowns, she said, "Relax and listen to what is being said to you."

"That's just it," I told her, "I don't know what's being said. I just kept hearing my name being called. Was it you calling me?"

"Yes, baby, but not only me. Someone else wants to talk to you."

As I jumped up off the chair in excitement asking who it was, I heard that soft, familiar female voice say, "Me."

I turned around to see my friend Aria, who passed a few years before and I really didn't get to say goodbye to her or have any closure. My eyes welled up; I ran to her and hugged her with all my might. I turned to Grams, who was smiling. She nodded and said, "Be well, my baby," and disappeared into the night air.

I turned to Aria. "What are you doing here?"

"I know you heard me calling you." She laughed and it was so heavenly.

"I had no idea it was *you! Oh my God!* How are you?"

She chuckled. "Calm down. I'm good. I really am. I'm at peace now."

"Yes, but...well, no buts. You're at peace and that's all that matters."

"See, I knew you were going to grow. I'm so proud of you. But there's something I need for you to do for me, though."

"Yes?"

"I need you to allow me to be at peace. You keep holding on to me, but in the wrong way."

I nodded. "Yes, you're right."

"I'm good." She caressed my face. "I promise you I'm good. I need for you to keep living and keep enjoying your life. I lived my life to the fullest. I'm fine. You have to let me go."

"But I...I just feel like you were robbed, and it makes me so angry that I want to fight and cry and fight and cry some more."

"Yes, I understand that, but God has the final say so. You know better. Let me go so that you can live. I mean it. Promise me."

"I guess I can try. I just miss you so much. And thank you for this. I needed this."

"I know. I'm always here if you want to talk."

"Okay. Thank you for saying that. But um, can I just say, bitch you are looking motherfuckin' flawless! Work it girl! What the hell kind of Juju Juice you got over there and why the hell yo ass ain't bring me none?"

She fell out with laughter. "That's the Christian I need back!"

"I'm just saying... Sis, you look *good!* But okay. I'll do better. I have no choice now. Especially if you went through all of this."

"No, you don't. And thank you for hearing me. Set me free, and you be free. I love you, Chubbz".

"I love you too, Apple. And tell Grams I said, *thank you."*

We hugged each other so tight. Then she slowly backed away from me. She smiled at me, blew me a kiss, and turned into an orb of bright lights and went on her way. I was instantly at peace. I now knew what that calming feeling was coming from. Not only did I know what it was, I knew where it came from. The two of them.

It was morning and I was awakened by the crew setting up for breakfast. When I asked what time it was, one of the employees told me six-thirty. Now you know I jumped my ass up and ran back up to that room, praying Danny wasn't awake yet. As I slowly opened the door and peeked in, Danny was sprawled out across the bed and knocked out. Yes, I did giggle as I took off my clothes and crawled in the bed beside him.

No sooner than he felt me beside him, he rolled over and snuggled up under me. Even, though I was pretty much ignoring him, because I was still thinking about what happened, when he wrapped his arm around me, I teared up with happiness. She finally came to me and set me free of so much anger I had been suppressing for her or because of her. Tears streamed down my face as I was letting it all go. She was good, my Grams was good, and now, I could finally say that I was good. As the sunlight gleamed through the window, I was thankful and filled with Joy. As it's said, "Joy comes in the morning", and that it did.

I managed to slide from under Danny, so I could go in the bathroom to get myself together. I turned on the shower water and started pinning my hair up. I looked in the mirror at myself and started crying again. I could not believe what I had experienced. Again, all tears of joy but mainly, tears of relief. I felt so much better and so much lighter. I turned my music on—low, of course—got in the shower, washed everything away and, by the time I got out, I was alright.

I came out the bathroom to Danny sitting on the side of the bed, looking hungover. He's one of those people that looks extremely rough when they first wake up.

"Well, good morning Lover. How are you?"

Through a deep groan, he managed to say, "Good morning, babe. How are you?"

"I'm good sugga. Did you sleep well?"

"I did until I rolled over and noticed you were gone. Where did you go?"

"Oh, I just went down to walk the shore. That's all."

"Yeah, I kind of figured as much. You good?"

"Yes. Why? Wassup?"

"'Cause I'm feeling like something." He got up and went to the bathroom to pee.

"Oh yeah? What are you feeling like?"

He came out of the bathroom. "You. Gimmie some love."

So, I'm sure as you could imagine, we had morning sex before breakfast. This time, it was just straight fucking though. I wasn't in the mood for that *be cute* shit, and I could tell neither was he. Not only was it good, but he started speaking Spanish and *baby, the orgasm was powerful!* Do you hear me? WHEW! Afterwards, we showered and went to breakfast. We worked up a serious appetite.

After breakfast, we went back to the room, stripped down, sat on the balcony and talked about nothing. I was coloring as we chatted until he got quiet. I looked up at him. He was looking back at me, smiling.

"What's good?" I asked him.

"Nothing, just loving you and the moment."

I burst out laughing and said, "Stop being cheesy." We both laughed. "I want to go back down to the beach before we leave."

He agreed, so we got dressed and bounced down to the beach.

Danny decided he wanted to just chill on the beach for a few. I got in the water and played with some of the local kids, while he laid on the chaise lounge, napping off and on. We stayed out on the beach for a good little while. By the time we came back in, it was time for lunch. We made sure we packed up everything so that after lunch, we could make our way to the port with no problems. I didn't eat much for lunch. I had a salad with seafood on the side. Danny's ass had a full-on meal, hunni.

As I was finishing my salad, I looked up and saw a Red Robin. The tale of the Red Robin goes, "Because of his red breast and this association with fire, like the Raven in mythology, the Robin is said to have brought fire from heaven. As such, in folklore, Robins are considered holy birds, and are beloved by gardeners; for they remind him of paradise and the legendary Garden of Eden."

I kissed Danny's face and said "I'll be right back." I walked over to the trees toward the Red Robin. When I looked up, I saw two of them. I started to smile when I heard Layalah, startling me.

"You want to feed them?" she asked.

"Where you come from?"

She smiled. "I was feeding them. It's one of my jobs here, is to feed the birds."

"Oh okay. They are so beautiful...and loud!" I chuckled. "I had no idea they were that loud."

"Normally they aren't. I think they like you. They're heavenly birds, so if they didn't like you, they would definitely fly away."

"So I've been told. Just so beautiful."

"Hold your hand out."

As Layalah poured seeds in my hand, they both flew down and began to eat out of my hand. One flew up to my shoulder and sat there for a few seconds before flying away.

It made me think of Grams and Aria. I knew it was them, re-assuring me that everything was well now on all levels. I hugged Layala and thanked her for that little moment.

I made my way back to Danny and we made our way back to the room.

"What was that about?" he asked.

"I just wanted to see the birds up close and she allowed me to feed them," I said, but I wasn't going to tell him the whole story. He's not ready for that much of me just yet. Although, I think he has a clue.

Now, back on the boat, we began our journey home. I swear it seemed like it took us less time to get home than it did to get to the doggone island. Once we were docked and he made sure his boat was secured, we headed to the car.

As the valet was packing our bags in the trunk, I sat in the car waiting for Danny to finish squaring away his business. It was about 6:30 p.m., and I was a little hungry and ready for dinner.

The sun was starting to set, as I looked out into the water. I thanked God for allowing me to experience my friend one last time. Just like clockwork, whenever I'm truly happy and filled with joy, the tears began to flow. I don't know what it is, but I just let it happen now. As I'm wiping tears and laughing, Danny walks out and gets in the car.

He looks at me. "Are you all right?"

I smiled and nodded. "Yeah, I'm cool. I just got off the phone, laughing at my sister," I said, thanking God for my quick wits.

"Okay," he said and leaned over to kiss my face before we pulled off.

We went to his place, where he had our dinner delivered and waiting for us—lobster, salad, and bread pudding. I told him I wanted some and my God was it good. It hit all my inner moist foodie spots hunni.

After dinner, we cleaned up and went outside for a dip in the pool. He wanted us to be completely naked like we were in the Bahamas, which I didn't mind but it felt like he wanted to say something or something was on his heart. As I was taking off my shorts, Danny jumped in the pool. I eased in the pool from the steps and made my way to him in the middle of the pool. I loved the way his pool sat in his backyard. When you walk down the white stone steps from his patio, which was off the sunroom, you followed the white stone pathway under the wooden arches, which led you right to the pool area. At night, the pathway was softly lit up with little circular solar lights. The trick was, they only light up when you trigger the sensors. They were just too cute.

I locked my legs around him and laid my head on his shoulder. He took my hair down and ran his fingers through it.

"What's on your heart?"

He simply said, "You know, I needed you this week in more ways than I realized. Thank you for simply enjoying every part of me and allowing me to be myself judgment-free. Christian, you have no idea what this means to me.

"Oh, sugga, you're welcome. You know I don't make people feel any less than what they should. Besides, I know you're a good man. We all need that love and support from someone we trust. Besides, when have you ever known me to turn down a trip to an Island?"

"See, that's what I'm talking about. You just live life, you love endlessly, and you make everyone around you laugh while staying positive and upbeat. That's what I love about you, baby."

"Why thank you. I love that about me, too." I chuckled. "But no, for real, thank you. I'm glad I could make you feel better, Mr. Daniel. We'll definitely have to do this again."

"Oh, we definitely are! I already know I'm going to miss you. I really, really enjoyed you, Christian. Thank you so much. I haven't felt this way since before my dad passed away. I actually felt alone for a good while. Thank you for making me feel love and loved. I'm serious."

You don't have to thank me for me being me, Danny. But again, I'm glad I could make you feel better. That's why I lead with my heart. It usually tells me how to handle people. I sensed you needed a hug and some love. Didn't bother me, that's just how I am. Not to mention, I needed this trip as well. It gave me a great deal of clarity on a few things I needed to deal with. So thank you! It's definitely all-good, boo."

"Cool. Glad I could help poppa. Now, you gone gimmie some or do I have to take it?

I laughed. "Boy! See? You had to mess up."

We had sex in the pool, or at least we started in the pool and ended up in the house in the living room on the floor. But he's just so passionate and good at it! I noticed with Danny, it might start off as "sex", but it *always* transitions into passionate sex. You know how some folks just fuck for the sake of it, just to get their nut off. It's nothing wrong with that, it's just not me. With whomever I decide to sleep with, there's always some kind of connection. I definitely have my moments, but even still, when I do, I have a connection with that person. Danny definitely gave passion with intimacy, which I should have known because his culture is like that.

Afterward, we laid on the floor, talking and joking a little more. I got up to use the bathroom and to put my nightshirt on. As I was coming out of the bathroom, he was sitting on the sofa chilling. He had turned the lights off and was drinking a beer, just looking into the backyard.

I sat down beside him. "Are you alright?"

"I'm perfectly fine."

I kissed his face and made my way up to the bedroom. I wanted to leave him in his moment of peace.

As I was repacking my bag, I decided to take a shower. I got out, slipped into his bathrobe and continued to pack. I heard him shuffling up the steps, grunting and groaning. I didn't even ask, I just continued to pack. He sat on the side of the bed, took off his shorts, and kicked his feet up. He watched me pack through his slightly opened eyes. I winked at him then told him to go to sleep. And he did just that. Once I packed, I crawled in the bed beside him.

The next morning, I was awakened by the smell of breakfast and fresh hot coffee. I went to the bathroom and freshened up before I bounced down the steps.

When I turned the corner to see Danny cooking ass naked in an apron, *I almost fell out!* He was jamming to his music and cooking. He was too cute and oh so comical, I couldn't stop laughing. He grabbed my hand and started dancing. I think he was more taken aback by my knowing how to salsa enough to keep up with him. The spin and the dip when I kicked up my leg sent him over.

After we ate the delicious breakfast, I went upstairs to get my bags to bring them downstairs. Of course, when I went back upstairs to actually get dressed, he grabbed me, threw me on the bed, pulled the robe off and um yeah. We got it on again. LOL!

He said he was not going to let me leave without one last romp, and baby, when I tell you he knocked the bottom *out! Whew!* I guess he figured he'd give me something to remember him by on my way home *and* at home. And *that*, he did. Hmph!

We showered together while having a very hot and steamy make-out session. Afterwards we got dressed and left for the airport. We pulled into the airport parking lot and he parked the SUV. We needed the space. Between my suitcase and his bags, it was the best option. Since I was fifteen minutes early for my check-in, we sat in the truck and had another make-out session while listening to music. I'm not gone lie; it was nice. When it was time for me to leave, he hugged me so tight. He just kept thanking me. He thanked me so much I had to make him stop thanking me. We both laughed, and I told him I'd let him know when I land and when I'm actually safe and sound in my house. Love, before I even took off, Danny texted me a dozen times to say thanks again and he couldn't wait for us to link up again.

I smiled at the messages, but I didn't respond until I got home. Once I was home and settled, I texted him, and he called right away. I told him I needed to finish unpacking and getting a few things in order and I'd call him before I went to bed. It felt so good to be alone in my place and in my own bed. You know how I am about my me-time. I stripped off my clothes and stretched across my bed and, for three hours, I listened to soft music and did absolutely nothing. It felt *so* good! I called him back about eleven o'clock and we talked for a half hour.

As I laid in my bed for the night, I thought about what I experienced. Not just Danny, but everything. I felt so good and so relaxed. I was glad to know that my Doll (Aria) was all right and finally free. She was still beautiful and still smiling. That was the ultimate for me. I had to go from DC to Abacos Island in order to find peace, and you know what Love? It was totally worth it. The times where I would cry or just wonder why everything happened. Why did it have to happen to her. Such a beautiful soul. But the fact that she came to me with my grandmother; that gave my soul such peace. Me talking to Danny all while helping him cope with his loss, gave my soul peace. Everything from this past week gave me comfort and peace. That's what it's all about for me. That's my ultimate end result. Comfort. Returned Love and Peace.

Okay Love,

I'm sleepy now. I'll talk to you later.

Love you much.

A MIDNIGHT TROIS

Love,

Oh my Love! I'm getting ready to burst at the seams! I couldn't wait to get home to tell you about Aden, the Arab guy I met at the Halloween party last year in DC. Chyle! Go get a drink heffa! This joker...! I know, I know. Ugh. I shake my head at me too sis. LOL.

Anyway, when I met Aden last year, I should have known it was gone be some shit with him. I mean when I met him, I was dressed in black from head to toe. I had on my "Aaliyah" hair (with the Chinese bangs), a black fishnet body stocking, a black leather choker, a Leather top, 9 tails whip, black thigh-high boots, with a black lace tulle skirt. I was dressed as an S&M participant. I wore a mask when I first came in, but that bitch got hot as fuck, so I took it off an hour later.

I remember seeing him when I came in because I thought he was so handsome! He didn't have on a costume and was sitting at the bar on the lower level. The way the club is set up, you walk into the lower level right at the bar. When I came in, he was sitting right in eyesight of the door. We managed to lock eyes before I made my way upstairs to the party area. He's five-foot-ten, Arab, tattoo sleeves on both arms, thick, full beard, some sexy juicy-ass lips with a little bad boy swagger and a hint of mystery. Just all kinds of sexy. Thick body about two hundred thirty-five pounds, but he was solid with some belly on him. I'm sure he saw me mouth, *Damn*, and lick my lips, before making my upstairs.

While upstairs, I ran into the fellas. We did our usual hug, laugh, crack jokes, snap on each other a little bit, and went straight to the bar for drinks. They couldn't believe my costume. You know me, I'm the more reserved one out of the group. So, for me to be dressed like that, they were *not* ready, which was what made it even funnier. Oh hunni trust me, I totally AM!

We had been upstairs for about a good hour before I took off my mask. It's bad enough the wig was making me hot, the mask was making it worse. I told the fellas I'd be back; I wanted to go put my mask in one of the lockers downstairs. I wasn't in the mood to take it outside and put it in the car.

I found an empty locker, locked my mask and wallet away, then headed back to the bar to get another drink. Before reaching the bar, I went over near the restrooms where the mirrors were. Chyle please. I was NOT about to leave my high-end mask just laying around unattended. TUH! A No Sir. So anyways, I needed to give myself a once over to make sure this old nasty piece of wig was still laid, baby. Of course it was. I just adjusted it a little. As I started moving towards the bar, I passed by *him*, not even paying attention. I ordered an Amaretto sour. When I looked up across the bar, he was staring me right in the face. I smiled at him. He got up off his stool to walk over to where I stood.

He introduced himself and pushed my hair out of my face so he could see my eyes. I peered up at him with a slight smile.

"I couldn't see your eyes. I need to see your eyes. I'm Aden." He extended his hand.

I put my hand in his. "I'm Christian, Aden, nice to meet you."

"I saw you when you walked in. I was going to find you before I left."

I chuckled. "I don't know if I'm creeped out or flattered."

"Oh, you're definitely flattered. I can tell by the way you're smiling at me."

"Really now?"

"Yes. Really. So wassup wit'chu, Christian? What are you supposed to be tonight?" He looks me up and down.

"I'm an S&M participant, and I'll let your imagination do the rest." I winked.

"Oh, shit." He laughed. "Okay for the imagination. Be careful, mine is very vivid and high def."

I laughed. "Alright for high def!" I then looked him up and down. "And what are you supposed to be, Aden?

"Oh, Aden is Aden. I was going to be super petty and dress like a Muslim with a bomb strapped to my chest, *but* that may not have gone over, too well." He smiled.

"Now that's not even funny," I said to him, while cracking up, but it really wasn't funny.

"Well I am Islamic, but still..."

"I could tell by your features that you were something. I just wasn't sure. And yes, I'm glad you didn't do that." I laughed, again.

"So, are you single, Christian? Or are you just walking around, teasing motherfuckers in this lil sexy ass get up you got on?"

"Uuummm, both!"

We both laughed.

"That's wassup. So, when can I get up under that skirt?"

"Straight to the point, huh? Hmph."

"I don't know any other way to be. I see it, I like it, I get it."

"Well, good for you. However, I do what I want, when I want. And this ain't no walk in the park, boo. You're sexy, though. I'll give you that. But you ain't that damn sexy."

"I'm saying. You're sexy, too. Let's fuck around a little bit." He places his hand on my thigh.

"Get...your hand off my thigh! And *no!* I'm going back to my friends". I leaned in close to him and told him to "Catch me later."

"My bad. Can I at least get those ten numbers?

So, I gave him my number and told him to text me. I drank my drink then went back to my friends on the upper level. We partied until about two in the morning, before we left to go get something to eat. I figured, why not? I was hungry any damn way and wasn't even remotely close to being sleepy. So hey, why not.

As we were eating, I was texting with Aden. He apologized about putting his hand on my thigh and being so straight forward.

I told him it was cool; I'm a firm believer in "mean what you say and say what you mean." He said he wanted to see me if I was up to it. I told him I didn't mind, but we weren't fucking. He laughed and said that was fine.

He really wasn't in the mood. He just wanted to see me. So, I told him I'd text him my address when I was leaving the restaurant.

Once we were done eating, we said our goodbyes, along with hugs, kisses, and whatnot's. I waited until I was home and changed my clothes before I texted him my address. He pulled up within ten minutes of my sending him my address. I was like, well damn! Once he texted me to tell me he was downstairs, I made my way down. As I was walking out the door of the garage, I saw flashing lights across the garage. It was *him*! He was sitting in a brand-new Porsche Panamera. *Baby*! You know my kitty was purring. I told you before "Mr. Spee" has one, and when he would turn the seat warmers on for me during the winter, YES GAWD! Butter baby.

Okay I'm back. LOL. As I walked over to his car; he unlocked the doors and I got in. He started smiling at me, took his blunt out of his mouth, and proceeded to ask a few questions.

"Why did I take my wig off?"

"Um, because I'm home and that bitch was *hot*."

He laughed and said he understood and that he liked my natural hair as well.

We sat in his car and talked for two hours before he pulled off. He was just so chill and so laid-back. I was feeling him for real. The conversation flowed naturally. By the time I went back into my house, it was around four in the morning.

Now, cut to the present day. We kept in touch with each other, had sex a few times; everything was going nice. Actually, everything was going well. I got a phone call from him one day asking me to help him host a party in New York. He gave me the rundown about the whole thing. It was a sex party for some of his high-end clients, which threw me for a surprise at first. But once we talked about it more, I caught it—he wanted me to facilitate. Now, Love, we both know I'm no stranger to that lifestyle, but I was just taken aback by him asking. Then again, I, thought about it, we did talk about it while having pillow talk a few nights. Just not to the extent of it being HIS clients. So, I agreed to help him, as long as we talked about everything upfront and there were no surprises later on.

However, he required, that I come dressed the way I did for Halloween. You know I'm thinking what the fuck? Why? Well he said that's what the environment was about, and he liked the look on me more than he should have. It made sense once I, thought about it. He would often ask me to put on certain things or pieces before sex or to get him in the mood. So him being in like company totally makes sense.

The weekend of the party, I hopped on the train and made my way to New York. He had it all laid out for me too. The hotel was near Times Square. He went all out. He did listen and pay attention after all.

He put me up in a very nice suite. Then when I heard him knocking on the door later on as I was unpacking, I noticed that *we* were in a very nice suite. I wasn't complaining. I just said, it is what it is, hunni. We went out for dinner later that evening. He took me to a very nice restaurant that overlooked the city. Of course, I love New York at night because of the beautiful city line and the way it lights up. I think the best part of our date was the walk down to the pier. We walked past a gay club that was jumping. It was *small as hell*, but they were in there living and enjoying life, hunni. I loved it. We stopped and partied with the fam for a few minutes before we continued on our way.

As we were walking down the boardwalk, we just talked a lot about life and what he was truly thinking and feeling at that moment. He let me in on another side of him. The private side of his heart, along with his inner most passionate, thoughts. He said something's I haven't heard anyone say since my uncle B was living. Not only what he was saying, but how he was saying it—with such conviction and passion. I'll say it again, it's amazing what we can discover about someone when we don't judge them, isn't it? Just LISTEN to them with an open mind ear and heart. The rest will flow and yield amazing results.

The day of the party, we had a great breakfast in our room, which was brought to us by room service. I knew he could eat, but *damn!* It was like he ordered everything off the top part of the menu.

After breakfast (and after we had sex), we went out to do some shopping. We met up with a few of his buddies. Come to find out, they lived in New York and would also be at the party. On our way back to the hotel to chill for a few minutes before the party, I get a text from a buddy of mine, who's a New York City police officer, telling me he was looking at me. You know my normal response, "CREEP!" LOL. I told him where I was staying and to come by when he was free. He agreed. I haven't seen Mr. Officer in so long; I was seriously excited to see him.

As time passed, Aden and I took a nap, and woke up to our growling stomachs. We went downstairs to grab something light. I wanted a salad and he wanted pizza. As we were ordering, Mr. Officer texted me to tell me he was on his way to me and his ETA was five minutes.

Once our food was ready, Mr. Officer texted me to tell me he was outside. I told Aden I was going outside to meet a friend. Although he said, "Cool," I could tell he felt some kind of way about it, which made me smirk.

Love, you know me; I greet everyone with open arms. We hugged right away. Not only did I hug him so tight, but I felt him when he exhaled. It was just so refreshing to see him. To be able to actually touch him and greet him in love. I hadn't seen him since he came back from Afghan in 2002. It was just bad timing. Every time I would come to the city, we would always miss each other, so I was more than happy to see his face. He was looking good and very happy, all of which I told him. As he and I were sitting in the lobby catching up, Aden managed to make his way over to us. I introduced him as "a friend of mine." They shook hands.

"I'll meet you upstairs," Aden said and walked off.

"I'll be right up." I could tell he was feeling some kind of way. Mr. Officer smirked; he caught it, too.

Now you know damn well he asked me who Aden was.

"Who the fuck was that clown?"

"Stop!" I laughed out loud. "He doesn't know. He's still learning me.

"You better school his ass on *who I am!*"

He had me in stitches, hunni. He had lots little smart-ass joke's. "Anyway! We're going to a party tonight, so that's why I'm in town."

"A party or a *party*?"

"Yeah. That second one." I chuckled.

"A'ight, cool. Make sure you hit me before you leave. I might need that whiff on my lip."

I smiled. "You get on my nerves. Bye!" Shaking my head, as I walk toward the elevator doors of the hotel.

He yelled, "I'm Serious! Text me later!" and pulled off.

I made my way back to our suite. I walked in and noticed his attitude. I took off my shoes then sat in the chair.

"Okay. Explain," I said to him.

"What?"

"Why you have an attitude or at least seem to be upset?"

He chuckled. "How you gone just call me out though?"

"Just explain."

"I don't know what came over me. I felt some kind of way when I saw you hug him like that. You don't hug me like that."

"You're right because I see you more than I see him. I haven't seen him in years. He's a very good friend of mine. I will always greet him that way if I need to."

"Okay, I see. I don't know. The shit just shook me a little bit."

"I could tell, and so could he."

"Damn. My bad."

"It's cool. Let me just inform you of one thing. I'm me. I'm going to always be me. You and I don't have labels. Even if we did, I'd tell you the same thing. So, I need for you to check your insecurities at the door when it comes to me, sugga. I'm not *that* person. We've talked about this before. So, chill."

"You're right."

"Now, I need to eat and prep."

"Forgive me. We good?"

"Of course."

After I ate my salad, I showered. Since we had a little time to kill, we lollygagged around the room for a bit. We talked about the whole situation and why he felt that way.

He told me flat out, "I have insecurity issues."

"I get it, but I'm going to help you work on that. We enjoy each other's company, so let's not ruin it with BS."

Again, he agreed.

As I was putting on my body stocking, he was looking at me, smiling.

"What are you smiling at?"

"You. Just admiring the view. That's all."

#Pause Okay Love. I had to sidetrack for a second here. What the fuck is it with these dudes and the whole drag thing. They fake like they don't like fem queens or drag queens etc., but baby, they go *in*! If you are put together right, they *love* that shit. I've seen it a number of times. I just look laugh and shake my head. Like yeah, okay. I see you with the shit's as well. *#Continue*

"Oh, okay," I told him. "I'll change at the party." I am *not* about to walk out this hotel in this get up." I laughed. "Ain't no telling who I'll bump into."

We both laughed, as he nodded.

"It's cool because we have a driver."

"Nope, I'm good." I laughed and continued dressing.

In the car, as we were riding through the city, I couldn't help but admire the lights and views again. I mean, it's New York City, how could you not? Our ride was only about twenty minutes from our hotel, but because of traffic and road construction, it took a little longer. As we pulled up to the party site, it looked like what appeared to be an abandoned building.

I looked at him. "What the hell?"

He laughed at me and said it wasn't. Of course, I should have known otherwise. That's how the meatpacking district is in New York.

We walked into the building, and it was immaculate. Pure genius the way it was set up.

From the outside, it was nothing more than an old abandoned brick building, with lots of windows. As we proceeded inside, I was taken aback because it was absolutely gorgeous. Exposed brick walls with crystal chandeliers lighting the way to the other hallways. I would not have expected any of it. The marble floors, oriental rugs... the works, hunni. It was definitely "Snobby" approved. I literally laughed out loud in *Aw*.

We made our way upstairs to the party location, which was a loft-style apartment, he stopped me in the hallway.

"Don't be afraid of what you might see."

I tilted my head. "I'm good... Unless there is something you're not telling me."

Then, the flood gates opened. "You will be the only one dressed this way," he said.

Even, though it didn't bother me because I was used to that as well, but something didn't feel right. So, I sat down on the steps and made him tell me *everything.*

"Okay. It's a room full of Big Money Fellas, who wants to be dominated by you and a few others."

Now this was making more sense. "Whatever," I said, "you gone pay the fuck down for this shit. This is *definitely* extra." He thanked me and agreed. "Mmhhmm, let's go."

When we went into the unit—it, too, was gorge—we were greeted by the owners and one of the hostesses, Asia. After Aden introduced me to everyone, Asia escorted me to the room where I was to change and finish my prep. I went in the room, put my bags down, then I told Asia to show me around so I could get familiar with the premises. She was more than happy to do so (as Aden had already informed her that I may want to do that anyway). I guess he was paying attention.

While walking around, I noticed two rooms with locked doors. I didn't think anything of it. It just meant that those rooms were off limits to guests. As we were finishing up the tour, Asia and I were walking down the steps where we were greeted by the other property owner, Mandel.

Love let me tell you... Umph, he was *fine as fuck!* I was hoping he would be one who wanted me all, to himself. No Lie, I was thinking, *Fuck, Aden. Mandel finna get this goddamn work!* Bitch, he was fine as frog hair! Baby listen...whew! I'm getting riled up again just thinking about that man. My God!

I extended my hand to shake his.

"Oh no, Christian, we hug around here. You're in my home so you're able to be trusted."

His big, strong ass hugged me and *bitch, I was over!* Baby, the way my culo was smoking! Goodness! He was about six-foot-three, two hundred thirty-five pounds, with solid football frame. He had a full beard and pretty chocolate skin. He smelled *so* good. You already know I was ready to straddle his ass like a seahorse and ride until I was seasick. He took me by the hand, then proceeded to show me around.

He showed me where the deejay would be set up, and then he took me to the area where the food and beverages were going to be. I suggested he set up the bartenders at two separate ends of the room. That way, there wouldn't be, too much congestion on one side. We all know alcohol is a hot button. He agreed, then hugged me again. Baby. I Just...HMPH. SMOKING.

We walked into the kitchen, where we sat and chatted a little more. Just to get to know each other a little better. He was nice and easy to talk to; his simple deep voice, his sexy lips, his sexy shape up, those brown eyes and, did I mention, how good he smelled? Oh.

Ok. LOL! After about 45 minutes of convo, I looked at my watch and told him I needed to finish getting ready.

"Aden told me you were a showstopper." He said with that thick Caribbean accent as he smiled at me.

"I don't know about all of that; however, I make it do what it do for me, but that's about it. Although, I *can be* a showstopper if I want, too." As I winked at him.

He smiled. "I just bet you can."

My dumb ass was so busy smiling and flirting, girl I tripped up the steps. OOP! I played it off like I was taking off my shoe. HA!

Anyway, I went in the room to change into my little all black number. As I was pulling up my skirt, Aden walked in to see if I needed anything and to bring me a bottle of water.

He saw me and said, "Oh shit," but I wasn't really paying him any attention.

I turned around to get my hair out of the bag, when this fool was standing behind me, rubbing his dick. If you could have seen my face.

"MF. Not right now!"

"Come on. You know that shit be turning me on. I just need like thirty pumps."

"Boy, get'cho ass on somewhere!"

"A'ight. Fifty pumps and no foreplay."

I laughed. "Aden! Bye!"

"My dick hard, though!"

"Stop rubbing it, you fool! You better go pee or something. Besides, his guests are arriving. So, no."

"Just French kiss it a lil bit for me."

"BYE!"

And I closed the door to the bathroom, so I could finish getting ready. As I was putting on my make-up, I heard him curse again.

"Aw. Lord, what now?" I went out to check on him. He had gotten deodorant on his black shirt. You know how that goes when you put on deodorant, too early? Yeah, that mess. "Calm down," I told him. It really wasn't that serious.

We switched shirts. Even, though I'm slightly bigger than he is, it still worked. I took his shirt and added a few slits in it across the front and made that shit work—and it did, too. He was blown that I had cut up his shirt, but he got over it. He ain't really have a choice.

I went back into the bathroom to finish my face and hair. I gave myself one final look, then we left the room.

As we were walking towards the steps, everybody stopped and turned. I don't like that kind of attention, so I stopped walking. "What?" I asked.

They all burst out laughing and a few people said, "You look Fucking Great!"

Mandel applauded me and whistled, which embarrassed me even more. It was cute, though. I'm not gone even lie; it did make me turn up. LOL. I motioned for Aden to go in front of me, so I could glide down the steps alone. I meeaannn might as well rick with it right? LOL. Oh, hunni, they loved it. Once I reached the bottom of the steps, Mandel took my hand, then went to introduce me to a few of his buddies. Very handsome, wealthy men of all ethnicities. They were all dressed in black T-shirts and black pants, looking like Mob goons. I chuckled under my breath.

I pulled Aden to the side. "Are they going to change clothes, or stay blacked out?"

"They will, once they are given the green light."

I said, "Okay," and walked away.

It was about a quarter to eleven; I was making my rounds, ensuring everything and everyone was alright. That's when Aden walked over to me, grabbed my hand, and told me to follow him. We went in the kitchen, where I sat down on the stool.

"What's up?"

"It's about to get live."

I laughed. "I'm sure I can handle it."

"I just want to make sure you're cool."

"Yes. This is not my first party; we already discussed this." I don't know why he was acting so weird. "Is that it? I need to get back to the floor and do what I'm being paid to do."

The music blared, the lights flickered and then lowered.

"What the fuck is that?" I asked him.

He laughed. "That's what I was waiting on. They should all be naked now."

I laughed. "Oohhhh..." That's what you were talking about. Cool".

Love, you know my nosey ass was ready to see what Mandel had to offer. I ran out that kitchen and around that corner so damn fast; I left Aden's ass sitting right there by himself. Baby I was G.O.N.E!

As I was coming around the corner, I bumped into Asia, who told me to touch up my lipstick and go kick ass. I did just that. I went to the bathroom, did a quick touch-up, fluffed my hair, and headed toward the main floor. Mandel grabbed me by the hand to escort me to the front so I could give my little speech. It was nothing major. I just introduce myself, told them the rules, introduced the host, and told them to enjoy. The male to female ratio was uneven; again, not that it shocked me, but it made me pay even more attention to detail. Also, everyone was either naked or in their underclothes. As I stepped down from the deejay stand, Mandel escorted me to the section of the party area behind a curtain. I didn't say anything, I just went with it.

There was an S&M area that consisted of sex swings, toys, lubes and various other sextras. That room was lit up with a red light and candles. Not only did it set the mood, it smelled good. You know how certain fragrances can stimulate the mind and body. As I inhaled and exhaled, a few of the fellas started filing into the room.

Mandel whispered into my ear, "It's all about you now, Sir Christian."

I knew what the hell that meant. It was time for me to switch hats and make it do what it do hunni. I made them all line up and strip. I went down the line to look at them one by one, while twirling handcuffs around my fingers. As the train from my black skirt flowed behind me ever so elegantly; I made sure each and every one of the fellas caught a whiff of my essence; while I touched and teased them so effortlessly.

I asked each of them what they wanted from me. They all said the same thing—"Whatever you will have me to do Mr. EssXtcy". They were open for anything. So, I tested them to see. I went and sat in the chair in front of them. The chair was perfectly placed in front of the alter. As I took my seat, I made two of them make out with each other, I made the other two perform oral on each other, and I made Mandel come over to me and massage my feet and kiss my legs until I told him to stop. This went on for about two minutes, and I made them all stop and line up again. By now, all their dicks were rock hard and, I must admit, once the blood was flowing, it was very impressive lineup.

I figured I'd take it up one more notch before I dismissed them. I got up, reached in the bag, grabbed the blindfolds, proceeded to blind fold them, and made them lock their hands behind their heads. I grabbed the leather paddle from the alter, I lubed up one hand, and I kissed each one on the lips as I massaged their balls while giving them slight hand jobs, all while spanking an ass cheek. Oh no, it's not as complicated as it sounds. All I did was alternate. Kiss, ass smack, ball rub, ass smack, dick massage, kiss again. I did this to each of them for one minute a piece. I didn't want to give them too much. I didn't want to make them cum just yet. Another words, I was "edging" them.

By the time I got to Mandel, I put in overtime for him. Now you know I was gone make sure he was good. He's the host and I was attracted to him. I made his knees buckle a little bit. Hey, it is what it is, remember? *wink* Once I was done, I dismissed them and told them to go find partners and I'd be out to check on them in a few minutes. Chyle, I'm not gone lie, I was not in the mood to go any further than that. I needed a drink and some music to really get me in *that* mind frame. So, I decided to go out and mingle with the others since I sent them on their way. When I walked out the backroom, Aden was having a conversation on the other side of the room, with a very attractive young lady. I didn't see her come in at all. But then again, I was preoccupied a number of times.

I could tell by their body language there was some flirting going on and they were into each other, which was fine by me. Like I said, we weren't a couple and I wanted some of Mandel anyway. Go on and do you papa.

Speaking of Mandel, I saw him watching me as I made my rounds to check on everyone. As I locked eyes with him, he gave me the nod, and we both know what that means. Um yeah, I walked over to him, he grabbed my hand as we walked up the stairs. I looked over and Aden was still talking to the young lady. Mandel and I went into the same room where I changed my clothes. We sat down on the bed; he grabbed my hand and kissed the back of it.

"Thank you," he said. "Thank you for being a good sport and for not judging me and my friends."

I smiled. "I don't do that, and all is well."

We sat and talked in that room for about an hour. We just talked and laughed. He was so sweet. He laughed at me because I kept looking at his dick. I couldn't help it. Even, though he wore speedos, baby, I could see that print. He had *meat. Whew!*

As Mandel and I were talking, guess who decided to walk in the room looking for me? Yup! He sure did. The look on his face was priceless. Mandel and I were facing each other when Aden walked in. You know how I always sit on my leg.

Mandel turned around to face him. "What's up?" he asked Aden. "Shit. What y'all up to?"

"We're talking. So, if you don't need anything, feel free to exit."

"Yes, sir," he said, grabbing his cell phone charger.

As Aden walked out the room, he looked at me with that "*What the fuck are you in here doing*" look on his face. Hunni, I wanted to crack up laughing. All I could think was "Excuse me sir, but wasn't you just all up in some heffa's face?

I smiled. "I'll be down in a few—"

"Maybe," Mandel interjected, without looking at Aden.

Aden closed that door with the quickness.

I giggled.

"I think your buddy is a little pissed, but he'll be fine," said Mandel.

"I think you're right."

"I wanna kiss those lips.'

"Then do it."

He leaned in to kiss me. His lips were so full and soft, on top of him smelling so heavenly. Of course, he wanted more than a kiss. I was rather hesitant at first, so I took the skirt part off and we talked a little more—until I was comfortable with him enough to go that far. Not that I wasn't turned on by him, because Lord knows I was, I just wasn't there yet. You know I gotta be warmed up unless I'm already ready. So, we laid back on the bed and talked for a few more minutes. At least until he pulled off the rest of my clothes and went to *work*. That man can kiss and do things with his mouth! The funny part is, after sex, and I was sitting on top of Mandel, and guess who walked in again? I turned to look at the door and the look on his face was as if he had just saw a ghost. As soon as I looked back down at Mandel, he sat up and started kissing me on the chest.

"Get out," he told Aden, "We're not done yet." All I could think was "OOP! BITCH! Well, alright now." Aden turned and kind of stormed out the room. The funny part, I wasn't even completely naked. I still had on my body stocking, wig and boots.

I sat on top of Mandel and we talked more while kissing in between.

We did that for about another hour, then we got ourselves together and headed back to the party. As we walked down the steps, he caressed the small of my back, skirting around my waist. I was thinking, *Aww, hell!* ...Exactly!

I went into the kitchen for something to drink and Mandel went to talk to his buddy. Two minutes later, he came into the kitchen as I was eating a strawberry. He smiled at me and walked over to me and ate the other end of the strawberry right from my lips, which led to another kiss.

Again, Aden was watching. By now, he was fuming. Mind you, he was still entertaining ol' girl. The kitchen had an opening over the sink, so I could see clean across the room with no problem and vice versa. All I could think was, *"This big head fuckka gone leave me at this damn party"* (smh). I played around for about another 30 minutes before I was actually ready to go.

I made sure the other fellas all found their partners and did what I told them to do. One of them wanted me to dominate him while he was fucking the other chick that was in the back room. Basically, tell him what to do, and before he cum's, finger pop him. He liked the explosive orgasm. I ain't mad at the player. He did that. After I was done with him, I made the rest of my rounds then cleaned up a little.

By this time it was about a quarter to three. I told Aden; I was going to go back to the hotel because I was over it. I wrapped up with Mandel, who wanted more kisses and quality time before I left (which was fine with me). He cashed me out, then called me a driver. Anyway, while I was changing my clothes, I turned my phone back on to check my messages. Mr. Officer had texted me and said he was waiting on me. He was working the overnight shift. Well since I wanted some of him anyway, I responded that I was actually on my way back to the hotel and he could meet me if he wanted to. Before I left I made sure Aden knew I was actually gone this time. Of course he was fine because he was still entertaining little "Miss Perky Titt's". I found Mandel and told him I was fully ready exit now, if that was okay with him. He said it was fine. He wanted my contact information. I agreed, then he called his driver to take me back to my hotel.

I told Aden I was leaving; I don't know why he thought that meant he had to leave as well. I told him he didn't have to. Then Mandel jumped in and told him he needed him to stay and help with the end process (whatever that means). Mandel walked me down to the lobby, kissed my forehead, hugged me, then let me go.

He told me to text him when I got back to my room. Again, I agreed. While riding back to the hotel, I texted Mr. Officer that I would text him when I was in my room.

I needed to shower and get the smell of Mandel's fine ass off me. Mr. Officer already told me he wanted some "Monkey Stump" as he put it. LOL! Like who even says that? Chyle, I ran through that lobby so damn fast; I was a streak of light. Literally after my shower, my cell phone vibrated. It was Mr. Officer asking for my room number. I gave it to him as I was spraying on my "good stuff".

Love, no sooner than I was putting on my robe he was knocking on that door. Not a moment to far after I opened that door, he was taking off my robe. The way he grabbed my body and snatched that damn robe off... baby, I was over, and my legs were *up, up, and away!* His sexy voice, with that "New Yawk" accent had me gone. That little scruffy faced otter, with his thick pink dick had me in ecstasy. As he were having sex, he was saying things like how much he'd missed me and to never make him wait this long again. All kinds of shit. It was hot until he asked, "Whose is it?"

I politely told him, "Depending on how much you offer, it could be yours." That just made him fuck me even harder because I was being a smart ass. I liked it though! Bitch don't judge me! LOL!

We went at it for an hour. Once we were done, we laid in my bed and laughed and talked about life. You know, the regular intimate after-sex talk BS. He got up to shower, I slid my robe on when I heard a buzzing sound. I looked over on the nightstand, it was his phone. Now you know my nosy ass was gone look at it. It was his ex-wife, telling him she will meet him in the morning with their son. Love, if you could have seen my face. I didn't even know he had a son. Well, I didn't know he went through with it. He talked about it but wasn't 100 percent sure. I read it but I didn't unseal my lips to him. He's the type to always tell me the truth whether I wanna know or not.

I just figured he'll tell me later or when he's ready. I know him well enough to know he'll mention it when he's ready. When he came out the bathroom, I was standing by the window, just enjoying the view of the city lights. He came over to me, kissed me, grabbed a water out the fridge, and proceeded to get dressed. I went to the sink to wash my face and put my hair back up, when I heard my phone going off. When I looked at the text, it was Aden telling me he was on his way back. I just responded, *Okay*.

"That must be old boy. Tell his soft ass he can come back now, but you smell like my *dick and you prolly pregnant!*"

I laughed at him and told him to get out. He can be *such* a jerk, but he's a sweetheart when he wants to be.

As Mr. Officer and I were getting on the elevator, he made me get on in-front of him. We had one hell of a make out session all the way to the lobby. Ironically enough, nobody got on. Although he was ready to get off again. TUH! Mind you, I still had my robe on. He politely threw my leg around his waist and went in. That mini kissing session was HOT AS FUCK! Yes, I was turned on all over again. HMPH. As the elevator neared the 1st floor, I got myself together and he adjusted himself (as I laughed), we got off the elevator, he turned to hug me and then he kissed my neck on the sly. I laughed and pushed him off me. Guess who was standing in the door of the lobby watching? All I could was shake my head, Love. Again, he had an attitude and I could tell. When Mr. Officer saw him, he smirked again. Then this fool starts walking away, then turns to me and yells across the lobby, "Thanks again, Wet-Wet. Next time don't wait so long. Ima keep it on my top lip. *Goodnight!*"

It was five-thirty in the morning and his ass was being messy... on purpose.

I laughed. "Skip yo' lil' ass up outta here Negro!"

As Aden and I were riding the elevator back up to our room, he didn't have much to say except that he was tired and ready to go home. I agreed. When we got to the room, he took his clothes off and hopped in the shower. While he was showering, I cleaned up my side of the room. I made sure all my things were packed up and ready to go. We were leaving later that evening anyway. When I was done packing, as I was plugging my phone into the charger, Aden came out the bathroom.

"So, are we gone talk about tonight or what?"

"Maybe once I get out the shower and I'm in the mood, we sure can."

"Oh Okay. So, it's all about you now?"

"If you want me to talk to you, you need to let me shower and gather my thoughts.

He grunts and groans like a child. "A'ight, fine."

I went to get in the shower and I politely took my damn time. I turned my music on low and enjoyed myself. Of course, when I got out the shower, his ass was asleep, which I kind of figured he would be. His eyes were red and he was rubbing them. I kissed his face, climbed in my bed, and went to sleep. Once I finally dozed off it was about 6:00a.m., only to be awakened by my phone at 10:00 a.m. Oddly enough, I felt like I was rested. When I turned over to see if Aden was still asleep, he was looking at me. I got up out of my bed, went over to his bed and laid beside him. He kissed my shoulder, then I mounted him.

"So, what do you want to talk about?"

"Why the fuck did you carry me like that? Twice."

"Twice?"

"Christian, stop fucking playing."

"I need for you to... Well, first adjust your dick. Your morning wood is poking. Secondly, explain the twice thing."

He laughed. "Well, shit! You da one that got on top!" He looked up at me. "*Yes, twice!* Once with Mandel and then with the cop dude."

"If memory serves me correct, she was five-seven, long flowing hair with a Farrah Fawcett blowout, caramel complexed skin, a gorgeous smile, pretty legs, perfect tits and was in your face most of the time. Not to mention I saw her when she was rubbing your beard and when she grabbed your dick. So, do you care to try again?"

"*Damn! Oh, shit!* You saw all of that!? *Goddamn!*"

"Exactly. Don't try me. You know better. You've been around me long enough to know better."

"Fuck! You right. And since you're sitting there, rub my balls for me."

I fell out laughing. "No! And you need to cut the shit. I asked you what the fuck we were doing. We don't have labels, so how can you get up*set? I didn't even stunt"Miss. Farrah" that was all over you. Matter of fact, I was watching you* to see what your reaction was going to be. You were loving every bit of it!" I laughed.

"Damn! Who's the creep now? Shit! Yeah, you right. We don't have labels."

"Exactly. So why are you so upset? Hell, I didn't fuck nobody in your face. You just so happened to walk in on me and Mandel. We didn't have sex until almost an hour or two later."

"What about cop dude?"

I smiled. "Wouldn't you like to know."

"Yes! You know what? Nah. Don't tell me."

"I wasn't."

"We gone fuck or nah? I mean, you already in position. Go ahead and slide it in and stop bull'shittin'."

So, um, yeah. We had sex. He was right. I was in position already. The sex was actually pretty good this time. I guess he was feeling some kind of way. Like he needed to prove himself. I wasn't mad, but he ain't *never* performed like that the whole time we've been kick'n it. *You go, boy.* No, I didn't tell him that. Are you kidding me?! He's already cocky as fuck. LOL. Nah.

After we were done, we ate breakfast and chilled in the room until it was time to go. I sent a few more text messages to Mr. Officer, chatted with Mandel for a few, made Aden's toes curl again, then we packed up and headed back to DC. Before we left, we stopped and got some pizza from one of his favorite spots. I had to go to the famous "Kat'z Deli" for my mother.

Catch this gag; Aden stayed at my place for a whole ass week. He politely made himself comfortable. By Wednesday, I asked him what the deal was. He said he just needed a break. When I asked from what, he said just from everything. I didn't go any further.

We hung out a couple days during the week and relaxed at home. He would drop me off at work and pick me up in the evenings.

While I was gone during the day, he would handle his business then be done by the time I was off work. I mean, it worked for about a week, then I told him he needed to go home. I needed my place back. He could come back in a few days. He agreed; and said he totally understood. Not that it was up for discussion, but okay. He went home for a whole three days before he was back looking me in my face. I think he was lonely and just wanted to be around someone. At least that's how it seemed to me. I didn't mind, I just needed my "me" time. I made that very clear to him. Which he also understood.

He and I still talk and hang out, but he moved to New Jersey, so I only see him when I go up there. He doesn't even come to DC anymore. I didn't ask him what happened, I just rolled with it. Some shit is just better left unknown. He'll send for me when he wants to see me, which I told him don't mind, as long as I'm free. We hang out in the city while just enjoying each other. He told me recently that he finally gets it. The whole "me time" thing and wanting to do whatever, whenever thing. We had a long talk about the party and what was really good with us. He seems more open and optimistic since he's been living in New Jersey. His growth is amazing. I told him how proud of him I was and how much I missed him. We decided to kick it up a notch and stay in contact a little more.

I went over to visit Mandel in Dubai a few times. I'll tell you about that later. Baaaybeeey! HMPH. Alright now.

Mr. Officer? Of course, I still talk to his little crazy ass. I've spent time in New York with him a few times after that weekend as well. We talk on a weekly basis now.

Okay, Love, I've gotta go now. My dinner guests are arriving. I'll keep you posted on Mr. Officer and Mandel. Girl he a *Hot mess!*.. But I Love his little ass. He's definitely good peoples. But that Mandel... "Big Daddy Mandingo". #SWOON

Anyways,

I'll talk to you later boo.

Love you much.

"NOT DURING WORK HOURS"

Love!

So okay, remember old boy I had been telling you about for the last two months? Yeah, well, shit popped off today. I had to come home and make me a cocktail. Shit, I'm lying, I drank a whole bottle. *Girl!* Not Marcus, Vincent. The Vincent with the big, thick bodied furry face. I'm about to tell you. Get you some wine and get ready. He got me, girl. HE GOT ME!

So, remember I was training at work with the other vets, right? Okay, remember I was telling you about Vince and how we often flirt with each other throughout the day? Well, come to find out, he was one of the other fellas who enrolled in the late training classes. It was hilarious when he saw me in the class. His whole face lit up. I was shocked he came into the aerobics class, to be honest. But in his defense, it was kick boxing aerobics, so hey.

When he joined us, we were in mid-session, so we were dancing already. Of course, he came in and stood beside me because I was in the back. I was only in the back because the women were in front and shorter than me. Besides, I could cut up in the back and not distract anybody. Our instructor was a retired Navy seal and he was rockin'! He knows Janet is my QUEEN so he would have special mixes for me to keep me interested. You know me hunni, once I'm bored, my ass is gone. We had a great class and called it a day.

So, as we were in the locker room, I was taking off my sneakers when I realized I still had my head band on. I walked over to the mirror to take it off the proper way. Last time, I was being fast and tried to snatch it off and damn near pulled my hair out. A hot mess (smh). This is where the GAG begins. Now remember, Vince and I have always flirted with each other since day one, but I just never paid him any attention. Not to *that* extent. You know how I am with these dudes. They be funny acting and mad stink at times, so I play them to the left (for the most part). When I was getting my bag out the locker, Vincent walked by me wearing a towel. Now you know damn well I saw him without even looking in his direction (yes, I'm that good). Ha!

I took my clothes off and grabbed my towel and shower shoes. As I was making my way down to the showers, I was looking to see which one was available. We had a full class so not very many showers up front were free. I just so happened to look up, and there was a shower directly in front of me that was empty. Go figure; it was the one next to him.

He stuck his big ass head out to tell me "Aye! You can use this one. It's Empty."

I smiled and said, "Thank you."

As I walked past his shower, he pulled back the curtain. "What kind of soap you got? I'm out."

Now Love, you know damn well this was click bait right?

So, I stopped. "I don't have body wash; I have my Bronner's bar today."

"dayum. That expensive ass soap. Well, let me hold it then." He smiled.

"I'm not given you my bar before I use it! GROSS!"

"Then hurry up and use it so I can use it," he said, while rubbing his body and smiling.

"Man, whateva. I'll let you know when I'm done."

I got in the shower. I had my little shower speaker with me, so my music was on and I was good. I didn't even realize how long I was in the shower. Love, why did he walk his box-head-ass down to my shower, *ass naked*, and pulled back my shower curtain? Bitch! I was done!

"Unhunh! What do you want?"

"Christian, why you playing?! Let me get that!"

"Boy, here!" I shoved the bar at him. "And close my damn curtain back!"

He snatched the curtain back open, then said, "See? You can't even bring it to me because your thick ass in here jammin' and dancin' and shit!"

I laughed. "Man, take this soap and be gone!"

"You betta stop playing with me before I fuck the shit outta you in here, *Oz* style."

"*Oz*? Oooh shit! Okay, you gotta stop playing now. I'm starting to get turned on. For real, for real. No bullshit!" I closed my curtain back. I heard him shout while he was walking away,

"I'm not fuckin' playing!"

"Oh my God!" I pulled back the shower curtain and poked my head out. "Why are you so loud?"

He turned to look at me, then said, "Ain't nobody in here, but us. I already checked. He smiled then bit his bottom lip.

I chuckled. "Oh I just bet you did," I said with a sarcastic tone.

"I did! I could get in there with you right now, fuck the dog shit outta you, and nobody would know."

I laughed. "VINCENT! Go get in the shower! Bye!" I snatched the curtain closed.

"That's a'ight. I'ma get that ass. Thanks for the soap though," he said, walking away.

I carried on with my shower. My heart was beating so damn fast! I think because I was turned the fuck on by his simple ass. You know that aggressive shit turns me on. Hmph! I rinsed off with the quickness. I said to myself, *Nope, I am not giving this fool the opportunity to get my ass caught up at work.* The sad part is, he wasn't lying. That locker room on that side of the building, is in the basement and secluded. So once folks leave, they can't hear shit back in that part of the building.

I went to put my clothes on. Now mind you, he was nowhere

on my end. No sooner than I pulled up my underwear and they snapped on my waist; his wide-back-ass came around the corner.

"Oh, shit! Those are nice. Let me take'em back off real quick. Won't nobody know?"

I chuckled. "Vince, carry your ass on." Love, I looked down and this boy was rubbing his damn meat. Like for real, I couldn't take my eyes off it. "And stop rubbing your dick! Shit! It's nice though. Dayum it's nice. But still! Stop!"

He burst out laughing. "You like this meat. Stop playing and gimmie some. Come handle it for me."

"I'm going upstairs sir."

I wanted to give his ass that monkey stomp so bad! LMAO! But not at work! After I got dressed, I grabbed my bag out the locker and was on my way back upstairs. It was almost time for me to go home so I wasn't tripping.

Anyway, the next day, I came to work to find someone had brought me lunch and left it on my desk with a note that read: *Please drop the soap one time for me.* I hollered! I knew it was his simple ass! I was getting ready to throw the note away when I looked at it again, to see his number was on the bottom of it. He told me to text him before the next class so he wouldn't be late again. The next class was the coming Friday.

Now, cut to Friday at 1:30 p.m. I texted his simple ass to tell him I was on my way down to the class. He responded, saying he was in the restroom and he'd be right down. I went down to the locker room, got dressed and was ready to go. He walked in laughing talking shit (as usual), I burst out laughing and told him not to start. He was eye balling me in my purple and black camo compression pants. Yes, they were fitting right too.

Yes, I wore them on purpose *wink*. We had another great class. It was really good. My body was used to it now. Once my muscle memory kicked in, I was kick'n ass! So, we were in the back of the class again working out. One of the moves, you do a spin and clap. That joker managed to spin, slap my ass in the process; then gonna say, "Oooh! No panties". I laughed because I had on a jockstrap actually. I burst out laughing and punched him in the arm (not that he felt it). Yes, the flirtation was REAL.

We had to stop playing around because the trainer was watching us. The trainer is handsome too, but he looks bat-shit crazy. We don't fuck with him like that. That joker been done jumped out the ceiling on us. Girl, I'm serious. He's cool, but I don't take him too far. He's great eye candy. Which is why so many women take the class as well. He has an ass that won't wait, accompanied by some sexy thick legs and thighs. That bald head fucker is *nice! WHEW!* I got sidetracked. Sorry. But yeah, we had a good class. LOL.

After class, I had to chill for five minutes before I went to the locker room. It was already the end of the day, so I wasn't too pressed to hurry up. Hell, the class ended at three o'clock. I leave at three-thirty, so I was fine. Vince sat beside me on the floor in the back of the studio and we watched the other class for a few minutes. We chatted for a few then jumped up to head to the showers.

Love, all I can do is shake my head. As we made our way back to the locker room. It was my fault for the slow walk. My legs were over it. I was sore! I told him I was going to sit in the sauna for a few, then I'd get in the shower. I wasn't telling him that so that he'd join me, I was just saying in general because we were walking, talking, and laughing. I took my clothes off, grabbed my towel and made my way to the sauna. How about this joker was already sitting in there? I didn't even see his chunky ass walk past me or through the area. He's already naked, sitting there, grinning. I laughed, shook my head, then I sat down on the upper ledge first and laid down. We talked and laughed a little more. Forty-five minutes later, we hit the showers.

I went back to my locker to get my body wash, which I brought on purpose this time, and my shower speaker. I switched towels and made my way to that same shower stall from last week. Vincent was behind me and went to the same shower he was in before as well. I turned on my music, dropped my towel and climbed right on in. It was cute until... somebody decided to join me in my shower. I was washing my face when he climbed in and kissed my neck. At first, I was startled, but then I burst out laughing.

"I told you I'ma get that ass."

"Boy, if you don't carry your ass on! And stop kissing my damn neck."

"I know it's your spot. You told me without telling." He kissed my neck again.

"No I didn't; you're just very intuitive."

"That, too," he said, grinding on my ass.

"You betta quit! I told you I was already feeling some kind of way."

"Then give in and stop bull-shittin'. You feel that grown man meat."

I turned around and faced him. "And what if I don't?"

"I'ma take it. Like this..."

Baby! The way his strong, wide, back black ass threw my leg up in that shower and slipped it in! *Bitch! Ovah! Baby listen!* When I tell you, he rocked the fuck out of me in that damn shower... And that's what I get! Vince hoisted my big ass up in the shower and bounced me off his dick like a got dayum puppet master! Then, he had the nerve to make me get loud on purpose. He wanted me to make noise; and I damn sure did. I made him put me down though. I was trying to run before he was done, and he was not having it. He fucked the breaks off me in that damn locker room. He had me on the floor, on the benches; we went back in the sauna and finished.

He laughed because when we were done, I got back in the shower.

I told him, "You had me all on the floor. Ew!"

"You're right," he said and got in the shower with me.

He was trying to low-key start back up again

"No, I'm going home."

"Can I go too?"

"You sure can. Just not right now though. Text me later."

"A'ight, bet."

We kissed, then I got dressed. We kissed again before I left the locker room. On my ride home, I had to check myself. Even though he and I don't work together, we are still in the same building. I don't do the whole inter-office relationship crap. Too many issues. I've seen it blow up, too many times. He texted me about 7:30 p.m. to get my address. I hesitated to give it to him at first, but then I thought about it and figured I'd talk to his ass when he got here. I cleaned up and made sure I was smelling good and all that good stuff. You know how I do.

He texted me when he was in the lobby and I buzzed him up. His eyes lit up when he walked in my apartment.

"So, this is the infamous Snobby Manor, huh? Very Nice!"

"I don't know about the infamous part but thank you."

He kept walking and looking around. I laughed. "There aren't any cameras in here. You're safe."

He laughed. "Please, I'm not even worried about that. You're popular, but you ain't that kind of popular."

"I beg your pardon! I'ma motherfuckin' celebrity slim!"

He laughed. "You sure are, but privacy is your thing. So I ain't even worried."

"You're right! And I'm glad you brought that up. I need for you not to act weird later on. I'm sure you won't, but we still need to talk about it."

"How so?"

"Just because I finally gave in to you and your sex desires, doesn't mean you have rights, or you own anything."

"Oh...nah, never."

"I'm just making sure we're clear. That's all. You know I'm not beyond looking at you like you're stupid and walking away. Won't even react or respond"

"I mean I can't make that promise, if you keep throwing those legs up like that. But shit, it's all-good. It's definitely *all-good!*"

"Mmhhmm. Now, come on. I wanna show you something." I winked.

He got excited like a kid in a goddamn candy store. "Now that's what the fuck I'm talkin' 'bout!"

He started taking his clothes off before he even got to the bedroom. Excited much? We had old nasty, raunchy-ass sex too. He wasn't lying when he said *Oz* style. You know I like my hair pulled and being choked. It was hella "Wild N Loud". There was hair pulling, growling, smacking, cursing, music, jungle noises and straight Hardcore FUCKING. Oh baby we did that! I must admit though, I didn't expect him to stay the night, but he did. Probably because we went for a few rounds. After a while, I made his ass get the fuck off me!

He wanted another round in the morning, but I was not in the mood. I pulled out the coconut oil on his ass. I hit that fool with the Kung-Fu grip and BOOM! He was good.

So okay, cut to present day. I moved to a different building and don't really see him that often. We would speak in passing, but neither of us really had time to get it in or talk. Between my being on travel and him being on travel, we were literally passing each other in the night (so to speak). Anyway, me and my girls were at dinner at the Harbor. Guess who the hell saw me before I saw him? He came right over to the table to make sure I saw him and spoke.

You already know those two had jokes. I told them later who he was. As the night went on, we laughed and joked about it. Again, they had more jokes. It was definitely comical to be honest. He gave NO FUCKS when he walked up to me hunni.

When we were done with our time together, I walked my ladies to their car before I made my way back to the side where I told my driver I'd meet him. By the time I was done with them, I got a text. It read: *I wanted to take you in that bathroom and fuck you silly one more time.* I laughed and responded with: *Then you should have said something.* He laughed-out-loud and told me: *Meet me by the Ferris wheel.* Which was fine with me because I actually wanted some ice cream. So since the ice cream booth was right there, I didn't mind meeting him. We talked, and he offered to take me home. I dismissed my driver and he brought me home and we fucked right in the garage. I mounted him the same way I used to mount B in his truck. I forgot how good he could kiss and how amazing his stroke was. *Whew lawd!* After the fuck was done, we just kissed for about a good 30 minutes off and on. AH! His kisses are just perfect. I LOVE when a fat boy knows how to kiss hunni. It just set's my culo OFF!

So, I got that *we need to link up more often* text the next morning. I smiled and replied, *I agree.* He said he didn't realize he missed our conversations so much until he saw me, and we linked up again. He's a total sweetheart. He's another one of those bully-on-the-outside-but-a-soft-teddy-on-the-inside type of fella's. If you don't know him, then you would think the worse about him just off of his appearance. Which is funny, because he and I started talking because I would always speak to him. I mean, when you're in the IT department, you're bound to have to speak to folks or interact. So hey. Besides, I'm naturally polite. I was gone speak to the man anyway. Him being *PHINE* a *"Black Bear"* was a bonus. Anyway, we've been talking a little more lately, but you know me, I'm all for action than words hunni!

Blah, all in a day! But yeah, Love, he *got me!* More times than I care to admit though. LOL. That's what my ass gets for flirting. I knew he had that hammer. I could look at him and tell what his sex was knocking on. It's all good. I'll take that "L" for now. HA!

Okay Love,

I'm on my way to New York for the weekend. Ill fill you in about Mr. "Arab Money" when I'm settled.

We'll talk later.

Eskimo Kisses!

THAT NORTHEAST REGIONAL BEARDY

Hey Love,

I went to New York to visit "Butta" and the family for a couple of days. I had a blast, as I always do. As usual, I rode the train up. Go get you a drink and let me give you the tea about this one. As I shake my head thinking, *Only me.*

So okay, like always, we had to wait in the waiting area in Union Station in Washington, DC, before we boarded, which was cool. But this particular time, there were so many cutie pies and handsome blue-collar workers. Again, I wasn't complaining. You know I'm all for the eye candy. Matter of fact, a few of them walked past me so much, when I said "Damn!" out loud, the lady sitting beside me burst out laughing and said, "Baby, I'm thinking the same thing. Ain't they fine tonight?"

"Yes Mayum they are!"

We both laughed, as we continued enjoying the sights.

It was time for us to board our train, so we lined up. Apparently, I didn't see the chocolate piece of man candy eyeing me. I was looking down at my phone, opening my app so I could have my ticket ready to show the attendant.

As I made my way to the front of the line, I saw a bag handler on the platform, just chilling on the cart. He was a sexy little chocolate teddy bear that had a full beard. He looked at me, smiled and flashed those pretty white teeth. I couldn't help but smile back at him. Now you know I winked at him as well. He had me feeling like something. Whew! I walked toward the train, trying to find a car to board that wasn't as crowded. It wasn't a full train, and I found my perfect seat. It was a window seat four rows back from the entrance and restroom. It was perfect since I would always sit by the window and close to the door.

I was settling into my seat when one of the crew members walked past me and spoke. I was putting my bag in the overhead compartment when he doubled back to help me.

Girl, I finally looked up and *damn!* He was fine too. I thanked him and he said, "No Problem. That's what we're here for. To help out and shit." Then he smiled and winked at me. *Baby!* I don't know what "Mutha Oshun" was serving in the universe, but I was here for it. Not only was he taller than me, but he also had a *body* and smelled so damn good.

Just a handsome chocolate full bearded Adonis. His name was Kevin. After helping me with my bag, he told me he'd catch me later. I said cool, then I sat down and made myself comfortable.

As was getting myself situated, I noticed more people began to filter through the car, yet it was still rather empty. I just chalked it up to it being an early trip. I pulled out my laptop and accessories, began my plug-in, and was ready to go, so I could get some work done. As the train began to depart from the station, the ticket taker walked past me toward the front. I knew what that meant. He had his little ticket scanning device in his hand already.

I knew they were getting ready to come down the line to scan tickets and, of course, I had to pee. I jumped up, ran to the bathroom, and when I came out, there was another cutie pie standing at my seat. He looked up and smiled at me. His name was Rico. He was so damn handsome. Again, I was thinking, *what the hell is going on today?* And again, *not* complaining. Basically, I need to start riding the train during this late night; early morning hours if I can help it; because Milk and Honey is being served. Anyway, Rico was Dominican; six feet tall, about two hundred twenty pounds, with a very nice body, nice shape-up on his beard and everything. You know I sized him up. Thick legs were *everything!*

"Is this you?" Rico asked, smiling.

"Yes. Hold on and let me bring up my ticket for you." I pulled out my cell phone to retrieve my electronic ticket.

"No rush. Take ya time. Train ain't even that full." He laughed.

"Thank you. And here it is." I smiled, showing him my ticket.

"Cool. Thanks." He looked around and then asked, "So how are you doing?"

"I'm very well, thank you. How about you?"

"I'm Good. No real complaints. I see you're getting off in New York, Christian. What's the trip for?" Let me find out he peeped my name off my ticket.

I tilted my head, giving him a look. All in my business and whatnot!

"I'm Rico, by the way."

"Yes, Rico, I am. I'm going to visit the fam for the weekend.'

"Cool. I gotta go make my rounds, but I'll be back to chat with you in a few." He smiled. "Yes, by all means, please do." I smiled and winked.

Rico stepped away to finish making his rounds, and I sat down and did some work. It's only a three-hour train ride from DC to New York. I always make sure I take time to look out the window to catch the view. It helps me to focus and reflect. It's always so beautiful. Especially when we're going over the bridge; the way the sun rises and reflects off the waves is so calming and peaceful. It's my favorite moment on the train ride. Once I was done reflecting, I went back to typing. I turned on my music, but I didn't put in my headphones. I mean, it was just me in the front of the car. Besides, the music wasn't loud or anything crazy.

I was jamming to Notorious BIG when Kevin walked back past me. I was jamming away while typing. Apparently, he had been standing next to me for at least a minute before I even looked up and noticed him. Girl, I know. I was in a zone. He knocked on the overhead compartment and started laughing.

"Aye, what'chu know about that?" he asked.

I chuckled. "I know a little bit. Wassup?"

"Nothing much. I was just seeing what was up with you."

"I'm enjoying my music and doing some work. I need to go get me some coffee."

"Then let's go then."

Let me lock my computer away first.

I locked my laptop away and we made our way to the dining car while briefly chatting. Guess who was standing behind the counter? Yep, Rico. I laughed and told him he was a jack of all trades.

He laughed. "Yeah, I get around."

Rico and I were talking so much that I didn't even notice that Kevin had walked away. Oops. Rico gave me my coffee, but I told him to hold it for me. I need to my seat to get my creamer. When I returned, he had jokes.

"How are you gone bring your own creamer, though?"

"What do you mean 'how'? Y'all ain't got none. And what you do have is gross and bland. I think the fuck noooot."

"Yeah, you right." He laughed. "What kind is that anyway?"

"It's International Sweet Cream. The only kind I drink."

Rico leaned in. "So, can I taste it?" His lips turned up into a devilish grin.

I returned his devilish grin. "Sure. Get a cup."

"I wanna taste you. I mean, yours." He smiled.

I smirked. "Well, you can't taste mine. I'll pour you some though."

"Yeah, okay." Girl, the flirty smile in his eyes held a flame.

"I'm not fooling with you, sir. I'm going back to my seat. Thank you."

"I'll be back there in a few. We ain't finished this convo just yet."

I laughed and said, "Whatever," as I walked away.

I was back in my seat, typing and jamming to my music, when I heard the conductor come over the intercom, announcing we were about forty-five minutes out from New York. I started packing up my things so I would be ready to jump off the train when it stopped.

I was packed up and ready to go when Rico walked up to my section and sat down in the seat across from me. He said he wanted to chat with me a little more, but he knew I was getting ready to exit. We swapped numbers, then he pulled my bag down for me while I gave my area one last once over.

As the train pulled into New York's Penn Station, I got up to put on my jacket. Rico got up to go back to his station.

"Can I get a hug?"

I smiled because you already know I love giving out hugs. "Sure."

He wrapped his arms around me, kissed my neck, and said, "I'll see you soon."

Baaybeeey! I almost gave him my body. He smelled so damn good; kissing all on me like that. *Shit!* I laughed and said, "Boy gone with all that before you get fucked on this train!"

During my stay in New York for the weekend, we texted each other. We had a great text convo. "Butta" was trying to figure out who I was talking to the entire time. Old nosy ass. Of course, I didn't say anything. He's always trying to get me married off to some dayum body. Rico asked me which train I was going to return on. I told him it was the eleven-p.m. train back to DC. Baby, listen, he made sure he was on the same train as me. I sent him a copy of my digital ticket on purpose. I didn't think he would be able to, but he did it. Again, I asked no questions.

I said my goodbyes to the family, before making my way to the train station. As I was standing on the platform, waiting for my train, Rico texted me and told me to make sure I boarded the last car because he saved me a good seat. Naturally, that made me smile. When the train pulled up, he greeted me at the door with nothing but smiles.

Looking sexy in his blue uniform, with his hat cocked to the side. So cliché, but so cute. I boarded, he hugged me again—smelling good—took my bag and told me to follow him. Walking behind him, I noticed he was bowlegged. Those legs were sexy! Whew! That walk was the business. I was getting hot and bothered just looking at him walk. I know. I laughed at myself too.

He did save me a good seat. It was one of the seats in the back near the door. I was getting ready to snap on him because I, thought it was near the restroom. It was quite roomy, so it definitely worked.

He turned to me, and in his sexy voice and that accent, said, "This seat is just for us."

"For us?"

"Yes, just for us." He smiled.

"Hmph. All right now. Well, thank you. I appreciate it."

"I said I was going to take care of you, didn't I?"

"Yes, you did."

"Then that is what I shall do. Would you like anything?"

"Actually, yes. A sweet tea with lemon and a cup of ice."

"Cool. But first, can I have a kiss?" he asked, smiling like a dayum Cheshire cat.

"Well, I did tell you that you could have one. I do keep my word. So sure."

He smiled and leaned down to kiss me. He had some soft, sexy, juicy lips. Good breath too. He laughed and thanked me. He went to go get my drink, and I couldn't help but watch him walk away. When he returned, he brought me back a brownie. A man after my own heart. He laughed when I told him, "I forgot I told you how much I love chocolate and sweets." He left me for a few minutes to go make his rounds.

Since we were sitting in the last car, it was easier for him to chat with me between his rounds. After a while, he came back and sat beside me. Only this time, he seemed a little different. He seemed more relaxed and a little more chill this time. He told me he had some wine while he was in the front to calm his nerves.

I laughed. "I knew it was something," I said. Even the way he was looking at me; his whole mood was different.

We sat and talked for a good hour before I had to pee. Baby that tea and ice was leaning on my bladder. I'm glad I had on my sweat pants. Speaking of which, when I came back, I noticed his clothes were looser.

"Um, are you alright?" I asked him.

He chuckled. "Yes. I'm good. Why?"

"Because you look like you were in a fight while I was in the restroom."

"My clothes were making me hot."

"That's that damn alcohol you were drinking." We both laughed.

"Yeah, I think so."

I sat down beside him in my seat, when I noticed he took my bag and pushed it further under the seat. No sooner than I looked up, he was on top of me. I laughed and said, *"Oh! Okay!"*

He pulled back. "Oh my God, Christian, I'm so sorry. I just wanted you so bad."

"It's okay. Just warn me first. Shit!" I chuckled. "It's cool. Breathe and relax, boo."

After a minute, I decided to take the initiative and mount him and began kissing him. *Why* did I do that? Baby he went all *in*. I mean, literally! Love! This MF lifted me up, pulled my sweatpants back, and let have! We were all stretched out across the seats and everything.

I stopped him. "What if somebody walks back here? I *do not* want you to lose your job."

"Everybody is sitting down or busy. We're good." Can you believe that shit? He told me

he usually uses this time to take a nap or a break anyway. I laughed then went for it. He beat the breaks off me in that back row. And yes, I let him have it too! Baby that Dominican went to *work.* It was fast and good, just the way I like it. Those thick bowlegs were *rocking*! The best part, his dick had a nice curve, and he was hitting *all the right spots*! Whew! - too much information, I know, but baaaaybeeey, I had *no* complaints!

I've noticed one thing about Hispanic, Dominican, Latino, and Afro Cuban men; they do everything with such passion. The way he was kissing me, the way he was gyrating his hips, the way he was touching me. Sex and quickies are passionate with them. At least the few I've been intimate with. I think that's why I'm so low-key attracted to them. I just see one and get all hot and bothered.

Anyway, after we were done, and he was done growling, we sat up and fixed ourselves. We both laughed.

"I needed that," he said.

I replied with "I wanted it, and I'm glad you delivered."

He laughed and I said look, you know I hold no punches (with his fine ass). We had another hour to go on the train ride, so we laughed, kissed and talked for the rest of the way.

When the train pulled into Union Station in DC, he helped me gather my things and told me to wait for him. I walked into the station to the coffee shop to buy bottled water. As I was texting him to tell him where I was, he was coming around the corner, smiling. He changed his clothes and that man looked damn good in those jeans.

"Follow me to my car," he said.

"My driver is waiting…"

"Cancel it."

BLOOP! Well ok.

He took me home and *bitch,* we had sex again! This time we were really able to spread out. Talk about having your back blown out. Geeze. I had water legs when we were finished.

"You are a Spanish Fruit Fly with balls of gold," I said.

"Christian what the fuck?!" Then he laughed.

We enjoyed every inch of each other's bodies. More times than I could remember.

I was so glad I had Monday off. I would have called out if I didn't. Ol' boy was *not* in the mood to leave any time soon. Honestly, I wasn't ready for him to leave either. By the time we woke up, which was around noon, we were hungry, so we ordered in and chilled. It was very nice. He didn't leave until Tuesday morning. There was plenty of sex, wine, movies, laughter, and passionate kissing. It was nice. Naturally, I didn't read anything into it. He dropped me off at work Tuesday morning and went on his way.

We keep in touch. We actually had sex in the bathroom on a

recent trip up to New York a few months ago. One look at each other and it was *on!* We knew. The funny part was, Kevin was walking past the restroom when the door opened, and he burst out laughing. Later on, he came to my seat asking if he could get next. *Boy, bye!* He was cute, but he ain't that cute. He was trying hard too. However, I did size him up. Very nice and very tempting, but he seemed a little loose and childish, so I passed. I told Rico and he confirmed it. Kevin wasn't wrapped, too tight. He was messy and all over the place. Anyway, that was that and *it* still happens from time to time. Hasn't in a good while. But hey, I'm good. If it's run its course, it was fun while it lasted. On to the Next Stop. OW!

Okay Love, I've got to go.

I'm on my way to Miami to meet Chef.

I'll fill you in later.

Eskimo kisses.

THE HEALING OF THE SACRED CLOWN

Hey my love,

Please forgive me. I know it's been a while, but I've been going through the motions lately. I wasn't sure what was wrong with me, but I had to take a break from everybody and everything. I needed to get away. I went to go visit Jerry. Yes, he moved to Ithaca, New York (finally). He has a beautiful home there. It was so funny how all of it happened. Remember I met him when I was sitting on the bench, feeding the birds in Central Park? I was waiting on Alana, to tell me where to meet her, only to find out she had a meeting at the last minute, so she wanted a raincheck for lunch (which was perfectly cool). So, we agreed to link up later, if we were both free.

I sat on the bench and continued to feed the birds when Jerry sat down beside me. I said right away, "Oh, my God, I love your cologne." Then it was an instant connection.

He laughed and said, "Amazing nose."

"I have a K-9 nose and I'm often teased for it, but I love it."

We talked for four hours and didn't even realize it. We left the park and grabbed dinner. Chyle, Alana called me back and I sent her straight to voicemail, I was enjoying him so much! It was like I was feeding off his energy and personality. He was a breath of fresh air for me. Ever since that day, we've been the best of friends. We always keep in touch. He always manages to call me whenever I need to get away or just really need to talk.

One day in the middle of October, I felt like I needed to get away from home and my surroundings really badly. Low and behold, he called me.

I remember saying hello, and when he said my name, I burst into tears. I remember crying and telling him I had no idea what was wrong with me, but I didn't know if I wanna continue to cry, fight, break stuff, be happy, laugh or what! I had so many emotions flooding my soul at one time all I could do was cry. He called me on a Monday evening, and I was on the train to him Tuesday afternoon. It was just *that bad* and *that serious*. Oh, hunni, I was a mess.

I remember not being able to talk to anyone about what I was going through because I couldn't put what I was feeling into words, which was making me even more frustrated. I know it sounds funny, but I was going *through it.* I wasn't snapping on anybody or anything, I was just to myself. I would stay in the house all day or in my room. I did not want to be around people, or if I had to, not for extended periods of time. So yeah, it was time for me to do something. I remember calling a cab to take me to the train station because I didn't want to leave my car at the train station for a prolonged period. I didn't know when I would be back, so that way, I knew where it was. I left a note on the fridge for my family that I'd be back. I just needed some time alone. That was one of the best decisions I had ever made in my life, concerning me and my wellbeing.

The train ride up was so beautiful. It was the fall season and I could look out the window to see the many variations of fall hues on the trees. The trees were so beautiful. That was the beginning of my relaxation. I felt my body when it slightly exhaled. It felt really nice. When the train finally stopped in Ithaca, and I was finally able to get off. I was so ready to see Jerry. I knew he would make me feel better. When I came around the corner and saw Jerry waiting on me, I slightly exhaled again. He got out his car, took my bags, placed them in the trunk, and came to hug me. I fell right into his arms. It was like I was pushed into him. Not physically, but more on a soul connecting level. He just hugged me so tight, then told me it was going to be all right. He was going to help restore and "fix me". I laughed, then told him "yes because I broke me and don't know what I did".

On the car ride to his home, we chatted a little bit about what was going on and how I was feeling. He said that I was going through; a lot and my reactions were very understandable. Having to bury a really good friend at such a young age, then having to deal with family drama and issues, on top of not understanding what was going on around me in the world.

I told him, I just felt like I was literally carrying the weight of the world on my shoulders. He told me by the time I was ready to leave, I'd have a better understanding as of WHO I was and WHAT I was becoming. I'm like, *yeah okay, whatever.* I was very dismissive of it. He knew I was and chuckled. The drive on the way to his estate was so nice and pleasant. Once we pulled up, I saw why he moved.

I stepped out the car to get a better glimpse of his home, because it was my favorite style of home. He lived in a gorgeous Victorian that sat on top of a hill by itself. It still had its original charm to it, but he definitely upgraded it. It had that super long front porch that went across the front, with the wooden swings on the both ends, those stained-glass doors, windows and wooden beams. Just immaculate. His home was surrounded by breathtaking views and the fresh air was so crisp. Just what I needed.

We walked into the house and we were greeted by his German Shepard "Zeus", who was absolutely beautiful. He was so big with a gorgeous fluffy coat. Just adorable. Jerry was slightly shocked because he said he had never seen Zeus take to someone so quickly. I told him he probably smelled Bella on me, so he knew I was okay. Besides, you know animals and babies are one in the same. They KNOW a good person right off the break. If your spirit ain't right, they have no problem with letting you know that they are NOT about to fuck with you. LOL. Yeah, I'm good with King Zeus.

Jerry laughed then showed me to my room and, Love, I pulled those curtains back and good Lord! Just beautiful. I had no idea he was sitting up on a hill like that. Like, I knew it, but I really didn't pay it any attention. The array of trees aligning the back field of his house, with all the fall colors, were just breathtaking. Again, I exhaled a little more.

I went back downstairs to where Jerry and Zeus were. Of course, they were in the kitchen. I walked down the hall to where they were while looking at the pictures of his family along the wall. Very handsome family. Jerry was easy on the eyes as well. He is about five feet ten inches (give or take a few), Native American with beautiful hair, and a grown man's body. Whew, Lord. Although he was handsome and super sexy (Lord knows he smelled good), I don't think of him in a sexual way. He truly and honestly is my friend. But being easy on the eyes never hurt anybody hunni. LOL. Whew! As I made my way to the kitchen, I walked through the doors and he was sitting at the island smiling.

His kitchen was to die for! When you walked into the entryway, that bitch OPENED UP! GOOD GAWD! It was a state-of-the-art chef's kitchen with floor-to-ceiling glass doors, which in essence were actually windows. It was accompanied by a deck that wrapped around the entire back of the house. Ah! I mean, just…I was in heaven.

You know I'm an Estate Whore. And I'll be that! LOL. Like I was saying, he was sitting at the island, smiling when I walked in. He laughed at my reaction to the kitchen space. Then I turned around and saw that stove and almost had a full body orgasm. Yeah, he already knew I was going to have some of that. Speaking of which, he asked me what I wanted to do for dinner, I told him COOK! He burst out laughing, then asked me what I wanted to cook. I told him it didn't matter as long as I could use every inch of that kitchen. He agreed, so we went to the market, got some fresh fish, veggies and ingredients for me to make a cake as well. Before I knew it, KA'BLAM! BITCH PUDDING! I was in the kitchen tearing it down! My shoulders dropped a little more. The moments of exhaling were becoming more and more frequent now. This time Jerry caught it, then spoke up about it.

"Christian, you've exhaled a number of five times since we've been together, and this time, your shoulders fell."

"Yes. You are absolutely right. I felt it."

"I'm glad I could be of service. I was going to wait, but since your soul is already at ease, I'll go into it now."

"Wait, huh?"

"What I mean is, you are relaxed enough to let your guard down. You think it's you, but it's not."

"Explain," I said, as I was seasoning the fish and preparing it to go in the oven."

Jerry explained to me what I had been feeling lately and going through. He said that I have the ability to soak up people's energy, then spew it back out. Be it good or bad. It's not something that's learned, either you're born with it, or you're not. I told him he was starting to freak me out a little bit because everything he was saying was making sense.

We talked a little more about it, then he told me he wanted me to meet his mother and aunt. They were coming over for dinner on Thursday.

"Okay, great! Thanks for making me uncomfortable."

He laughed and then told me I'd be perfectly fine with them.

So, as you guessed it, Thursday came, and I was so nervous. Not in a bad way, but I was rather antsy to see why he wanted me to meet his family. Which I thought it was cool because Jerry is so cool and laid back so I could only imagine what his mother was like. Jerry and I had been having a ball all week. He took me to all kinds of markets, popular landmarks, restaurants and my favorites were the culture shops. I found so many little trinkets, fabrics and nick-knacks. I was in heaven. I know, right! None of my materialistic whorish ways surfaced at all. I just had so much fun. Not to mention fall is my favorite time of the year. It was just so nice!

My bad, I digress. Oh yes, back to the family. I was in the kitchen baking a lemon pound cake (Jerry told me that was one of their favs) while dancing to some music. You know, doing what I do, when

I heard some giggling behind me, followed with, "Don't you hurt nothing over there, young man." Oh, my God! I turned around and burst out laughing. I was slightly embarrassed, but hey. That's what I do, hunni. Jerry introduced us. Naturally I hugged them both. When I hugged his aunt (Giselle), she looked at his mother (Diyani) and said, "Uh-huh. You did good Jerry. I like this one."

I was looking confused, trying to figure out what they were talking about. Jerry winked and smiled at me. I just said, "Okay."

They sat down at the table, and I made sure I gave them some cake while it was still warm. They wanted to talk to me because apparently Jerry had told them so much about me, because he felt as though I could benefit from talking to them in person. Again, I had the confused face. Once we were through the ice breakers, they went in on me! I was NOT READY. Oh hunni, they wanted to know what makes me happy, what makes me mad, what pisses me off, what makes me cry, what irritates me. I mean just a slew of emotional questions. I didn't get it at first, until later on that night.

Jerry had disappeared somewhere in the house and left us in the kitchen talking. We decided to move to the sofa with more cake, a bottle of wine and a cheese tray. Oh hunni, we were having us a grand old time. I was enjoying them telling me everything I needed to know about me and my situation.

Apparently, I was born with the gift of being extremely intuitive. Amongst those questions they asked me, one of them was: Do I constantly feel guilty for things that are beyond my control? Like poverty, war, etc. And I DO! I told Diyani, me just walking through the market or grocery store, I'd began to cry, or my eyes would well up with tears. I'm blessed and able to grocery shop or have those options, when so many others are starving or have NO options. Again, they looked at each other and smile.

This time I spoke up. I asked them, what does that mean? That's the second time they did that in my presence. SPILL IT! They both burst out laughing and told me flat out. I would be considered a "Atlas or Planetary Healer"; or in some cases an "Heyoka". They explained that people like me (because there are more like me) are prone to feel this way on a regular basis.

Now you know doggone well I felt like this was a crock of bull, but that lasted for all of a split second. It was quickly subdued by the look of seriousness on their faces. They explained to me what that title was and now that I was aware, how my life was about to change. Right! UGH! Not ready for that...Or was I? They told me I needed to have my center realigned so that I would have better control over my "powers" (so to speak). Honestly though, it was no laughing matter. Everything I was going through had been turned up times one hundred on an emotional level. Not only because of my own emotions, but because of other people around me emotions. I was taking on the burden of carrying their emotional baggage and not even aware of it.

Jerry, Diyani and Gisele were masters of their craft. They knew what it was like to be an emotional wreck and not understanding what was going on within you. They spent the rest of the week working with me, teaching me various exercises, ways to cope with things, and ways to bring myself out of a trance if I happen to end up in one. Everything we discussed and talked about taught me a great deal about myself. I told them what was driving me crazy to the point I needed to leave. Jerry's phone call was right on time. Now that I think about it, I see why he was right on time (smiling).

I filled them in on the whole story about burying one of my BFFs, then having my grandfather drop dead shortly after her, then, not having a very loving relationship with my mother at the time because of our constant fighting and bickering, then worrying about others in my family with their personal issues; all while crying over things in the world (see). Everything was happening all at once. The more I tried to fight back my tears and emotions, the worse it got. The more I tried to subdue it, the bigger and more out of control it got until I broke. As I was giving them detail after detail, I began to cry and get emotional all over again. That's when Gisele took me by my hand and I immediately began to change.

I stopped the tears and everything. It was like I could feel her energy flowing through my body. It was all positive emotions. Everything from love to compassion to hope. Diyani took my other hand. I exhaled and then there was a burst of energy that flowed through my body like I was being reborn into this new spirit. I felt like the Phoenix in me was rising again.

At that moment, I knew what I needed to do. As I turned around to hug Gisele, I looked up to see Jerry standing in the doorway, drinking his tea and smiling. I hugged Gisele. She laughed and then said not to pay him any attention.

Jerry has had his own bouts with the struggles of self-identity and aura cleansing. From my understanding, he went through the same exact thing. That's how he was able to pinpoint me and spark up a conversation. Jerry later told me that night, after his family left; that he sat beside me on that park because I was glowing. The energy I was radiating that day drew him right to me. He told me my aura was so bright and loud that he couldn't resist me. There was no doubt in his heart and soul that he had to get to know me.

I said, "So you basically set all of this up?" and laughed.

He told me that I was a part of a secret society, and I might as well get used to it. I laughed it off and told him to be careful. He went on to tell me, "Not many people are like you or are able to have the kind of heart that you do. It goes beyond the physical." Which is very true. I look at your heart and soul. Then and only then will I look at your physical appearance. If your aura ain't clean or something about you doesn't rub me the right way right off the break, then I won't even bother with you. You just may be the kind of trouble I don't want to be bothered with.

Now, I'm so good; I know how to activate it when I need to. I never fully turn it off because I can't. Its apart of my WHO. And I'm okay with that. I've learned how to lead with love. When you live a judgement free life, the possibilities are endless. The universe will provide you with everything that you need. All you have to do is ask. Ask and it shall be given unto you. I left Jerry feeling renewed, ready and free. I keep in touch with him and his aunt. His mother passed away and all is well. At the end of my experience with them; it was confirmation for me. You never know what God has in store for you. Be open, be ready and always be willing to let the old die in order to make room for the new to be born.

"When you follow the crowd you lose yourself, but when you follow your soul you will lose the crowd. Eventually your soul tribe will appear. But do not fear the process of solitude." I'm so free and I LOVE IT!

They are forever and always my Soul Tribe.

Okay Love,

I'll talk to you later.

Eskimo Kisses.

Printed in the United States
By Bookmasters